Roger Roemmich

DON'T LET YOUR CLIENTS EAT DOG FOOD WHEN THEY'RE OLD!

Don't Let Your Clients Eat Dog Food When They're Old!

A Financial Professional's Guide to Retirement Cash Flow Management

Roger Roemmich

DON'T LET YOUR CLIENTS EAT DOG
FOOD WHEN THEY'RE OLD!
A FINANCIAL PROFESSIONAL'S GUIDE TO
RETIREMENT CASH FLOW MANAGEMENT

Copyright © 2014 Roger Roemmich.

All rights reserved. No part of this book may be used or reproduced by any means, graphic, electronic, or mechanical, including photocopying, recording, taping or by any information storage retrieval system without the written permission of the publisher except in the case of brief quotations embodied in critical articles and reviews.

iUniverse books may be ordered through booksellers or by contacting:

iUniverse
1663 Liberty Drive
Bloomington, IN 47403
www.iuniverse.com
1-800-Authors (1-800-288-4677)

Because of the dynamic nature of the Internet, any web addresses or links contained in this book may have changed since publication and may no longer be valid. The views expressed in this work are solely those of the author and do not necessarily reflect the views of the publisher, and the publisher hereby disclaims any responsibility for them.

Any people depicted in stock imagery provided by Thinkstock are models, and such images are being used for illustrative purposes only.
Certain stock imagery © Thinkstock.

ISBN: 978-1-4917-4371-3 (sc)
ISBN: 978-1-4917-4372-0 (hc)
ISBN: 978-1-4917-4373-7 (e)

Library of Congress Control Number: 2014913957

Printed in the United States of America.

iUniverse rev. date: 07/31/2014

I've got all the money I'll ever need, if I die by four o'clock.
—Henny Youngman

Contents

About the Author ix

Acknowledgments xi

Introduction xiii

Chapter 1 Missteps and Blunders: Common Client Mistakes . 1

Chapter 2 Screaming from the Room: Retirement Timing . . 14

Chapter 3 The Taxman Never Retires: Taxes and Retirees . . 33

Chapter 4 The Taxman Cometh: Retirement Accounts and Client Debt 52

Chapter 5 Gather ye Rosebuds: Traditional and Alternative Investments 68

Chapter 6 The Sequencing Factor: Sequencing Risk and Client Draw Downs 93

Chapter 7 Social Security 101: Safety Net Essentials 116

Chapter 8 The Wizard behind the Curtain: Social Security Timing 138

Chapter 9 No More House Calls: Medicare and Retirees . .160

Chapter 10	Elephants in the Room: A Case for Long-Term Care. 188
Chapter 11	Concepts in Play: Case Studies 213
Chapter 12	Appendix: Quick Facts at a Glance 237

About the Author

ROGER ROEMMICH IS CHIEF investment officer of ROKA Wealth Strategists (www.rokawealthstrategists.com), a registered investment advisory firm serving affluent individuals in and around Atlanta, Georgia. The company offers a wide range of financial services, but its emphasis is on retirement planning for baby boomers still in the accumulation phase of their financial lives, and on cash flow management for retirees. Roemmich is also the CEO and founder of the Retirement Cash Flow Education Group, a Web-based educational services provider on retirement issues for individuals and financial professionals (www.retirementcashflow.com).

Roemmich is a certified public accountant, a certified financial planner with FINRA Series 7, 31, 63, and 65 designations, and a long-term care professional. He is also licensed to sell a variety of insurance products. Recognized as an elite financial advisor with nearly four decades of experience in finance, Roemmich holds a PhD in accounting from Michigan State University. His academic positions include a tenured professorship at the School of Accounting at the University of Georgia in Athens, Georgia, where he taught for ten years. Roemmich founded the Certified Retirement Plan Specialist (CRPS) Program, and he is one of three founding members of the Life Insurance Advisors Association. In addition, he served as executive vice president of the largest trainer and consultant to the trust industry, Cannon Financial.

Acknowledgments

No author ever writes a book in a vacuum. The help and support of family, friends, and colleagues is essential to the effort. As I learned long ago, it takes a team to do anything worthwhile, and I couldn't have hoped for a better one! First and foremost, I'd like to thank my beautiful fiancée, Candace Fennell, for reading the manuscript and offering sage advice on its content. Together with assistance from my esteemed business associate, Kari March, I was able to sort through what to cut and what to keep while determining the best way to organize the material so that it would be of maximum help to financial professionals as they work with clients on retirement planning and management. A special thanks goes to the good people at iUniverse, especially my ghostwriter, David W. Shaw.

Last but certainly not least, I thank Allan and Elsie Roemmich. You both have been wonderful parents, and I wouldn't be the man I am today without your love and guidance. My son, Todd Roemmich, and my daughter, Kerri Roemmich-Hammond, are blessings dear to my heart. And my dog, Beau, a furry friend I cherish, fills my life with laughs and smiles.

Thanks to you all!

Introduction

THERE'S NO DOUBT ABOUT it—money ranks among the most personal of all topics for most of us. For some people, it's even more personal than sex! It's almost as if money lingers like some deep and dark secret nobody wants to expose in their lives. If a person has lots of cash, it's not likely a subject that will come up over cocktails at the country club in any truly revealing way. If a person is of modest or limited means, the lack of financial freedom and wherewithal is very likely a painful subject that can launch an episode of depression accompanied by feelings of inadequacy. Let's face it. In America, the dollar is king. It's how we typically measure success in life, whether that's wrong or not.

As a financial professional, you know this is true. People get prickly when it comes to sharing details about their money, and when the chips are down, they often don't think straight about how to preserve capital and plan for the future. How many times have you had clients who got emotional when their stocks took a nosedive, and then the clients put in a sell order against your emphatic advice? How many times have you had an elderly couple sit across the desk from you and glibly say that they haven't informed their kids about where the money is, let alone how much has or has not been socked away over the years? How many times have you simply shaken your head and wondered how otherwise intelligent individuals could make inherently silly decisions about their finances because they failed to take responsibility for their own financial future?

We've all been there! As a financial professional in academia and in the trenches for almost four decades, I know I have. In fact, like you, I've pretty much seen it all. What's truly worrying to me now is that I'll be seeing more and more situations where a client has built a financial rat trap that will end up fostering fiscal suicide in retirement. With approximately seventy-eight million Americans in the baby boom generation, the broad and complicated issues associated with retirement planning during the accumulation phase and cash flow management after retirement in the distribution phase are going to become an increasingly common part of our lives as financial professionals serving an aging population.

The statistics relating to the financial ill health of retirement in the United States are sobering. According to a June 2013 study from the National Institute on Retirement Security, 45 percent of workers across America have absolutely nothing saved in a retirement account, or the equivalent of roughly thirty-eight million people! The study, based on data from the Federal Reserve's Survey of Consumer Finances, indicated that the median amount in retirement accounts was only $12,000 for workers nearing retirement age. A 2013 study from the American Association of Retired People found that credit card debt for workers over the age of fifty was higher than for younger workers, an average of $8,278 for the former and $6,258 for the latter.

The savings rate was low before the Great Recession kicked into full gear in the last quarter of 2008. When the recession ended, the financial meltdown had stripped Americans of 40 percent of their personal wealth. Some sources indicate that the total loss in individual retirement accounts and 401(k) accounts during the economic collapse amounted to $2.8 trillion, or roughly 47 percent of their value. Granted, some of that wealth is back from the recent stock market rally, but many boomers who got burned in the crash panicked and sold at a staggering loss. Then they lobbed what was left of their money into fixed-income investments, many of which haven't even kept up with inflation in our present economy.

Yes, the prospects for some future retirees in America are dim indeed. Incidentally, I blame the prolonged, totally unnatural low-interest environment that resulted from the Federal Reserve's response to the Great Recession for a lot of the mayhem we're currently seeing. Even before the crash, boomers were taking on more risk than they ever should have by chasing risky high-growth stocks. When the world economy blew up, well, let's just assume you already know what a mess that was, especially if your clients invested mainly in the financial sector. It's gotten even worse since then, as the returns from once safe and predictable investments in savings accounts, certificates of deposit, and money market accounts plummeted to historic lows.

In a sense, then, retirees and those approaching retirement have been put through the wringer, suffering the double whammy of lost or severely eroded principal, and the lost opportunity in stocks and mutual funds that would have given them a higher return as the market indexes hit record highs in 2013 and 2014. Let's also not forget that half of Americans don't even own stocks or bonds. These individuals are the ones whose sole locus of wealth was in real estate, and we all know how that went. Home values are starting to rebound, but many low-income homeowners can't even get banks to refinance their mortgages at the current lower interest rates. Retirement for these people is a pipe dream.

From where I'm sitting, I can only characterize the current status for retirees and those hoping to retire someday as a full-blown retirement crisis that virtually guarantees that most baby boomers and those of younger generations will face nothing short of a dire existence in their so-called golden years. For the first time, we will have millions of Americans living retirement, if they're even lucky enough to be able to retire, that engender a quality of life far inferior to the sort their parents and grandparents enjoyed. Most will have to rely on Social Security alone for basic subsistence, and that's what life will be. Subsistence.

With the average annual draw of $15,000 in Social Security for an individual, and between $22,000 and $30,000 for couples who held jobs squarely in the middle class, the future looks bleak. For late boomers in their early fifties and those in Gen X and the millennial generation, Social Security may well not be there for them in its current form. It'll be there, of course, but with the current gridlock in Washington, the reforms may not come in time to guarantee 100 percent payment of promised benefits. Add the fact that expenditures for health care beyond the basics of Medicare tally up to approximately $250,000 per couple over the twenty to thirty years of retirement, and that fewer than 25 percent of current retirees have any sort of long-term care protection. The bleak scenario just gets even worse.

The companion book to this one—*Don't Eat Dog Food When You're Old!*—addresses the core issues associated with retirement from a layperson's point of view, with the hope that readers will be armed with the information they need to work with financial professionals on a sound plan for the accumulation and distribution phases of their financial lives. It provides all that's needed for you and your clients to have an educated conversation. Combined with this book, which contains far more technical information related to retirement issues from the point of view of financial professionals, you'll have a formidable arsenal of knowledge to work with.

Over the years, especially recently, I've found that the majority of financial professionals only know about retirement issues directly related to their chosen field of expertise. It's no big surprise, really. After all, we only know what we've been taught. Accountants know about taxes and all manner of accepted accounting practices for individuals and businesses, but they probably know next to nothing about the various ways a client could secure some manner of long-term care protection. It's simply an issue that's outside the ken of most CPAs. Financial advisors and stockbrokers know about investments, but do they know about the intricate nuances of Social Security and Medicare? Insurance agents know about products that may be more suited for a would-be retiree. Chances are they know little or nothing about nontraded real estate investment trusts or other alternative investments. Obviously, tax attorneys zero in on taxes.

The bottom line is very few of us are working from a big-picture view of the entire gamut of interrelated subjects that go into sound retirement planning and cash flow management for clients. Even if you're not allowed to counsel clients on, say, taxes or estate planning, having the knowledge is your first step to advising clients on what they need to know and where they should look for the advice you can't offer them for whatever reason. Just because you can't actively advise a client about one of the many apples in the retirement basket doesn't mean you shouldn't know what those apples are and where the worms are hiding inside!

If the boomers and their younger counterparts fail to get the comprehensive retirement advice they need, they're going to face the unpleasant consequences of a declining quality of life as principal diminishes and cash flow dries up because of inflation pressures, or, just as possible, because of the astronomical costs associated with long-term care, even if that care is received at home. Long-term care is the leading cause of poverty among seniors without sufficient coverage to mitigate costs when one or both spouses end up in a nursing home. Negative cash flow is something we're all going to see a lot more of in the coming years for our clients, and it's not going to be nice.

We have many clients that may or may not be familiar even with the basics of finance. You'd be surprised at how many millionaires on my client list don't have a clear picture of all the pieces of the puzzle they can fit together to create a far brighter financial picture in their retirement. In my view, such complacency embraces a lack of knowledge that is tantamount to lethal danger. We have clients who haven't saved enough in many cases.

Compounding the problems we face as financial professionals is the fact that many people don't like to talk about their money, much less getting old and sick after they retire. Many are too busy or lazy to learn what they need to know to have the best chance of avoiding potentially devastating financial pitfalls on their way to retirement or after they retire. What we've got is a disturbing trend that is impacting millions of Americans already, and it will impact an exponentially expanding number in the years to come.

As a retirement specialist, I have over the years made it my business to study at great length the core issues that my clients are facing or will face in retirement. I've studied arcane tax laws that affect seniors directly, the minutiae of Social Security, the complexities and incongruities of Medicare, the frequently obscure or counterintuitive options for inflation safeguards, and the constantly changing landscape of products for long-term care protection. To help potential retirees and the retired today means we all need to have a working knowledge of these issues as they relate to retirement, and that's what this book is meant to do. It's meant to give you a foundation to build on as you advise clients from a retirement planning and retirement cash flow management perspective.

One of the core tools at your disposal is something I call a CAMP Score. It's basically a highly sophisticated retirement calculator we at the Retirement Cash Flow Education Group developed to help individuals and financial professionals assess retirement readiness. Visit our website (www.retirementcashflow.com) to log on for a tour of the CAMP Score. I think you'll find it may become an integral part of your business as you work to advise clients about retirement timing, Social Security timing, Medicare, long-term care, taxes, and investments.

In the appendix, you'll find a series of pages complete with tables and comparison charts written and formatted as client primers. They're meant as handouts you can copy and use during discussions with your clients about key retirement considerations and strategies. You can also download the primers at our website (www.retirementcashflow.com).

You'll find lots of other interesting and helpful educational information designed for you and your clients.

If you are a certified financial advisor, a stockbroker, a certified public accountant, a tax attorney, or a professional in insurance sales, you will inevitably be dealing with increasing numbers of individuals whose central financial issue is retirement. It's essential for you to know what mistakes you can avoid (there are many) as you advise these clients, and it's essential for you to know that even clients of limited means need not despair completely. With the right overall financial strategy coupled with an array of products suited for the unique needs of the individual's time horizon, the way forward will be clear for you and your clients.

Retirement in America today is a steep, rocky road for most people. For some, it may not be possible to fully retire at all. Working part-time when you're in your midseventies is fast becoming commonplace. The issues grow more complex every day. As a financial professional, you have the power to change lives for the better. You have the ability to assist clients in their quest for freedom and quality of life during retirement. All it takes is a solid plan based on the best possible information available. That's what you'll find in the pages of this book and on our website!

I

Missteps and Blunders
Common Client Mistakes

> You can be young without money, but you can't be old without it. —Tennessee Williams

AT THE RISK OF sounding arrogant, I have to say that sometimes our clients are their own worst enemies. They mean well, naturally. They want what's best for them and their loved ones. They crave the ability to live life in retirement without financial worries, but they often make mistakes leading up to retirement and in retirement that tilt the odds against them. In a sense, we have to save them from themselves. Just as important, it's essential for us to know which life ring to offer when the financial waters get rough. To do that requires us to look at how we serve our clients in ways that differ greatly from those of the past. We can't stick to what we've always done. We have to look carefully at our own practices to avoid giving advice that can end up hurting the people we are striving to help.

That's easier said than done in many cases. It's human nature to stick to the familiar path that offers the course of least resistance. The familiar is comfortable. It's what we know, and it's also often the cause of real harm when it comes to the formulation of an integrated plan to assist our clients in their efforts to accumulate sufficient wealth to retire.

In the years subsequent to retirement, the familiar emphasis on asset retention without giving due consideration to retirement cash flow is a common misstep.

Likewise, failing to fully include tax considerations in the cash flow package can lead to unpleasant financial consequences. The intricacies of Medicare and long-term care are all part of the puzzle as well. Of course, I'll discuss professional insights in the coming chapters, but let's start out with the typical blunders clients frequently make before and during retirement. If you know the nature of the missteps, you can help your clients avoid stepping on a financial landmine or two.

The most common client blunders

Blunder 1: Retiring too early

The single worst mistake your clients can make is leaving their jobs too early. Typically, your clients are at the peak in terms of earnings toward the end of their careers. That means they can maximize their contributions to qualified retirement vehicles—traditional individual retirement accounts and 401(k) accounts, or they may contribute to Roth IRAs (in lieu of traditional IRA contributions). Contributing to traditional IRAs and 401(k)s eliminates taxes on capital gains and other forms of growth on the investments. Some financial advisors recommend against maximum contributions in favor of reducing debt on home mortgages, which is a bad idea. If you don't recommend that clients make the maximum contributions that they can afford, especially in the end years of their working lives, you're not pushing clients toward an opportunity to truly leverage their assets for long-term cash flow during retirement. Similarly, the Roth IRA is often ignored when it shouldn't be.

When your clients say they want to quit work, they're also likely going to say they want to collect Social Security before reaching full retirement age. That's sixty-six for boomers born before 1960, and it's sixty-seven for boomers and younger people born in 1960 and beyond. Most of us fully understand that is a mistake because it substantially decreases benefits. Retiring at sixty-two instead of sixty-six will cost clients born between 1943 and 1954 a whopping 25 percent of their benefits for life! With life expectancies now firmly trending to the mideighties for men and women, at least according to some insurance company actuarial tables, the long-term cash flow benefits of Social Security represent the most valuable lynchpin in a retirement package for most clients, especially those on the verge of retiring.

Urge your clients to defer Social Security for as long as possible! For example, if they defer until they're seventy, they'll earn an 8 percent bonus per year after age sixty-six for boomers born between 1943 and 1954 on top of the benefits they'd receive at full retirement age. Over time, that really adds up! In later chapters, we'll talk about spousal benefits and bonus deferment benefits if clients put off collecting until age seventy. We'll also talk about paying back Social Security benefits and why that can be a smart move for some people if they do so within twelve months of beginning to collect benefits.

Blunder 2: Retiring with too much debt

It comes as no surprise that most Americans have debt. What does surprise financial professionals is how many people want to retire while they're still carrying debt on homes, boats, cars, and high-interest credit cards. Clients may also have to pay for alimony, the care of an elderly parent, or even college tuition for their kids. Debt should be viewed in arbitrage terms. Is repayment a better after-tax use of assets than making an investment when capital gains are factored into the decision?

Generally speaking, clients should have no debt other than a low-interest mortgage of 5 percent or less. Selling investments to pay off high-interest debt nets a gain far in excess of the returns on most traditional investments today. Yet, some financial professionals advise clients to keep the investments anyway. I've never been able to figure out the logic of that, but life is often quite illogical, so I guess nothing should really surprise me.

The problem may arise from the fact that many clients and some financial advisors focus almost exclusively on capital retention. Keeping the pile of gold intact becomes almost an obsession. Thus, the idea of selling a stock to pay off high-interest debt sounds counterintuitive, as does the idea of securing a low-interest home equity loan to do the same thing. Of course, it isn't! Also counterintuitive is the inclination to prepay the mortgage, but the higher return from leveraging the capital with proper investments is a better use of the assets. Essentially, the entire debt-to-asset ratio comes into play. Few clients really understand how it all works and how debt can seriously reduce total cash flow. It's up to us to explain it all in simple terms the average Joe can understand.

Blunder 3: Failing to prepare for maximized cash flow during retirement

Asset accumulation and retention is often the Holy Grail of clients and financial advisors. However, cash flow is really the key consideration before and after retirement, not asset accumulation and retention. For example, if the client has a pension, that pension has value for cash flow, but a surprising number of clients don't view it as a valuable asset because it's an intangible until they start collecting. Social Security falls into this category as well. Yet, from a cash flow perspective, the one in five Americans who still have some kind of pension are truly in the catbird's seat!

If the client has an annuity, the value of that product is in its ability to deliver cash flow for the client for life, and with life expectancies trending ever upward, the annuity could provide a key leg of the proverbial financial stool. Clients may balk at the notion of sinking $100,000 into an annuity that promises only $5,000, or 5 percent, in returns per year, thinking that it would be better to simply leverage the assets instead. What the client doesn't understand is that the right *variable* annuity can offer a basket of benefits in addition to the 5 percent annual lifetime guaranteed payment.

Financial professionals often under-appreciate the advantages of tax-deferred annuities with living benefits, such as the ability of the client to access payouts for long-term care costs in the event that the client is no longer able to complete two of the six designated activities of daily living. Diversified dividend-paying stocks, short- and midterm bonds, and dividends from alternative investments, such as a real estate investment trust, are other buckets clients can put in place for enhanced retirement cash flow.

Your clients may think they need less cash flow to pay expenses when they retire, but, in my view, they actually need cash flow for 100 percent of their current expenses. Tax savings do provide a part of cash flow after retirement for most clients. Some industry experts say they'll need only about 70 to 80 percent of their current cash flow. I disagree. Retirees need to have positive cash flow with a built-in safety buffer to protect against the inevitable unforeseen bumps in the road and to fight off the erosive impact of creeping inflation.

Although some may say it's self-serving, it's important for you to steer your clients toward investing their money in sound and stable financial instruments. A steady blue-chip stock that pays a reliable 3 to 4 percent dividend is well worth a look, as opposed to taking a flier in the tech or pharmaceutical segments of the market on stocks that go up and down like a yoyo whenever the wind shifts on Wall Street. If your clients aren't invested, they'll never make their money grow beyond the pressures of inflation, even those of ordinary times. We're not living in ordinary circumstances, not since 2008 when the world's economy changed dramatically from what it once was.

Blunder 4: Not making maximum contributions to tax-deferred accounts before retiring

Many clients, especially those nearing retirement, will want to siphon discretionary funds away from contributions to tax-deferred accounts like an IRA or a 401(k) when in fact those years just prior to retirement are important ones for this type of contribution. Some clients and financial professionals may argue that the taxes will have to be paid later anyway, so it makes little sense to defer now because you'll have to pay the piper at some point. However, with the right basket of investments, it's possible to defer the taxes until the bracket is reduced from a client's peak earning years. Drawing down a Roth IRA first is a good example of how clients can put off paying the taxes on qualified retirement accounts for as long as possible. Without you to help them, clients might draw down a traditional IRA before they draw down a Roth IRA. Or, worse, they'll reinvest in a low-interest taxable certificate of deposit while taking distributions from a 401(k). The point is the retiree will need to have maximized all tax-deferred income for as long as possible during the accumulation phase to enable implementation of cash flow strategies that minimize tax liabilities during retirement.

Blunder 5: Ignoring taxes on investments and Social Security before and after retiring

It's very common for clients to put blinders on when it comes to various tax issues, such as income taxed as ordinary versus capital gains. It's also very common for financial professionals to make the false assumption that retirement tax issues parallel tax issues during a working career. They don't. Thus, the tax situation can get out of hand very fast. Tax treatment of investments becomes the second great discriminating factor for the quality of retirement life. Most financial professionals fail to recognize that net cash flow after taxes and protecting net cash flow after taxes are the two most important financial variables in the financial quality of retirement life.

For example, your clients are not likely going to fully understand the taxability issues surrounding their Social Security benefits, and yet protecting those benefits from as much tax as possible is an essential key to bolstering retirement cash flow. Finding ways to keep the modified adjusted gross income levels below the tax threshold through distributions from Roth IRAs, reverse mortgages, and partial or full distributions from fixed or variable annuities with values below their tax cost are highly advantageous for clients. So are home equity loans in some cases, especially in earlier years of retirement when deferment of Social Security benefits, annuity withdrawals, and distributions from tax-deferred accounts can add up to big bucks later.

Blunder 6: Not including long-term care protection in retirement strategies

Long-term care is a very touchy subject for nearly all of us. We detest the idea of living out the last of our days in some hellhole of a nursing home. Incontinence, bedsores, terrible food, physical frailty, Alzheimer's disease, lack of mobility, it all comes together to create a depressing nightmare of old age that's easier to ignore than face head on. Your clients are very likely to scurry away from a discussion about long-term care protection, and it will be up to you to gently steer them to some of the stark realities they need to take into account as they plan for their retirement.

According to the American Association of Long-Term Care Insurance, in the next twenty-five years or so the number of seniors with disabilities, many of which will make them candidates for long-term care, is projected to double, impacting about twenty-one million of us. One out of four retirees will likely require some form of long-term care during their retirement years, and that's a conservative estimate. Other sources put the figure at closer to 70 percent of all retirees over the age of sixty-five. Rest assured, though, when you bring up the subject of long-term care, your clients are likely going to say they don't need protection.

Tell them to guess again! Unexpected long-term care costs are the leading cause of poverty among senior citizens who were otherwise able to make ends meet. Long-term care in a skilled-nursing setting, like a nursing home, averages a little over $72,000 per year, says the US Department of Health and Human Services. The numbers from the 2012 Genworth Cost of Care Survey puts the figure at $81,030. In metropolitan areas, the costs can soar to the low six figures without batting an eye. Millionaires on my client list would be hard pressed to keep up with these costs for any length of time. Sadly, long-term care lasts a year or two in most cases, and sometimes the patient lingers on far longer than that. In short, individuals can't afford to pay the costs, and many can't afford to pay the costs for protection either.

We'll take a close look at the various options available today, including traditional long-term care insurance and annuities and universal life insurance that build long-term protection into the package, usually for an extra fee. Even partial coverage is better than no coverage at all. As noted, the sad truth of the matter is that fewer than 9 percent of seniors over the age of sixty-five have any sort of long-term care coverage. Premiums for traditional long-term care insurance are soaring, sometimes in excess of 40 percent per year or more.

What's more, many clients refuse to request CPAs to issue a W-2 Form to those whom we're paying for at-home long-term care, thereby eliminating any potential tax breaks they're entitled to along the way. There are also tax breaks for kids footing the bill for parental care, if certain criteria are met. The long-term care issue can't be ignored, but it's going to be one of the toughest nuts to crack for you as a financial professional as you pursue an integrated plan for your clients during the accumulation and distribution phases of their financial lives.

Blunder 7: Playing cheapskate with Medicare supplemental insurance coverage

For clients operating with very limited retirement cash flow, the idea of shelling out close to $5,000 per year for supplemental Medicare and other health coverage really presses a hot button. Clients get angry. They wring their hands and say they can't afford, say, Part D in Medicare to help offset the expenses for prescription drugs. They'll typically go for the cheapest options, namely Medicare Advantage plans, falsely thinking they don't need more than the minimum.

Of course, they're wrong about that! Unexpected increases in health care costs not covered with some form of insurance, including Medicare, represent a financial danger to clients, second only to the ruinous costs of unexpected and unplanned for long-term care. The present state of Medicare and the options open to your clients are complicated even for financial professionals. Imagine what it's like for your clients. They're going to become confused, frustrated, and frequently annoyed about the entire issue. In spite of this, encourage them to make the effort to do all their homework *before* enrollment time approaches, and to include in the cash flow equation payments for the best possible health care coverage that they can afford. Medicare Supplement plans represent a huge bargain that retirees should buy unless they are financially destitute and forced to rely on Medicaid.

Blunder 8: Falling prey to inevitable inflation

As financial professionals with a passion for economics, we all know that the basics of financial markets always—and I mean always—include inflation in the equation. No matter what goes on, the dollar of today won't have the same purchasing power as the dollar of thirty years hence. While your clients would agree with you, they're much less likely to actually take your advice and plan for inflation as they work with you on their retirement grand plan. It's your job to point out the weakness in a long-term strategy that fails to include inflation pressures that will slowly but surely creep up over time.

So, the question is, what can truly safeguard against inflation? The answer is actually a bit depressing. There's not a lot out there that can guard your clients from the stealthy wolf at the door. Certain annuities do have built-in guaranteed increases in income that guard against inflation. The cost of the product is higher, but it is well worth the money. Some traditional long-term care insurance policies offer an inflation rider. Most government pensions have cost-of-living increases, whereas many corporate pensions do not. Of course, Social Security increases a small amount, if at all, based on rises in inflation. As we all know, in this low-interest-rate environment, the cost of living adjustments in Social Security benefits do not happen every year.

Based on reality, most of your clients will need to factor inflation into the actual rate of return they're expecting from investments, even if the clients are still working. So, if clients have a cash flow based in part on a 5 percent return on, say, dividend-paying stocks or an annuity without guaranteed income increases, then in the long-term we've got to deduct from 1 to 3 percent from that return per year to account for inflation. I assure you, when (not if) you bring this up, your clients will not be pleased. Yet, the sad truth of the matter really is that a dollar today will buy more than a dollar thirty years from now. Don't ignore inflation. It's the silent killer, just like high blood pressure!

Blunder 9: Failure to account for sequencing risk and drawing down the wrong way

Sequencing risk is often overlooked, but it's important, as in what to draw down first during the distribution phase. Corresponding rises and falls in the market truly do have a serious impact on the financial health of a recent retiree. We'll get into much more detail later, but suffice it to say here that if your clients get hosed in the markets during their early years of retirement, like so many Americans of late, they're going to lose vast amounts of principal that could have otherwise generated some cash flow. If they are forced to draw down principal when the markets are low, the problem becomes even worse. Once the principal is gone or drastically reduced, it's almost impossible for a retiree to make up those losses. Their time horizon is basically gone, as is their earning power.

While I strongly argue against an overemphasis on asset accumulation and retention during retirement at the expense of exploiting all assets to maximize cash flow, I do equally emphasize the essential strategy of balancing sequence risk whenever possible. Thus, moving capital from risky stocks or bond funds in the few years before retirement makes sense if you can stagger the sequencing risk in doing so. For example, if an annuity is in the offing, that would reduce potential losses in a market downturn because of built-in guarantees within the contract. Investment in a nontraded real estate investment trust could also mitigate risk, though such investments bring inherent risks of their own. Simply moving from high-yield corporate bonds to tamer bonds could provide still more mitigating coverage in the event of a bear charging into the marketplace.

If retirees get hammered early, they're likely going to have to go back to work. If the retiree has a cash flow strategy that's not solely contingent on the traditional stock or bond allocations in taxable and qualified accounts, there is a possibility of reducing sequencing risk that could decimate retirees before they get out of the starting gate.

The other serious issues are when to draw down from the asset pool and what to draw down first. Naturally, we all know that the magic number for mandatory distribution requirements is 70.5 years of age. That's when that pesky taxman comes calling on a portion of all that tax-deferred income every year thereafter. Chances are, especially today, your clients will have been drawing down from those accounts before reaching that magical tax age, but if it is at all possible for them to do so, clients should put off taking any money from tax-deferred accounts before they're actually forced to take it. That means having other financial instruments in place, like annuities, income from REITs, wages, and qualifying dividends. These can help beat the taxman at his own game. You and your clients will never win a contest against Uncle Sam, but prolonging the plundering of tax-deferred accounts is a wise bet in nearly every scenario. The Roth IRA is a fabulous weapon to use as your clients bide their time until they're absolutely forced to begin drawing down their tax-deferred accounts.

Blunder 10: Ignoring your superb advice

Sometimes you can lead a horse to water, but you can't make it drink. We've all been there! You can talk until you're blue in the face, and certain clients won't pay any attention. These individuals either think they know it all already, or they're angry and full of despair because deep in their hearts they know they should be saving but aren't. They know they can't retire, but they're likely to do it anyway.

When you're ignored, don't get mad. Be gentle. Remind clients that the buck stops with them in terms of their financial lives. Let them know that you are well aware of how prickly some get when it comes to money, or the lack thereof, and that you're only looking out for their interests. Financial professionals get up close and personal with clients, so you're bound to experience some blowback now and then. If this happens, and it surely will, try to determine the cause of the hostility, and then try to fix it. More often, you'll have no clue about what went wrong, and the client won't tell you even after you've given them every chance.

Ours is a field of mathematical predictabilities. We understand how the universe breaks down into a complex tapestry of arithmetically perfect formulas, and so playing the role of the head shrink makes us feel uncomfortable. I'm not saying you need to wear that hat all the time. I'm just saying that the role you've chosen is one that requires a balancing act between the cool, cold facts of math and the warm, fuzzy, and frequently insane works of human emotions.

Parting words: We may be in the numbers business, but when the rubber meets the road, we're truly in the people business even more. The going can get tough and messy at times because we're dealing with the very essence of identity and self-worth on the part of those who come to us for guidance. Understand that it's all about psychology and that you'll need to come to grips with that as you seek your own new take on the old way of looking at retirement in America. It's not all about assets. No, it's about retirement cash flow! It's about how to build it when the client is deep into the accumulation stage and how to maximize net cash flow after taxes once that client punches the clock for the last time. It's about you, essentially! You have the power to change lives, if the horse will only take a sip of the sweet water under its nose.

2

Screaming from the Room Retirement Timing

The best time to think about retirement is before the boss does.
—Anonymous

THE SCENE IS ALL too familiar. A dapper couple in their midfifties sits in my office, their eyes gleaming with anticipation. I've worked with them for years, and I know what's coming. I can just sense it.

"Well," Jack says as he leans back in his chair and shoots me a big, toothy smile, "Jill and I are ready to call it quits at work. We've got our eye on a really nice condo in Tampa. It's just a short drive to the golf course and the marina. It's everything we've worked for! *We can't wait!*"

I ask, "Calling it quits? You mean you're saying you want to retire? *Both* of you plan to retire?"

"That's right!" Jill says. "We've had it with the rat race. We've just had it. Life isn't about work. Life is about living!"

I inwardly cringe. I've heard it all a thousand times. I look them both in the eye and tell them to hold their horses. They look disappointed, even a bit angry.

"What do you mean 'hold your horses'?" Jack asks. "I don't want a horse! I want a Sea Ray!"

Oh, boy! I think. *Here we go again!*

Sound familiar? I bet it does! Let's face it. Many people hate their jobs, or barely tolerate the work and their bosses. Work is something people do to pay the light bill. If they didn't have to work to get money, most people wouldn't punch in at eight o'clock and stalk off to the factory floor or the cube farm. They'd kick back and do what they've dreamed of doing all their lives, whatever that might be. It most assuredly wouldn't be work, at least not for the vast majority of people.

If you're in love with numbers as much as I am, you probably love your job. You've also got to like or even love people, even when they're a pain in the neck. But if you're doing what you're doing, I'll roll the dice and say you love it! Sure, some things about your work might bother you, but by and large, don't you count yourself lucky?

Whenever a couple like Jack and Jill spring the news that they're ready to retire too soon, I try to see the world through their eyes. Jack's the typical nice guy who just wants to chuck it all and go tooling around the bay in his powerboat with his pretty wife, and maybe even bring the grandkids along for the ride sometimes. He and she want to play couples golf and then enjoy a tasty dinner at the country club. It broke my heart, but I had to make the exceedingly unwelcome pronouncement that Jack and Jill weren't going up the hill to the nineteenth hole for a long, long time. They simply could not afford to retire yet.

Retiring too early can devastate lives

The desire to retire is bound to top the hit parade of client interest. You'll get tremendous pressure from clients to find a way to make it possible for them to leave their jobs, collect Social Security at age sixty-two, and cash out tax-deferred accounts in the first years of retirement. You're not your client's keeper in the truest sense of the word, but you do have a responsibility to steer them away from making mistakes that could ruin the rest of their lives. Retiring without sufficient cash flow is a recipe for disaster, and yet a surprising number of people take the plunge without giving cash flow enough thought. They tell themselves that they'll reduce expenses to make up for shortfalls, usually a very serious mistake because the expense reductions almost never happen. In fact, health care issues often ratchet up expenses beyond what retirees experienced when they were working.

Financial professionals often miss the boat as well. They focus on asset retention and liquidity when cash flow is really the most important consideration. If you tie up funds in a nontraded real estate investment trust for a few years that delivers returns of 6 or 7 percent in dividends that are then reinvested at a discount, I'd argue that the cash flow is more important than maintaining the liquidity of the sum invested.

In addition, as you counsel clients on everything they need to consider before they actually retire, you're bound to get lots of frustrated and confused looks when you tell clients that their health care isn't fully covered under Medicare. Yes, most intelligent people know that, but most won't have done the numbers and will be shocked when you tell them that Medicare Supplement insurance packages providing the most comprehensive coverage can cost more than $800 per month for a couple when that number includes deductibles, co-pays, and other health-related costs. That's a lot given that combined annual Social Security payments for a couple that took benefits at full retirement age amount to an average of $22,000.

The Social Security Administration estimates that Social Security covers only about 40 percent of the total amount needed to live comfortably during retirement, and health care is a big money siphon. It's likely to be even more so in coming years. Then when you mention the looming prospect of long-term care in a nursing home and just how expensive that can be, well, let's just say many clients would rather have a root canal than talk about that!

Clients will see the upside of the retirement lifestyle—golf, tennis, canasta, wine tasting, travel, time for hobbies, whatever pushes their pleasure buttons. Clients won't see the downside of the retirement lifestyle—diminishing assets and cash flow, increasing health care expenses, erosion of buying power due to inflation, physical and mental frailty, the death of spouses and close friends, and the inevitable realization that their own football game of life is in the fourth quarter. That's why you'll need to handle clients like Jack and Jill with tender, loving care, but always with the view toward providing them with the realistic advice they need to make educated decisions about their financial lives.

The retiree's quality of retirement life is frequently influenced by the client's attitude toward the process. Retirees who refuse to study retirement issues and adapt to required changes in their thought process may experience unnecessary retirement problems. Retirees find it difficult to grow their cash flow. They need to know that future cash flows will outpace future cash outflows! It's the outpacing cash flow against outflow that truly matters. It means the difference between a comfortable retirement and one rife with misery and stress.

A classic retiree mistake is deciding to retire when they want to retiree—as opposed to when they can afford to retire. Retirement should begin only after most retirement variables have been explored and any medical and/or cash flow exposures have been addressed. Quitting one's job should only occur once steps have been taken to ensure an appropriate margin of safety. Projected monthly retirement cash inflows should exceed retirement cash expenses unless the retiree or retirees (a couple) are willing and able to consume capital (principal).

Human capital should not be squandered

Human capital remains a greatly under-appreciated critical value. Choosing when to retire frequently affects retirement quality for twenty or more years. Spouses, loved ones, and even friends may also suffer or benefit from the decision. "Human capital" may be viewed as the discounted cash flow from a worker's efforts. A high percentage of people earn their highest wage or income just prior to retirement. Therefore, retiring too early may not be a reversible decision if the retiree discovers too late that their retirement cash flows do not allow them to enjoy their desired retirement standard of living.

Many athletes and business executives attempt comebacks every year. These persons discovered they did not want to or couldn't afford to give up their high compensation. A few return to former glories and former income, but many do not. I believe the average Jack or Jill may risk more "retiring early" than the high-powered athlete or executive. Many years ago, I advised two married, highly successful real estate agents not to retire in their very early fifties. They were in a situation quite similar to Jack and Jill's. They chose retirement to the mountain paradise of their dreams. Unfortunately, my fears were well placed. Within a few years, they realized they couldn't afford retirement and attempted to return to their previous world. They divorced (many fights over finances), and each returned to work, but both struggled to resurrect the success they had previously enjoyed.

Although clients don't want to hear it, they probably should defer retirement for as long as possible. Doing so will enable them to take full advantage of their human capital, maximize contributions to tax-deferred retirement accounts, build their payments into Social Security, obtain full benefits from Social Security by waiting to reach at least full retirement age before collecting, and put in place the appropriate basket of investments that promise cash flow during retirement years. Variable annuities and dividend-paying stocks are among two of the many options your clients may choose.

Even after retiring, seniors frequently must work part-time, a simple reality of the currently harsh economic climate. As you evaluate cash flow for potential retirees, factor in part-time work if the clients say they intend to stay in the labor force on a limited basis. However, plug that cash flow into the margin of safety, not the essential cash flow stream. Health problems and job loss can easily wipe out cash flow from part-time work.

Important point: Despite the risks of health problems or job loss, sustained part-time work can allow clients to retire with fewer assets because the added cash flow will make up for the deficiency. Continuing to work part-time can also help clients grow assets, as opposed to spending them down. Your clients may envision themselves in a part-time job that smacks of the odious, like a greeter in a big-box chain store. Not all part-time work is at the minimum wage. Some part-time work can actually be quite rewarding.

Make sure to point out the concept of marginal income when it comes to part-time work during retirement. For example, a person earning $1,000 per month who gets a 10 percent raise has $100 of marginal income. If this person does not raise his or her spending level, that $100 becomes savings. Thus, marginal income from a second job or working during retirement can have a powerful effect on the quality of retirement life.

Retirement cash flow is king

As you counsel clients, bear in mind that they are very likely to have a skewed view of cash-flow vehicles. In short, they won't see the inherent value in them, whereas they will see the perceived value of a stock or a bond because it has a clearly established sum attached to it in terms of principal and returns from dividends. When evaluating whether clients can afford to retire, make sure to point out that there are many cash flows that potential retirees may enjoy that are incorrectly viewed as having no investment value. Included in this category are:

1. Human capital (income from working full- or part-time)
2. Social Security

3. Corporate pensions

4. Government pensions

Social Security may provide cash flow to retirees, their spouse, their surviving spouse, their former spouse, their children, and occasionally even to surviving parents. Frequently, little or no value is attached to Social Security because it does not have a lump sum option. The monthly benefit is increased annually *if* the cost of living increases. Economists describe the increase as maintaining purchasing power. Note that a constant cash flow from interest on certificates of deposit and/or bonds loses purchasing power when inflation exists, and yet clients often think these are more valuable than a pension!

Those fortunate retirees with substantial retirement cash flows generally experience the best quality of retirement life. Cash flow—*not* assets—should be viewed as the central premise (variable) for planning retirement, and this is where the traditional thinking among financial professionals runs right off the tracks. We simply have not been taught to think in a new way. We have not been shown why a fixation on assets versus cash flow is just awful for our clients. You can have a plot of land worth $20 million, but if you can't generate income from that land, what good is it?

Sufficient cash flow allows retirees to:

1. Meet physiological (food, shelter, and health care) needs

2. Buy Medicare Part D drug coverage and Medicare Supplement insurance OR elect an appropriate Medicare Advantage Plan

3. Interact socially with friends and family

Protecting against adverse cash flow expenses may be more important than producing cash flow income. That's saying a lot! Let me repeat. Guarding against health care calamities is as important—or more important—than a focus on cash flow! Drop the ball in the health care liability arena, and it's usually game over. Medicare and long-term care protection (not necessarily insurance) should be considered *essential* to a good retirement plan. Failure to protect against these risks endangers *quality of life* for the retiree and those close to the retiree.

Estimating future cash inflows and outflows is both complex and worrisome. I typically inflate client expense projections and deflate their income projections. *I want the surprises to be positive not negative*, which is why I build in a margin of safety into anticipated cash flow needs. Building a margin of safety into retirement projections hopefully enables clients to enjoy retirement because their physiological needs are met *and* they feel able to pursue growth needs because their cash flow needs have been met. Developing new interests and/or pursuing old interests should be one of the joys of retirement.

Inflation is a major retirement consideration

Maintaining purchasing power becomes a critical goal in successfully planning a Quality Retirement. Purchasing power risk can be minimal during low inflation periods, especially over a short time frame, but over an extended time (retirement is an extended time) it is one of the most important investment risks.

Obviously, with life expectancies for men and women reaching age sixty-five now well into the mideighties (the official life expectancy number from the Centers for Disease Control and Prevention for men and women is seventy-eight), people are spending twenty years or more in retirement. Projecting cash flow meeting or exceeding cash expenses should always contemplate potential risks of an inflationary future. Note that projections reflecting a surplus cash flow provide a margin of safety against both inflation and underestimation of retirement expenses. Inflation can easily erode a retiree's quality of life. Investments and distribution choices should take care to build in either purchasing power increases or a margin of safety sufficient to meet inflationary pressures. As noted, future cash flow increases must outpace future cash flow needs.

Take a look at the following table. As you see, some cash flow vehicles provide the possibility that cash flow can increase over time to keep pace with inflation, and others don't.

Table 1

Type of vehicle	Potential for increasing cash flow
Social Security	Yes
Stocks	Yes
Corporate bonds	No
Treasury bonds	No
Treasury inflation protected bonds	Yes
Federal pensions	Yes
State pensions	Maybe
Local pensions	No
Stock mutual funds	Yes
Bond mutual funds	Maybe
Fixed annuities	No
Variable annuities	Yes
Nontraded REITs	Yes

Savvy retirement advisors recognize that seniors, loved ones, some advisors, and government/industry regulators place too much emphasis upon liquidity and not enough on cash flow considerations. I always try to carefully plan and explain cash flow sources and cash flow expenditures to clients like Jack and Jill.

Evaluating client retirement readiness

Retirement readiness is very difficult to measure both at retirement and during the course of a long retirement. There are all kinds of variables that typically slip through the cracks when thinking of retirement in a traditional way. The new approach I am arguing for incorporates the entire gamut of issues—projected cash flow from various sources and cash outflow, Social Security, Medicare, and long-term care. Within these main sections are subsets of related issues. They all impact each other and your clients in differing ways, but the most common element among them all is the potential impact on positive or negative cash flow during retirement.

For years, I struggled with the biggest issues that would influence the quality of life of my clients during retirement. Eventually, I came up with a formula, or a set of criteria, to use as I evaluated whether clients were ready to retire or not. Most investment advisors say a person needs to have cash flow in retirement that equals between 70 and 80 percent of income earned while working. That's a big-picture general statement and doesn't always reflect the unique situation of many clients. I wanted to drill down even further to determine precisely how ready a client really was for retirement. For example, if a potential retiree was a low wage earner, the lack of accumulated assets could mean the individual wasn't retirement ready even if enough cash flow was available to cover 80 percent of the income earned while working.

Thus, I approached the question of how much cash flow my clients need based on what I call a CAMP Score. It's a bit like a credit report on a client's retirement readiness that takes into account the four biggest issues that positively or negatively impact the quality of life for retirees. Monthly income, medical expenses, funds for emergencies, and contingencies for long-term care all rank at the top of the list of client concerns.

CAMP Score

C = Cash flow
A = Aging

M = Medical expenses
P = Purchasing power

Cash flow: Retirement cash flow is measured as a percentage of preretirement cash flow. If your client needs cash flow of $5,000 per month to meet expenses while working, and retirement cash flow is projected to equal $4,500 with medical coverage, long-term care protection, and purchasing power increases, then the CAMP Score is only 90. The client would need to match working cash flow and cover aging, medical, and purchasing power concerns (what's brought in now to meet expenses while working) to get a CAMP Score of 100. If the client doesn't score 100, then the individual can't afford to retire with enough of a financial safety margin.

In fact, a CAMP Score of 90 percent means the client is in considerable risk of financial duress in terms of long periods of high inflation, rising health care costs, and an event that triggers the necessity of long-term care. And just forget about the cruise to Alaska. That's just not going to happen for your clients without sufficient cash flow during retirement!

Important point: A minimally prepared (no margin of safety) retiree has a CAMP Score of approximately 100. Ideally, none of your clients should retire without a CAMP Score of 100 percent or more.

Aging: With life expectancies on the rise, retirees can expect to live twenty years or more in retirement. This means that expenses for in-home care, assisted living, or even long-term skilled-nursing care are more than likely. When evaluating the retirement readiness of your clients, factoring in whether any type of long-term care insurance or other coverage is in place becomes vital. How much is the coverage worth? The average nursing home runs more than $72,000 per year, and often twice that in major metropolitan locales. If no such protection is currently in place, the costs of getting and maintaining that coverage must be figured into overall cash outflow balanced against cash inflow.

Fixed or variable annuities and/or life insurance with long-term care riders are an option that we'll discuss later, but those can be expensive and out of reach for many Americans. By far the majority of care needs are considered personal and not urgent, meaning most retirees are going to need to pay for assistance in meal preparation, dressing, grooming, toileting, and so on as categorized in the six activities of daily living that factor into the dispensation of benefits and the approval of tax deductions for service when a doctor certifies that the retiree is unable to execute two or more of the activities of daily living (ADLs). The costs for prolonged long-term care among seniors with no form of protection are the leading cause of poverty among the retired. It is your absolute duty as a financial professional to counsel your clients about the dangers of ignoring the long-term care monster in the closet.

Protection generally is long-term care insurance or urgent care riders in life insurance or annuities that guard against increased need for personal care during retirement. Personal care is not medical care for health insurance or Medicare purposes but is defined as medical care for tax purposes if the retiree requires at least standby assistance with two or more of the ADLs. Service providers must be issued a W-2 for tax purposes for both parties, but that's a discussion for later.

Medical: Linked with long-term care are the routine expenses associated with health care. Prescriptions, co-pays, deductibles, premiums, and other costs all must be considered. As noted, Medicare doesn't cover everything, so the cash flow every month must be enough for clients to buy the very best supplemental Medicare insurance coverage they can afford. While there are regional differences for medical costs, Medicare with Part D (drug) coverage, and Medicare Supplement Type F coverage, total monthly costs, including Medicare Part B, typically run between $300 and $400 per month for an individual. Skimping on the supplemental insurance coverage to augment Medicare is a huge mistake many retirees make, exposing them to potential medical fees that could prove disastrous if one or both spouses get really sick.

Purchasing power: As I've said, protecting purchasing power against inflation is an essential consideration in determining whether clients are ready for retirement. If only the Social Security benefits are protected through the cost-of-living adjustment that becomes automatic if inflation rises, then the other sources of cash flow are vulnerable to decreasing purchasing power over time. The creeping, erosive force of inflation can hurt retirees. For example, most corporate pensions do not include an inflationary pension increase. Thus, $3,000 per month at age sixty-six may look great, but at age eighty-six, this same $3,000 per month doesn't look as good. Building in cash flow sources that account for inflation is very important. Most agree that accounting for 2 to 3 percent rates of annual inflation is an acceptable safeguard against the erosion of purchasing power. If you get creative, you can help your clients increase cash flow to hedge against inflationary pressures, but you have to put inflation high on your list of priorities.

Visit my website to calculate your clients' CAMP Scores: As noted earlier, I've put together an easy-to-use CAMP Score calculator on my website (www.retirementcashflow.com). All you have to do is input the key client information, and the calculator will come up with retirement readiness scores for your clients! The CAMP Score calculator is an impeccable retirement readiness barometer, and it's the most comprehensive tool of its sort available on the Internet. I encourage you to take a look!

Client debt delays retirement

If your clients are carrying high-cost debt, it's best to counsel them to pay it off prior to moving forward with retirement plans. It's shocking how many clients retire with debts of all kinds. When they do that, they start off at a distinct disadvantage. They add to cash outflow that detracts from their overall CAMP Score. Those approaching retirement while carrying high-cost debt reduce or totally eliminate their ability to fully fund tax-deferred IRA or 401(k) accounts. Nor can they contribute the maximum amount to a Roth IRA to build a tax-free source of cash flow for use in advance of drawing down assets that trigger tax liabilities.

Credit card debt is a great example of what clients should pay off first, though car and boat loans are another cash outflow to carefully look at as well. I cited these numbers earlier, but they bear repeating. The American Association of Retired People found that workers over age fifty carry an average of $8,278 in credit card debt! The money paid in interest to service the debt will almost always exceed the return on most sensible investments. So, carrying the debt and investing costs money because more is paid in interest than the investment can earn. This is particularly true if your client's investment is subject to capital gains taxes or adds to ordinary income, which is taxed at the federal level and in most states at the state level. Rental income is a good example of investment returns that are taxed as ordinary income. Stocks and mutual funds are taxed as capital gains. It's important to take a few minutes to explain this to clients because the tax liabilities truly do matter.

Low-cost debt, like a mortgage, is a different case, at least in these days of historically low mortgage-interest rates. At present, a portion of mortgage interest is deductible from federal income taxes, lowering the actual percentage of out-of-pocket expenses to service the mortgage loan. In other words, mortgage debt is usually pretty cheap. It's not as difficult to find investment vehicles that will provide a better return on invested money than servicing the mortgage loan. If the investment is in a 401(k) or other tax-deferred retirement account, the client's contribution is deductible from federal income taxes as well! That makes it a no-brainer. Advise your client to invest the money instead of paying off low-cost mortgage debt prior to retirement. Indeed, tell your client to sink as much cash as possible into tax-deferred retirement accounts, including after-tax Roth IRAs.

Example: A 4 percent per year mortgage rate is approximately 2.8 percent net of tax in most states. Assume the investment is in a tax-deferred corporate or individual retirement plan that is deductible. If the annual earning rate on the investment is a modest 5 percent per month, the tax-deferred investment comes out as a big winner!

Let's take a deeper look at retirement readiness debt issues. We've all heard of the power of compounding interest, but defining how it works for and against your clients is well worth the effort. Keeping basic economic tenets at the forefront of sound retirement planning solutions goes a long way to preserving and growing retirement assets and cash flow for your clients.

Compounding interest works for and against your clients

Credit card debt typically runs anywhere from 1 percent per month to 2.5 percent per month. Even the lowest monthly credit card rate compounds to over 12.6 percent per year. The calculations below illustrate compounding at 1 percent per month on a debt of $1,000.

Table 2

Month	Beginning Principal ($)	Interest ($)	Ending Principal ($)	Compound Annual Rate
0			1000.00	
1	1000.00	10.00	1010.00	
2	1010.00	10.10	1020.10	
3	1020.10	10.20	1030.30	
4	1030.30	10.30	1040.60	
5	1040.60	10.41	1051.01	
6	1051.01	10.51	1061.52	
7	1061.52	10.62	1072.14	
8	1072.14	10.72	1082.86	
9	1082.86	10.83	1093.69	
10	1093.69	10.94	1104.62	
11	1104.62	11.05	1115.67	
12	1115.67	11.16	1126.83	**12.68%**

Take a look at the twelfth month. Notice that the client now owes $115.67 on the original debt from a year back. Most folks do shortcut math without calculating compounding interest on debt. They say, "Well, 1 percent of $1,000 is $10." What they forget is that it's $10 for the first month and that it keeps going up from there! Even the best of investments don't earn 12.68 percent per year net of tax over the long run. It is absolutely critical to get rid of high-cost debt when planning retirement solutions.

Important point: If the cost of a debt is more expensive than the rate than can be earned on an investment, then paying off the debt is the preferred investment!

Taxes are another key consideration when assessing retirement readiness issues related to paying off debt or choosing to invest the money instead. The taxation of most investments is either ordinary income (currently federal tax rates of up to 39.6 percent) or capital gains (currently federal rates up to 23.8 percent). So, that means if the client invests and gets taxed on the return of that investment, the tax liability should be factored into the decision-making process regarding whether or not the debt should be paid off. Notice that a fixation on asset retention can lead clients to cling to investments that would be better to liquidate to pay off high-cost debt before or during retirement.

Let's assume an investment earns the same 1 percent per month that the client would pay on the credit card debt. The 1 percent per month return on the investment will result in a capital gains tax equal to 15 percent, the most common rate and tax on investments. Check out the calculation below in table 3.

Table 3

Month	Beginning Principal ($)	Interest ($)	Ending Principal ($)	Compound Annual Rate
0			1000.00	

1	1000.00	10.00	1010.00	
2	1010.00	10.10	1020.10	
3	1020.10	10.20	1030.30	
4	1030.30	10.30	1040.60	
5	1040.60	10.41	1051.01	
6	1051.01	10.51	1061.52	
7	1061.52	10.62	1072.14	
8	1072.14	10.72	1082.86	
9	1082.86	10.83	1093.69	
10	1093.69	10.94	1104.62	
11	1104.62	11.05	1115.67	
12	1115.67	11.16	1126.83	**12.68%**
		Net of Tax	1095.12	**9.51%**

Note that I have ignored state income taxes. Approximately 80 percent of states tax interest earned. Retirement of debt would compare even more favorably with investments if state income taxes apply. If the state tax is 5 percent net additional cost, then the net of tax interest return is only 8.88 percent.

Clearly, ignoring taxes is a huge mistake. The investor return from paying off a 1 percent per month credit card adds 12.68 percent to the investor's bottom line per year. By contrast, earning 1 percent per month by lending money only nets 8.88 percent to the investor's bottom line per year. Assuming the same 25 percent federal tax rate and an additional 5 percent per year state tax, the investor would have to earn a gross 18.11 percent per year since they would only net 70 percent of this return after taxes.

Some financial professionals don't give better advice when it comes to assessing what to do with debt as clients approach retirement, in part because their personal compensation is affected. I have had financial advisors literally scream at me because I advised their client to sell an investment earning 6 percent before tax (4.2 percent net of tax assuming

30 percent taxes) to pay-off 18 percent nondeductible credit card debt. The client selling a $10,000 investment to pay off $10,000 of credit card debt saves 13.8 percent or $1,380 per year (18.0 percent minus 4.2 percent)! Note that it takes a little over four years to even make one year of credit card payments (four times 4.2 percent is 16.8 percent)! Wouldn't clients be better served if every financial advisor used the principle of comparative advantage in giving clients financial advice? I think so, and I suspect you do as well.

Parting words: You're going to get pressured to green light the retirement of many clients that simply are not in a financial position to quit their jobs and live the so-called good life. The reality of America these days is that pensions are like anemic dinosaurs, and retirement savings rates thrash in the tank, and yet people can't wait to bolt from their jobs because they're typically underpaid and under appreciated. Add to the equation that grabbing Social Security early robs clients even more, and they're not fully aware of the very real financial gaps in the Medicare program that they'll have to pay for over the course of twenty years or more just to get adequate coverage.

In short, the social fabric of the times is tattered in terms of retirement security. In fact, we're seriously roaming into the realm of the *Emperor's New Clothes*, and it isn't pretty. As a financial professional, you understand the way it is, and you're going to have to push back gently as you quietly and intelligently inform your clients about the true reality of their unique financial landscape. You're just going to have to tell them like it is.

The good news is the automated CAMP Score calculator can help determine whether your clients are retirement ready or not. From there you can work out what can be done to bring the CAMP Score up to 100 percent or more if there is a shortfall. Typically, the lack of a cash flow margin of safety, inadequate funds for comprehensive Medicare supplemental insurance, and nonexistent provisions for long-term care represent the core reasons for CAMP Scores falling below 100 percent.

If your clients are weak in these areas, retirement may not be an option at the moment.

Naturally, part of the CAMP Score process also entails taking a hard look at the debts your clients are carrying. In fact, debt-to-earnings ratios are among the first areas of discussion I have with new clients. Taking out a low-cost home equity loan or cashing in an investment to pay off debts prior to retirement will improve the retirement readiness CAMP Score. The bottom line is people want to retire, but many never will be able to. Many others will want to scamper away from the workplace too soon without taking cash flow, routine health care, and long-term care into consideration. In today's stark economic landscape, it's important to make sure your clients are truly up to speed on the precise benefits and liabilities they face when they decide to retire. If they're truly not ready from a cash flow point of view, then they should keep working.

3

The Taxman Never Retires
Taxes and Retirees

In this world, nothing is sure but death and taxes. —Benjamin Franklin

It's tempting to continue our in-depth discussion about retirement planning and cash flow management in a highly traditional way. First, we'd look at what clients should do during the accumulation stage of their financial lives to maximize wealth through the acquisition of various types of assets, chiefly stocks, bonds, and mutual funds allocated in tax-deferred and taxable accounts. After all, we can't help people if they don't have any money. A lack of financial wherewithal robs our clients of choices, leaving them swinging in the fickle winds of the markets and vulnerable to the calamitous life events they're likely to face in retirement due to health care issues, both the routine costs and the bugaboo of long-term care that can and does hurtle otherwise financially secure retirees into the abyss of poverty.

But the key to effective counseling for retirees lies in a new way of thinking about all the interrelated issues. It's not enough for you as a financial advisor to pick hot stocks and urge diversification of portfolios, though that admittedly is pretty sexy for you as a person who loves numbers and the inner workings of financial markets. It's not enough for you as a certified public accountant to input data from clients into your tax software and remain content with a cookie-cut result. In fact, it's the one-size-fits-all approach that often gets clients into trouble when it comes to retirement planning and cash flow management.

Many investment advisors and other financial professionals emphasize the need to have a multitude of investment baskets or buckets during the accumulation phase prior to retirement. Unfortunately, most if not nearly all these same financial professionals fail to recognize the dramatic difference these buckets can play in providing cash flow for retirement in an efficient manner. Theorists suggest that two investment managers with the same investment style and the same investment period will get remarkably similar results. Financial professionals often use this research as a crutch to defend their one-size-fits-all approach for their clients. Implicit in their approach is that sequence of returns and taxes play little role in investment decisions during accumulation and distribution phases.

Nothing could be more incorrect! Sequence of returns, strategies for drawing down assets to maximize cash flow as opposed to retaining assets, proper funding of Medicare Supplement plans, life insurance, long-term care protection, and inflation and tax safeguards are all equally important. By virtue of the unique nature of each individual's financial landscape, all of your work will be akin to a dressmaker fitting a beautiful wedding gown for a radiant bride-to-be. You can't give the bride an off-the-rack gown from a discount store if she is to truly look her best as she walks down the aisle. The same goes for a tailor. The man in the fine suit looks best when the suit really fits. Likewise, you can't ignore all the working parts of the retirement machine in favor of the ones that turn you on, or the ones that you're most familiar with.

Thus, we need to start out in seemingly an upside-down manner, one that faces the taxman head on first. If we don't have a clear idea of how taxes impact retirees, we can't help them navigate the baffling tax code during the distribution phase. We can't help them buy the right investment vehicles while they're still working that will mitigate tax liabilities and enhance cash flow later. Congress has been making noise about reforming the federal tax code for decades. If it does, I'm all for it, as long as the code is simpler and fairer! But with the current gridlock on Capitol Hill, I wouldn't hold my breath. Therefore, we've got to work with what we have now, however ponderous, confusing, and frustrating as it may be.

Every financial advisor and CPA knows how integral taxes are when considering ways to maximize and retain wealth. However, what's often overlooked in both the accumulation and the distribution stage is a sound strategy built around provisions in the tax laws that favor seniors. For example, if your client or your client's kids are paying for homecare for a senior citizen, those costs can be wholly tax deductible if certain conditions are met. The deduction can be substantial. I teach tax seminars for CPAs, and I'm consistently amazed at how few of them know about this particular provision in the tax law. It's not that the CPAs don't care. They just never knew about it!

If your client has a negative cash flow event in a given year, you could realize long-term income for your client through the conversion of some or all of a traditional IRA into a Roth IRA, thereby capitalizing on the negative cash flow event to create future cash flow free of taxation. The sale of appreciated stock or a larger-than-usual withdrawal from a traditional IRA both represent other options in a negative-income scenario during a given year. Many families and way too many financial professionals either think it is great when retirees have a negative taxable income or believe there is no tax planning to be done when income is negative. When I conduct seminars for tax professionals, I plead with them to fight this kind of thinking. As I just said, negative taxable income provides an opportunity to realize income with no tax cost. Tax realization occurs when there is a triggering event that makes the tax consequence attributable to that year.

To recap, the following examples illustrate ways to **realize** income:

1. Withdrawals from an annuity

2. Withdrawals from a traditional IRA account

3. Conversion of a traditional IRA into a Roth IRA

4. Sale of appreciated stock or real estate

Note that realization of income should cause no tax when other income is negative and often saves thousands or even tens of thousands of later taxes. The examples above represent cases where there is a future tax expected even if the retiree dies without having realized the taxable event. Appreciated stock or real estate may realize **stepped-up basis** on the taxpayer's death. These are just a few instances to show you how a savvy advisor or CPA could make a big difference for clients in situations guaranteed to create major stress in the lives of the people counting on you for guidance. The complexities of all this aren't so much in the details, though the details certainly do matter. It's more in how all the details fit together.

Taxes on Social Security benefits can knock seniors flat

We're going to naturally spend quite a lot of time talking about Social Security. For example, when to take benefits is of vital concern. Yet, can we truly discuss when to take benefits without knowing the tax liabilities of doing so at any age beyond sixty-two? I'd say not. So let's take a look at an illustration that should give you some food for thought on the issue of taxes and Social Security benefits.

Illustration 1

The Social Security Administration estimates that the average retiree benefit is approximately $1,250 per month. It also estimates that this $1,250 per month constitutes 40 percent of the cash flow an average retiree would need to live comfortably. Thus, a senior couple receiving

$30,000 per year of Social Security benefits would need another $45,000 per year to meet their needs. A working pool of $75,000 for a retired couple to live on is not out of line when you consider costs for Medicare Part B and Part D, as well as supporting Medicare Supplement plans to cover gaps in the current Medicare program. It's also not out of line when you consider the ongoing rising costs of long-term care protection in the form of traditional insurance plans, or boosted premiums for a universal life insurance policy that contains a long-term care rider. Let's not forget a vacation or two per year, gas for the car or golf cart, dining out, and a trip to see the grandkids.

The big question is where does the extra money come from? I've already given you statistics that show many boomers sitting across the desk from you probably can't afford to fully retire. One or both spouses are going to have to work at least part-time. The temptation of both clients will be to grab Social Security early, or even at full retirement age, to give them that $30,000 base to build on. We'll talk about when to take benefits later, as I've said, but the tax issues remain salient for our purposes here. If the couple isn't working, they may be lucky enough to have cash flow from other sources to make up the missing $45,000. It doesn't matter where the extra money comes from—wages, interest, dividends, capital gains, and so on. The tax liabilities on Social Security benefits remain largely the same when you run the numbers to get your client's modified adjusted gross income.

The maddening MAGI

An individual or couple's modified adjusted gross income is used to determine when taxes on Social Security benefits apply. Some sources of income are taxed at a lower rate than others, but collectively when you reach the magic number of allowed provisional income, you're talking the same relative liability regardless of the source of the non–Social Security taxable income. Let's take a quick look at wages first.

Many seniors will have to continue to work to get that extra $45,000 needed for their lifestyle. If the $45,000 extra cash flow results from a job or jobs, the federal taxes would be approximately $900 to $1,000 per month, leaving only about $65,000 for the couple's living expenses. A 10 to 15 percent reduction in available net cash flow due to taxes should not be dismissed lightly. The $45,000 of wages would incur federal and state income taxes and result in $25,500 of the $30,000 of Social Security benefits being taxable. Up to 85 percent of Social Security benefits can become taxable, which means your clients really need to understand that their gross projected Social Security income won't represent actual cash flow if they have other sources of income that will accrue to boost them over the allowed threshold to where Social Security is taxed based on their modified adjusted gross income.

Not surprisingly, the senior worker would continue to pay employment taxes into the very system that is paying them Social Security benefits, and Medicare benefits if the person is sixty-five or older. Now, isn't that a good argument for deferring Social Security benefits for as long as possible? If your client has to work and can get by without Social Security benefits, then that's something he or she needs to consider before actually taking those benefits. If the person is going to work anyway, why take on additional tax liabilities? Why not defer to build up Social Security contributions and enjoy a bigger payout later?

If the client has sufficient investment vehicles to generate some or all of the $45,000 above the $30,000 base provided by Social Security, then why not work to make up the base revenue of that Social Security and use the income from investments to fill the gap? These are the kinds of questions I encourage you to ask your clients.

Taxability of Social Security benefits can be a very confusing topic for financial professionals, individuals, and even for most tax professionals. Social Security benefits become taxable when a taxpayer's modified adjusted gross income (MAGI) exceeds an allowed level. The allowed level is $25,000 of provisional income for single taxpayers and $32,000 for married couples filing jointly. Provisional income includes taxable income plus nontaxable municipal bond interest. One half of Social Security benefits are initially included in provisional income. Wages, interest, dividends, capital gains, alimony, and taxable distributions from retirement plans are part of the computation of MAGI.

MAGI exceptions

Unrealized capital gains, deferrals within retirement plans, and deferrals within annuities are not included in MAGI. Likewise, distributions that are characterized as return of capital are not part of MAGI. The most common form of return of capital distributions not included in MAGI are:

a. Distributions from REITs that are offset by depreciation

b. Some preferred dividends that are offset by depreciation (most are includible in income)

c. Distributions from annuities that are not from unrealized growth but that come from contributed capital (i.e., the investment is losing money)

More calculations

Social Security benefits become includible only when the taxpayer's provisional income exceeds $25,000 for single taxpayers and $32,000 for married filing jointly individuals. At this point, the lesser of one half the Social Security benefits or the amount over the allowed threshold is taxable. Assume Jack is single and has $23,000 of MAGI plus $12,000 of Social Security. His includible Social Security benefits would be $4,000.

The computation is as follows:

1. Adjusted gross income $23,000

2. Plus one half of SS benefits $6,000

3. Provisional income is $29,000

4. Less base amount $25,000

5. Excess above base amount $4,000

6. One half of SS benefits $6,000

7. Amount includible in gross income is the lesser of 5 or 6

When provisional income exceeds $34,000 for single taxpayers or $44,000 for married filing jointly taxpayers, the includible portion of Social Security benefits in the formula for calculating the taxable portion of Social Security benefits rises to 85 percent received. The computation below provides the numbers for our hypothetical couple with MAGI of $45,000 and $30,000 of Social Security.

1. Adjusted gross income $45,000

2. Plus 85 percent of SS benefits $25,500

3. Provisional income is $70,500

4. Less base amount $44,000

5. Excess above base amount $26,500

6. Eighty-five percent of SS $25,500

7. Amount includible in gross income is the lesser of 5 or 6

Important point: It makes no difference if wages or investment earnings supply the needed $45,000. The tax result would be largely the same in either case, with certain exceptions detailed below. Any difference would be attributable to employment taxes paid. The Social Security benefits would be 85 percent taxable (i.e., $25,500 per year), and a total federal tax of $900 to $1,000 per month results even if the money comes from investments.

Investment earnings that would trigger the tax event include:

1. Interest income from a savings account
2. Withdrawals from a traditional IRA
3. Income from a bond mutual fund
4. Dividends from a REIT (real estate investment trust)
5. Dividends from a preferred stock

Once again, the senior couple would net only $65,000 after federal tax to meet living expenses. State taxes due will vary tremendously. Most states tax Social Security benefits, but some don't. A few states do not have a state income tax.

Important point: If the source of the $45,000 came from capital gains or qualified dividends, there would be almost no additional tax liability resulting from the added cash flow. The Social Security benefits would be taxable as before ($25,500 taxable), but the capital gains and nonqualified dividends would not be taxable in the lower tax brackets, and no federal tax would be due on income from those sources. Personal exemptions and standard deductions would totally or substantially offset the tax effect of the Social Security. Thus, cash flow from capital gains and qualified dividends is better than cash flow from interest or other forms of ordinary income. The core concept here is to find the best balance between Social Security, which would be taxed based on MAGI, and sources of cash flow that are taxed at the lowest possible rate, or not at all, depending on your client's tax bracket.

Spousal benefits (more on these in chapter 7) are part of the Social Security taxability determination for the parents' joint return when family benefits are being drawn to include children. If the family's modified adjusted gross income exceeds $32,000 for married filing joint status, the benefits will be directly taxable. Children's Social Security benefits are seldom taxable (if the $32,000 modified adjusted gross income standard is exceeded) to the parents, because children's benefits are almost always attributed to children though paid to an adult parent or guardian payee.

Long-term capital gains and qualifying dividends represent the lesser evil of income taxed as ordinary

Many financial advisors are aware that there are tax advantages for capital gains and qualifying dividends, but few realize how important these advantages are to taxpayers over sixty-five. These taxpayers are less likely to be working, or if they are working, the job is part-time and not generating enough annual revenue to push them above the 10 percent and 15 percent tax brackets where capital gains are not taxable. Remember also that qualifying dividends are taxed as long-term capital gains. Thus, a 4 percent dividend from Coca Cola or Microsoft is much better than a 4 percent certificate of deposit (CD) or 4 percent bond interest, if a 4 percent CD even still exists. These latter two sources of cash flow are taxed as ordinary income. Four percent qualifying dividends remained common among very strong stable US companies in 2014, and they are well worth a strong look when suggesting stock picks for your clients.

Many dividends do not meet the criteria for "qualified dividends" treatment. Nonqualified dividends receive ordinary income treatment similar to wages and interest, making them less attractive from a tax standpoint, depending on your client's tax bracket. Dividends from money market funds, REITs and Business Development Companies (BDCs) do not generally receive qualified dividend status. Money market funds and BDCs derive their income from interest. Taxation generally requires "looking through" the investment vehicle. For money market and REITs, this results in the fund itself not qualifying to provide qualified dividends. Qualified dividends are defined as resulting from the paying entity doing something to create goods or provide service. Investing activities, including REITs, do not qualify.

Tax changes effective January 1 of 2013 make tight control of the amount and type of cash flow critical. Financial professionals will frequently confuse cash flow with income. However, I would cite the following examples of classic cash flow generators, which are **not** income (and therefore do not cause Social Security to become taxable):

1. Distributions from Roth IRAs

2. Partial or full distributions from fixed or variable annuities with values below their tax cost

3. Lump-sum or monthly distributions from a reverse mortgage

4. Partial or full liquidation of stocks or real estate below their tax cost

Seniors who can get their needed retirement cash flow without paying approximately 20 to 25 percent of their Social Security in taxes have much better retirement prospects than seniors who pay too much in taxes. When counseling your clients, it's important to know the whole story of their financial landscape. If you don't, ask questions! You might find out about an otherwise hidden tax opportunity, such as a negative income year or an annuity that's below tax value, which could furnish a temporary spurt of cash that wouldn't pose a tax liability from a Social Security standpoint.

It also bears noting that your clients should seek to utilize losses during peak income years. Retirees can typically expect lower marginal tax brackets. Utilizing losses during retirement fails taxpayers because taxes saved pale in comparison to lost opportunities from working years.

There was a major revision in the Internal Revenue Code in 1986. Before 1986, there were only two major categories of income/losses. These two categories were:

1. Earned income from labor plus dividends and interest plus/minus rental gains/losses. No distinction was

made between earned income (from work) and investment gains and losses from real estate investments and nonparticipative investments in businesses. These "passive" investments (from real estate and nonparticipative investments) were being used to create losses/deductions to reduce taxable income from wages and active small business ownership.

2. Capital gains/losses from investments in stocks, bonds, real estate, and other investments seeking "capital appreciation."

The pre-1986 tax code was motivating taxpayers to make investments to reduce taxes even where there was little chance of getting capital appreciation. These tax-motivated investments were frequently called "tax-sheltered" investments. The revisions in the Internal Revenue Code in 1986 created three distinct types of income/loss with minimal opportunity to use losses from one category to offset income from another category. The three types of income are:

1. Active or earned income

2. Passive losses and gains

3. Capital gains and losses

Tax harvesting nets retirees valued gains

Another area that's worth looking at from a tax point of view is known as the annual tax harvesting in some circles. It's all basic economics. More clients and financial advisors don't take advantage of tax harvesting because not enough capital is on the line, or everybody is just too busy. Usually, it's the former. I'd argue, though, that a good bead on any way to reduce a client's tax liability is part of our duty as financial professionals, no matter how small or large the payoff is for the client, and no matter how busy we may be.

Essentially, you can offset capital gains for those in brackets that will require tax payments on those gains by taking losses on poorly performing investments prior to the close of the calendar year. You can always recommend that your client buy those investments back in a new tax year if the prices remain attractive and you're willing to consider a break on commission to avoid the appearance of churning. Either that or the tax savings had better nicely exceed the commission amounts, or your client would be better served by sitting pat. At any rate, sometimes it's better to sell and realize tax savings than it is to hold a stock or mutual fund and hope it goes up enough to offset losses in the market.

Let's say your clients really did well this past year and realized capital gains on their stock holdings. As the year draws to a close, you suggest culling some loss positions from their portfolios to offset taxes already paid or currently owed on the capital gains. By taking losses on these loss positions, your hypothetical taxable capital gains could be reduced from $22,000 to $7,000.

However, I've seen pushback on this tactic. Some brokers object, saying the positions may recover the losses soon, so clients are told to sit out the tax harvesting advantage. Failing to take advantage of tax loss harvesting can cost clients lots of money. Over time, studies show that tax loss harvesting may make a difference of 1 percent a year in terms of returns. Modest increases in assets over time can often mean the difference between retirement readiness and being unable to retire at all.

Tax credits offer overlooked options

High individual earners and businesses can benefit enormously from buying tax credits to reduce tax liability. Yet few financial professionals consider this as an option. Frankly, that puzzles me, but so do a lot of things in today's financial markets. I'm not ashamed to admit that either! One thing I do know is that tax credits can make a big difference for affluent clients who have open minds. So, let's take a quick look!

Let's say your client just sold a farm held in the family for sixty years in the great state of Georgia. The family's CPA says that your client can expect to pay $36,000 in state taxes. After your client swallows hard and asks if there's any way to reduce the tax liability resulting from the sale, their CPA smiles and suggests that they consider buying state tax credits.

Your eyebrows arch just a little, and you say, "Interesting proposition! Tell us more!"

The CPA continues, citing an example from Georgia as a way to make the point about how tax credits can work in some cases. She says that individuals and businesses can benefit from purchasing tax credits in certain circumstances. An increasing number of states now use state tax credits as incentives for corporations doing business in the state, making the opportunities to take advantage of tax credits more numerous every day. Georgia allows corporations making films in the state to sell film credits granted by the state. The client's CPA recommends purchasing film credits for a 10 percent discount. If your client bought $30,000 of film credits for $27,000, the client would save $3,000.

Of course, everyone in the room loves the idea of saving $3,000, but you and your client are concerned about the risk of buying the film credits. The CPA says that there's very little risk, and so you advise the client to go for it.

Important point: Only the most sophisticated and conservative clients take advantage of the opportunity of buying tax credits. If you have a high-rolling client who expects to owe $25,000 in state taxes in any given tax year, you should investigate state tax credits. Clients with liabilities of $25,000 or more should buy state tax credits even if they have withheld $25,000 during the year to pay the taxes. The states typically refund overpayments quickly. Clients may save 10 to 20 percent when they buy tax credits, resulting in a tax refund of $2,500 to $5,000 in the money already paid to satisfy the tax liability of $25,000.

Illustration 2

The arbitrage factor

As a financial professional, you've no doubt studied the concept of arbitrage. Indeed, I suspect many of you apply the concept to the benefit of clients every day. Arbitrage does come into play when planning and managing retirement cash flow. Most of your clients won't have any idea about what arbitrage is, but perhaps it would be a good idea to fill them in, if it's to their benefit.

Here's an example that can help you sum up arbitrage for clients:

Ann never takes advantage of sales and never uses coupons. Ann would buy gasoline at her regular station even if a new station opened across the street with the same brands selling for ten cents less per gallon. Her sister Nancy works in high commerce and always looks for value. Nancy has tried to explain to her sister the concept of arbitrage, but Ann is having a little trouble putting all the ducks in a row.

Important point: Arbitrage is the practice of taking advantage of a price difference between two or more markets and then acting to capitalize on that difference.

Nancy expands her illustration. She uses the example of two cities that border each other. The Georgia city gas stations sell gas for 10 to15 cents per gallon more than the South Carolina city gas stations. Nancy lives in Georgia but within two miles of the South Carolina border. She buys all her gas in South Carolina because she can buy exactly the same gas for less in South Carolina.

The technical definition of arbitrage requires the possibility of risk-free profit at zero lost. Therefore the product must be the same, the timing must be the same, and there must be no risk of loss from choosing to buy product A rather than product B.

Nancy notices that Ann still looks confused. She sighs and takes another stab at elucidating.

She says, "Okay, Ann! Uh, like, well ... So, you choose to order pizza from your favorite pizza parlor. When you start to pay, the cashier asks you if you have a coupon. The cashier then offers you a coupon that will allow you to buy the pizza at a discount of $1.50. Since you were planning to buy the pizza, the coupon is a risk-free gain of $1.50. The pizza is the same pizza purchased at the same time, but it is $1.50 less expensive with the coupon. So is it *really* the same pizza?" Nancy asked. "Yes and no," she answers before Ann can utter a peep.

Ann smiles and says that she'll take the same pizza she wanted already at a discount, as opposed to paying full price. Both ladies laugh and swap talk about the stupidity, or apparent stupidity, of constant sale days at big-box retailers. But they both still prowl the sales floors whenever they get the chance at buying something they want at the lowest price.

Savvy financial professionals like you will recognize that many situations occur in every client's financial picture where the client has the opportunity to profit from recognizing near-equivalent opportunities. There are many of these situations. I acknowledge the effort required to ferret them out, but I can say emphatically that you should go for it, at least for certain high-end clients.

Most of the examples of arbitrage occur with investments. In the purest form of arbitrage, the same investment may sell in two different markets at a different price. When this occurs, savvy arbitrageurs can take advantage of the pricing difference by buying in the low price market and selling in the higher price market at a profit. Obviously, you may not be able to do this for every client, but it's good for your top moneymakers to know that you're on the ball with arbitrage!

In the real world, there are many opportunities for arbitrageurs where the investment products are similar but not identical. Mergers often occur because a large company listed on a major stock exchange purchases a smaller competitor at an attractive price (for the smaller competitor) and realizes gain because the larger competitor earnings are valued more highly by the market. Encourage your clients to look for midsized companies with a unique niche that will be attractive to larger companies as we go forward into a financial world with rising interest rates and the distinct possibility of increasing inflationary pressure. I recommend paying particular attention to the technology and pharmaceutical market sectors.

A preliminary word on Roth IRAs

Few financial advisors understand how valuable Roth IRAs can be to senior citizens. Both the principal and income from Roth IRAs are nontaxable. Because Roth IRA distributions are not includible in MAGI, any distributions made from Roth IRAs do not result in taxability of Social Security benefits to senior citizens because they are not considered income. Ironically, Roth IRA distributions receive more favorable tax treatment for senior citizens than capital gains. Capital gains, though not taxable to senior citizens in marginal tax brackets below 25 percent, are part of the determination of modified adjusted gross income. Thus, even when nontaxable, their existence may make Social Security benefits taxable. That's something to keep in mind as you wade through the tax implications of investments on Social Security income, and the tax implications of those investments on net cash flow after taxes are paid.

I think Suze Orman put it best when it comes to the value of a Roth IRA for retirees. She said, "I love the Roth IRA. Tax-free income in retirement is truly a great deal."

Illustration 3

Here's a brief look at some scenarios you will likely encounter as you advise your clients. Our three hypothetical couples have three different sets of financial circumstances, each of which would lead to a variation in the tax liability outcome.

1. If Couple 1 has $30,000 of Social Security and $60,000 from interest income, they would owe federal taxes of approximately $9,000.

2. If Couple 2 has $30,000 of Social Security and $60,000 of capital gains, they would owe federal taxes of approximately $600.

3. If Couple 3 has $30,000 of Social Security and $160,000 of Roth distributions, they would owe no federal taxes. Naturally, the $160,000 is meant to illustrate the fact that your clients pay nothing in taxes on distributions from Roth IRAs. At present, a married couple could stash $13,000 per year into two Roth IRA accounts, which means they could accumulate $160,000 in just over twelve years.

Some tax professionals might be inclined to dispute my statement, but under current tax law, a nondeductible IRA contribution can be immediately converted or converted later to a Roth IRA. I often advise clients to pile up years of nondeductible IRA contributions with plans to convert them at little tax cost after retirement.

Obviously, the tax advantages of a Roth IRA could make all the difference for a retired couple needing to make up for some or all of the $45,000 above Social Security that we discussed before. Substantial distributions from the Roth IRA could enable one or both spouses to stop working part-time, and those same distributions could lower or eliminate taxation of Social Security benefits and additional cash flow liabilities from federal and state income taxes. The net result would be more net cash to work with, which is always a good thing!

Important point: No amount of nontaxable Roth distributions would cause Social Security benefits to be taxable. Roth distributions are not part of MAGI. Thus, Roth IRA distributions do not cause Social Security benefits to be taxable.

Parting words: Chances are more than probable that your clients will have to pay taxes on as much as 85 percent of their Social Security benefits based on their MAGI. Deferring benefits for as long as possible shields those benefits from taxation while maximizing the amount of the monthly payout. It makes sense to defer for both reasons. If your clients are drawing Social Security, then cash flow from capital gains and qualifying dividends is preferred, even if the income itself is counted in MAGI that can trigger taxation of Social Security benefits. The lower tax rate for those investments and the fact that capital gains are not taxed in brackets below 25 percent makes them ideal for retirees.

4

The Taxman Cometh
Retirement Accounts and Client Debt

> The hardest thing in the world to understand is the income tax. —Albert Einstein

IT'S NO SECRET THAT many current and future retirees in America have it tough. Pensions are disappearing, which accounts for some of the trouble. The most recent statistics from the US Bureau of Labor show that the percentage of workers participating in defined benefit pension plans fell from 38 percent to 20 percent between 1980 and 2008. In the past, a corporate or government pension comprised one of the three legs of the proverbial retirement stool, with the other two being savings and Social Security. When unions were strong and when federal, state, and local governments were more solvent than they are now, a large number of Americans enjoyed the financial security of a pension. They also had savings to fall back on.

Back when interest rates were high enough to provide returns of 5 percent or more on a savings account, certificate of deposit, or a money market fund, the savings part of the stool was easy for most retirees to manage on their own. So, retirees had a pension and a relatively predictable way to save with the modest assurance that interest rates would remain stable. There was also some assurance with these investment vehicles that seniors wouldn't lose their principal in a bloodbath on Wall Street. The Social Security leg was a no-brainer.

Today, though, many of our clients are missing two legs of the three-legged stool. Only one in five workers has a pension, and the number is dropping every day, particularly in the corporate sector as companies ditch pension benefits in favor of offering the inherently cheaper and lower-corporate risk benefit of an employer match in a company-sponsored 401(k). That trend began in earnest almost as soon as Congress enacted the Revenue Act of 1978 that amended the tax code to include 401(k) accounts. As I already mentioned, the retirement savings rate for most Americans is so low that few can ever hope to retire without relying solely on Social Security, plus whatever part-time work they can get to supplement that income. Contributing to retirement accounts is therefore more important now than ever before.

I don't mean to strut about like a financial Chicken Little. The sky may look like it's falling hard and fast, but it isn't, at least not for all retirees. There is hope even for those with somewhat limited means, provided that those clients receive the advice they require to navigate the difficult American stage of retirement today, not yesterday, and provided that those clients take your advice and pursue the suggested strategy with unflinching discipline stretching over a decade or more. Preferably, clients will start saving for retirement as soon as they start working, though that might be easier said than done.

Sure, things don't look as good as they once did, but change is a singularly reliable constant in a chaotic world. It's inevitable, and it need not all be for the worse. It's our job as financial professionals to impart confidence and hope as much as it is to give clients a realistic view of their own unique set of financial limits and strengths. We must sing out about the necessity for Americans to save and save some more for their own retirements! And we must educate our clients about the power of compounding interest and the very powerful advantages of the tax-deferred retirement accounts that Congress set up to help alleviate the financial insecurity that resulted from the demise of the American pension, and to guard against the possibility that Social Security won't pay 100 percent of promised benefits due to Washington dropping the ball on the management of the program's finances.

The tax-deferral pushback

The single most valuable tool we have as financial professionals when counseling our clients is the ability to show the astonishing power of tax-deferred retirement savings through traditional individual retirement accounts and 401(k) accounts. Ancillary to this is the vital role Roth IRAs play in the tax game of retirement. These tax-preferred investment instruments truly constitute a new leg of the wobbly stool, along with the personal pension option available through variable and fixed annuities that can provide predictable cash flow over the remaining lifetime of the retiree. I'm sure you've mentioned these options to clients, and I'm just as sure that you've received pushback.

Clients say, "I'm just going to have to pay taxes on money drawn from my 401(k) anyway, so who cares when I pay? I doubt I'll be in a much lower bracket anyway, so I might as well pay now and have the money instead of saving it for later in a tax-deferred account I can't touch without penalty prior to age fifty-nine-and-a-half."

Or more common, "I can't afford to put money into my retirement account! I have college tuition to pay for my kids right now!" Insert any other excuse about why clients justify not putting money into tax-deferred accounts. There are as many excuses for failing to save for retirement as stars in the sky.

Or, "Hey, what good is a Roth IRA anyway? I've already paid taxes on the money! I doubt the investment will grow that much over time, so who cares if the growth, if there is any, won't be taxed?"

If you're like me, you try not to sigh and shake your head when clients talk like this. It's hard not to sometimes, but I manage. I can safely assume that you know the intricate workings of standard retirement vehicles like an IRA or a 401(k). That's not so much the case with the Roth IRA, which I've found gets lost in the shuffle among financial professionals for some strange reason. Just one example of the worth of a Roth IRA from a tax perspective is that your clients can draw it down first, thereby deferring taxes on their traditional IRA or 401(k) for as long as possible. Also, as mentioned in the last chapter, distributions from Roth IRAs aren't included in MAGI calculations, meaning they're not a tax liability when it comes to taxation of Social Security benefits. Can't you just see your clients' eyes glazing over when you start trying to explain these things?

Clients will say, "Uh, what's a MAGI?"

Many clients are very smart people. They have worked hard all their lives, and they really want to live with at least a modicum of dignity and comfort in their old age. But they don't live in our wonderful world of numbers. They're not passionate about them. In fact, numbers intimidate rather than enlighten most people. Therefore, the pushback you receive when advocating for maximum annual contributions into tax-deferred retirement accounts, and Roth IRAs, is understandable. While the pushback is obvious in the horrifyingly low savings rate among Americans over age fifty (and worse for younger people), the new way of thinking about counseling clients before and during retirement is going to include a healthy dash of psychology in addition to a new way of thinking about the intricate workings of all the associated issues yourself.

And, admit it, if someone balks at patently sound advice, don't you feel inclined to take the path of least resistance and just give up? You say, "Well, okay then! I really think you should do this, even if you have to cut back on eating out a little. But it's ultimately your call."

Don't give up too easily! The financial lives of your clients are on the line.

In an ideal world, your clients would have the financial wherewithal to max out annual contributions to their 401(k) accounts. The average maximum contribution in 2014 was set at $17,500, or $23,000 for individuals over the age of fifty. In addition, clients in the ideal world would max out their Roth IRAs, which in 2014 amounted to $6,500 for an individual age fifty or more. If your clients did not have a 401(k), they could still have deferred $6,500 in taxable income in a traditional IRA, or fully fund the Roth IRA as well. Making sure to highlight the figure for the maximum contribution limit in any given year is a great way to nudge your clients toward maximizing retirement savings.

People in the 15 percent tax bracket or lower aren't taxed on long-term capital gains, so the tax savings on growth isn't of any consequence, and the break from Uncle Sam amounts to only 15 percent of the contribution, or $975 off the $6,500 for a max on an IRA. Still, it behooves clients to contribute to tax-deferred accounts anyway because of the tax deduction and because the gains could otherwise be taxed in the event the client moves into a higher tax bracket. Explain this to clients when they bark at you, saying they have no good reason to contribute.

Important point: Encouraging a balanced split between traditional IRA or 401(k) contributions and contributions to a Roth IRA is a viable option well worth considering even when your clients have more limited resources and can't max out. If they're in the 10 or 15 percent tax bracket, the long-term benefits of these accounts are slightly reduced, but the accounts are still worth funding. In the case of clients in the lowest tax brackets, totally funding a Roth IRA as opposed to a tax-deferred IRA or 401(k) remains another option to consider.

In my experience, few financial professionals strongly suggest that their clients establish and fully fund Roth IRAs as early as possible in the accumulation stage, and keep fully funding them until the worker retires. It's almost as if a Roth IRA constitutes the stepchild of the traditional IRA or 401(k). Yet, Roth IRAs are an extremely powerful tool for cash flow during retirement because of the inherent tax advantages that go with them. While tax-deferred accounts are also powerful financial instruments for long-term retirement strategy, they should not rule the roost, as it were. In fact, I would argue that the short-term tax deduction for workers due to making a tax-deferred investment should not completely eclipse the long-term tax savings for workers during retirement if they diverted some after-tax annual cash to a Roth IRA on a consistent basis over an extended period of time.

The gentle art of persuasion

Most clients are reasonable enough individuals. They may not like what they're hearing from you, especially if they lack abundant financial resources, but they'll listen if the reasoning behind your advice is presented in a way that sets up the least amount of resistance. Think of yourself as a financial dentist. Sensible people go to the dentist even when they don't want to because they know if they get a cavity, or some other even more painful dental malady, it's going to hurt physically and cost more financially later.

What you're doing is similar. You're trying to help people avoid financial cavities that will inevitably result from neglecting vital moves in planning for and then managing retirement cash flow. The worst thing you can do as a financial professional is to advise clients not to defer as much money as possible from taxation when they're closing in on retirement, and, as I know is becoming quite clear, I argue that maximum contributions to tax-deferred accounts while clients are working should be a pillar of all the interlocking strategies you can bring to bear to assist people as they sort through the very complicated issues they face when contemplating old age. This is particularly true for people in higher tax brackets.

Important point: Deferring taxable income makes sense because in most cases current tax rates for clients will typically be higher than or equal to retirement tax rates. Plus, the money in the retirement account works harder than money in a taxable account. For example, in the combined federal and state tax bracket of 25 percent, every four dollars deferred grows five dollars ($4 deferred, plus $1 tax-deferred). As noted, people in the lowest brackets don't fare as well.

So, let's take a look at two related illustrations that you can use as the basis for a convincing argument in favor of maximizing tax deferrals before and during retirement. Remember, the new way of looking at the big picture of retirement hinges on an emphasis on cash flow. Conversely, emphasizing asset accumulation during retirement may lead to bad decisions. Examples of these bad decisions include:

1. Not buying a Medicare Supplement or buying a Medicare Advantage plan when a Medicare Supplement plan protects much better but has a higher cost

2. Choosing not to defer because taxes are inevitable and the client or, worse, the financial professional believes it is better and easier to pay the taxes now rather than later

Illustration 1: Return to cash

Here's what happens when the emphasis focuses upon translating assets into cash equivalents during retirement without giving due consideration to tax deferrals and cash flow over the long term.

Flawed reasoning: I could defer $20,000 into a retirement account resulting in tax savings of $6,000 currently assuming 30 percent combined state and federal taxes. However, when I retire in two years, I will also be in a 30 percent tax bracket, and I will simply pay 30 percent taxes on the balance then. There appears to be little difference and some hassle, and I don't believe it is worth the effort.

Fair enough! I can see how a person might think that, even though it makes little sense. Consider the table below based on a hypothetical tax-deferred investment of $1,000 growing at a steady 6 percent annually over a twelve-year time horizon. Adjacent to the figures for the $1,000 are figures that show an investment of $700 using the same parameters. No taxes are included in either column, but the $700 reflects what's left after paying 30 percent taxes on $1,000 that could have been put into a tax-deferred retirement account to avoid the tax liability.

Forgive me for the interest rate of 6 percent. I know that's high, but clients will have an easier time envisioning a higher rate of return. The older they are, the more accustomed they are to the higher returns that were vaporized in the economic collapse that began in the last quarter of 2008. Also, higher returns are available in a variety of investment vehicles, so 6 percent isn't all that outlandish, depending on what you're in. The benefit of tax deferrals will become clear as you study the tables below.

Another key consideration with these illustrations is Rule 72. While some attribute it to Albert Einstein, a careful investigation indicates that he never said anything about compounding interest being the eighth wonder of the world. However, the economics of Rule 72 are definitely something to keep in mind. Table 2 shows that it takes an additional five years to double an after-tax investment of $700 based on our current scenario, but with the taxes on interest figured into the equation. Both tables clearly reveal that deferring taxes on that $1,000 will enable clients to end up with a much larger sum for use during retirement.

Table 1: Return to cash

Year	Beginning Principal ($)	Interest ($)	Deferral Part One Return to Cash Ending Principal ($)	Return to Cash Value ($)
0			1000.00	700.00
1	1000.00	60.00	1060.00	742.00
2	1060.00	63.60	1123.60	786.52
3	1123.60	67.42	1191.02	833.71
4	1191.02	71.46	1262.48	883.73

5	1262.48	75.75	1338.23	936.76
6	1338.23	80.29	1418.52	992.96
7	1418.52	85.11	1503.63	1052.54
8	1503.63	90.22	1593.85	1115.69
9	1593.85	95.63	1689.48	1182.64
10	1689.48	101.37	1790.85	1253.59
11	1790.85	107.45	1898.30	1328.81
12	1898.30	113.90	2012.20	1408.54

Note the following about these calculations:

1. When the initial deferral of $1,000 is made, all $1,000 is earning at 6 percent. Absent the deferral, $300 would have been paid in taxes, leaving only $700 to earn 6 percent. The earnings of $42 after the first year would then have been subject to 30 percent taxes, leaving only $29.40 or 4.2 percent after-tax return. With the deferral, the client would have $1,060 versus $742. Plus, the client would have benefited from a 25 percent reduction in federal tax liability in the calendar year the contribution was made. Recall that the other 5 percent of the 30 percent total tax liability derived from state taxes, which vary widely throughout the United States. Obviously, $700 won't earn as much as a $1,000 over a twelve-year period.

Clients will know this, of course! But they may not process the numbers. It's easier to put the numbers out there, as in table 1, to enable clients to actually visualize the difference between a growth rate of 6 percent on $1,000 that was tax deferred compared to the growth rate of 6 percent on $700 after taxes.

Based on Rule 72, after twelve years' growth at 6 percent after-tax the original cash of $700 would have doubled, but the $1,000 would have doubled as well, leaving the client with $2,012.20 versus $1,408.54, or a difference of

$603.66. Now let's zoom that $1,000 up to an investment of $100,000. That paltry six hundred bucks seems a bit more substantial when you're talking $60,000! If you put it to your clients that way, they'll sit up and lean forward in their chairs, their interest suddenly piqued.

Illustration 2: Tax liability

Now, let's look at the tax aspects of our scenario, as well as the extra five years it will take for the $700 left over after taxes to double based on Rule 72 when the interest is taxed at 30 percent. In table 1, it's clear that the after-tax money produces less return than would have been possible had the initial $1,000 not been taxed at all. However, based on Rule 72, both will double at the same time at an earnings rate of 6 percent. It's just that the tax-deferred investment of $1,000 would be worth just over $600 more because the interest was shielded from the taxman during the growth period.

In table 2, we'll look at what happens when the client chooses not to defer taxes, leaving the $700 of the $1,000 to invest at the same 6 percent earnings rate on the investment itself. However, we'll throw in the fact that the interest on the $700 is subject to the 30 percent tax as ordinary income under our current scenario. The investment growth would be reflected in the following example, which shows that the actual return drops from 6 percent to 4.2 percent because of the tax liability, thereby extending the time it takes to double that same after-tax $700 by five years!

Table 2: Tax liability

Year	Beginning Principal ($)	Deferral Part Two No Deferral Pay Taxes As You Go Interest ($)	Taxes On Interest ($)	Ending Principal ($)
0				700.00
1	700.00	42.00	12.60	729.40

2	729.40	43.76	13.13	760.03
3	760.03	45.60	13.68	791.96
4	791.96	47.52	14.26	825.22
5	825.22	49.51	14.85	859.88
6	859.88	51.59	15.48	895.99
7	895.99	53.76	16.13	933.62
8	933.62	56.02	16.81	972.84
9	972.84	58.37	17.51	1013.70
10	1013.70	60.82	18.25	1056.27
11	1056.27	63.38	19.01	1100.63
12	1100.63	66.04	19.81	1146.86
13	1146.86	68.81	20.64	1195.03
14	1195.03	71.70	21.51	1245.22
15	1245.22	74.71	22.41	1297.52
16	1297.52	77.85	23.36	1352.02
17	1352.02	81.12	24.34	1408.80

Note the following about these calculations:

1. As I said above, the $700 earns at 6 percent, but taxes of 30 percent will apply to each year's earnings.

2. After seventeen years' growth at 4.2 percent after-tax the original cash of $700 would have doubled! So, it's clear that the application of Rule 72 takes longer under this scenario. The important point is that the interest is taxed, creating less growth and more tax liability over a longer time.

Important point: Deferral of earnings before tax into a retirement account results in after-tax earning rate equal to the earning rate of the investments! Note that after twelve years per $1,000 deferred into the retirement account, the accumulation is 22.82 percent greater than it is if taxes were paid on the interest.

Find creative ways for clients to maximize tax-deferred contributions

Given the power of tax-deferred retirement accounts to deliver substantially greater growth over time than provided by after-tax investments, we financial professionals need to assist our clients in every way possible to take full advantage of IRA or 401(k) accounts. This is especially true as clients near full retirement age and earn in higher tax brackets. While I argue that maximum contributions should be made throughout the accumulation stage of a client's financial life, if at all possible, I also strongly believe that maximizing contributions is even more vital as the client approaches retirement.

Important point: Taking a home equity loan or drawing down savings slated for emergencies is a way for clients to make maximum tax-deferred contributions when approaching retirement age. Think outside the box!

If investors do not have excess cash flow to make the deferrals, they should consider utilizing an equity loan to make the deferrals. Get the home equity loan in the years just prior to retiring. In addition to helping to maximize tax-deferred contributions, the home equity loans may provide a means to delay drawing from other retirement cash flow sources. These include:

1. Social Security
2. Variable annuities with living benefits
3. Cash flow from nontraded REITS

Important point: Once earned income decreases due to retirement, it becomes much more difficult to qualify for an equity loan. That's why clients considering this option should get one early, even if they don't need it right away.

The pros of tapping home equity

1. Equity loans are a very low cost of capital during low-interest-rate environments.

2. Equity loans may be used to replace short-term cash flow when maximizing contributions to qualified retirement plans during the last working years.

3. Equity loans can also be used to defer drawing down tax-deferred assets.

4. Equity loans may be used to reduce higher cost debt. Note that this increases both current and future cash flows.

Some of you might disagree with me about encouraging appropriate clients to consider tapping their home equity to fully fund retirement accounts in the last years of their accumulation stage. However, if you think about it, the tactic frees up cash otherwise locked away in real estate that can be borrowed at a relatively low cost, far lower than the potential returns on some traditional and alternative investments. If the cash delivers a greater long-term return that enhances long-term cash flow, then the decision to counsel clients in favor of this option should be easy!

The 401(k) piggybank syndrome

It's great if you can gently nudge your clients to channel as much money as possible into tax-deferred retirement accounts and into Roth IRAs. However, many will resist or even argue about the merits in spite of your efforts to showcase the tax savings and long-term growth potential. The fact is millions of workers are unable to save the recommended 10 to 15 percent of annual income for retirement. Many save nothing at all. Worse, those who have put money into tax-deferred retirement accounts, however little that may be on a national scale, frequently turn to those funds for nonretirement needs—mortgages, emergency health care, credit card debts, utility bills.

In a study released in 2013 by the financial advisory firm HelloWallet, based on data from the Federal Reserve and the US Census Bureau, the stark realities of what I call the 401(k) piggybank syndrome came to light. The study's survey results indicated one in four Americans raid their 401(k) plan in part or in total prior to retiring. At the time of the study, early withdrawals from 401(k) plans totaled a staggering $70 billion per year. One of the most surprising findings pointed out that only 8 percent of those cashing in their 401(k) accounts did so because of job loss, whereas 75 percent of the survey respondents said they raided their accounts to deal with routine financial challenges.

The study prompted many financial experts to once again question the value of tax-deferred accounts if people can't, or won't, fund them at levels that will ultimately make a difference during retirement. Others pointed out that many of the early withdrawals would have been avoided if the individuals had been better educated in the basic fundamentals of sound money management. There's no question about it. Many Americans don't know the first thing about finance, and that deficiency of knowledge is creating social problems that have real consequences for workers.

As I look at statistics like those above, I can't help but worry about the quality of life many baby boomers will face during retirement. Declining standards of living seem the most likely scenario. So, when clients come to me asking about cashing in an IRA or a 401(k) prior to retirement, I resist the urge to shout or fume. I don't need the high blood pressure! I simply ask lots of questions to find out why the early withdrawal is so necessary, or seemingly necessary, and I work hard to find alternatives for the client to consider. No doubt you've encountered the same situation with some of your clients. The bottom line is clients need to be better educated about what they give up when they cash in early. They need to know they are putting their financial lives in even more peril down the road when they will be less able to recover from losses and build for their financial futures.

A preliminary word on tax-deferred annuities

The advantages of tax-deferred annuities are frequently under-appreciated by many financial professionals, and I urge you to take a closer look at them when putting together a comprehensive plan to shield clients from the taxman before and after retirement. Historically, these tax-deferred annuities were sold based largely on their tax-deferral characteristics. Lower tax rates for the period from 1980 to 2012 diminished the tax-deferral role of annuities. Insurance companies responded by making annuities a source of guaranteed cash flow in retirement. This assumption of investment risk by the insurance companies has become very popular with investors who must provide for more of their own retirement with the rapid decline in corporate and government pensions.

The insurance company guarantee of future cash flows is frequently characterized as a "personal pension." Many of your clients may eagerly utilize this "living benefit" feature of annuities to build their cash flow sources for retirement. I sincerely believe the guaranteed living-benefit feature of annuities should make them a part of most retirees retirement planning. We'll discuss annuities at greater length later.

Parting words: The power of tax-deferred retirement accounts of all kinds ranks at the top when it comes to building a winning financial strategy for clients in the accumulation stage and after they retire. The immediate federal tax benefits for the worker, especially those in higher tax brackets, the growth of tax-sheltered principal and gains, and the ability to defer taxes even longer with the help of a well-funded Roth IRA represent immense potential value for clients.

It's a shame that so many don't understand what they're losing when they don't maximize annual contributions or when they raid their retirement accounts for nonretirement needs. It's up to us to show clients just how valuable tax-deferred accounts can be. It's our duty as financial professionals to gently but firmly inform our clients about the realities of today's harsh climate for present and future retirees, and to make it clear that these accounts may be all that stand between a life lived solely on the $22,000 annual average for a couple on Social Security in 2014 and a life with added cash flow from retirement accounts that could make it possible to play a round of golf or go see the grandkids in Topeka.

5

Gather ye Rosebuds
Traditional and Alternative Investments

I advise you to go on living solely to enrage those who are paying your annuities. It is the only pleasure I have left. —Voltaire

ALTHOUGH IT MAY SOUND obvious to a financial professional, I must say right up front that the accumulation and distribution phases of a client's financial life differ greatly. While the individual is working, emphasis is generally placed on aggressively growing assets and reinvesting returns to build capital. Risk tolerance is usually fairly high among more savvy clients, and loss of capital in downturns is seen as part of doing business, though naturally we all strive to put our clients into quality investments that are the least susceptible to the cyclical corrections that routinely occur in stock and bond markets.

The problem is that many of us fail to realize that the approach we used to advise our clients in the accumulation stages isn't necessarily the right one for clients in the distribution stage during retirement. Investments still remain important, of course, but the philosophy of capital preservation at all costs while ignoring cash flow and taxes can end up costing clients financially and from a quality of life perspective. Sometimes it's fine, or even wise, to touch capital, especially if doing so will reduce tax liabilities. For example, drawing down capital from a certificate of deposit makes more sense than keeping the capital intact and paying taxes on the interest as ordinary income. This is particularly the case if the taxed income might bump the client's modified adjusted gross income over the threshold established to determine whether or not Social Security benefits become taxable. Drawing down the CD is better than cashing out a dividend-paying stock that could be taxed as long-term capital gains. Sometimes it's wise to sacrifice liquidity for enhanced cash flow, so a low-return money market is another pot of cash to seriously consider drawing on if your clients require a burst of funds to cover an emergency.

During the working years, after meeting their current basic needs, prudent people save money to help meet future needs, including emergencies, college tuition, changing career paths, and retirement. In early working years, most people make financial mistakes, but they have plenty of time to correct errors. When seniors approach retirement or actually are retired, they're far less able to overcome mistakes and bad luck. That's a fundamental point that appears obvious, and yet many clients and some financial professionals do not factor time horizons and the ability to recover from mistakes into their financial strategies over the course of the accumulation stage. Risk tolerance rightly decreases the closer a client gets to retirement age, so aggressive growth opportunities should be pursued during the earlier phases of asset accumulation. For risk-averse clients, this approach can be a hard one to sell, but if the logic is explained, most people will see the sense of it.

Another obvious point is that financial advisors and their clients should always understand that unless projected retirement cash flows match or exceed retirement cash expenditures, principal will be consumed to meet monthly cash flow needs. Replacing cash flow is very difficult once a client retires. That means the accumulation phase of a person's life may require extending beyond the current Social Security full retirement age of sixty-six or sixty-seven.

In other words, your clients may not be able to retire when they want to, and it will be up to you to tell them and explain why they need to continue in accumulation mode until things change for the better from a cash flow perspective. Maybe the client could retire if he or she moved to a state with cheaper property taxes and a lower cost of living, and the client found gainful part-time employment to offset the lack of financial resources. The solution could be that simple, but it probably won't be. We as financial professionals need to keep an open mind and look for solutions that could help clients retire with enough cash flow to meet their needs. I've already explained the concept of the CAMP Score. It's a vital component to consider when designing a comprehensive strategy for your clients in both stages of their financial lives.

Accumulation strategies

As I've pointed out, the majority of baby boomers have saved little or nothing for retirement. That's a shame, but it is the reality we now face after two stock market crashes, a real estate bust, and stagnant wages for the middle class that have lasted for well over a decade. According to the US Census Bureau, the median household income of retirees today is approximately $35,000. With the average combined payout of $22,000 per year in Social Security for a couple, it's clear that Social Security now provides the lion's share of retirement cash flow for most Americans. However, if you look at that median cash flow, it's also clear that half of retirees have more to work with. Those that do were careful to save their money and plan for the future. These clients are the ones you can help during the accumulation and the distribution phases. Are the poor left behind? In a sense, they are. Full- or part-time work after normal retirement age is becoming reality for an increasingly significant portion of seniors. Again, the economic reality in America is harsh and unforgiving. Your clients need to keep that in mind when they come to you saying they want to retire when you know they're not ready from a cash flow standpoint.

During the accumulation stage, preparation for retirement should be given by developing different buckets of assets for use during retirement. Each bucket should be designed to meet needs during retirement, which means you always need to structure client investments with an eye toward the future. In early years, more emphasis on aggressive growth makes sense. As the client approaches retirement, scaling back to less aggressive investment vehicles will help preserve principal, but returns will likewise decrease. When seniors focus on assets rather than cash flow, they underestimate Social Security, pensions, and annuities, so you'll need to manage their realistic expectations and point out that there is more to the picture than mere investment returns. As noted, the key concern should be the amount of cash flow provided from all the various investments and assets.

Important point: If clients have sufficient cash flow from various sources to easily cover at least 100 percent of the cash flow they earned while working, meaning they likely have a CAMP Score of 100 percent or better if long-term care and inflation protection has been built into their plan, then it makes sense to keep some investments on the more aggressive side, as opposed to giving in to risk aversion that will translate to lower returns and less cash flow. No financial strategy is a one-size-fits-all silver bullet. Your clients may not realize this and push you to temper investments to an overly conservative position simply because they're afraid of losing capital when they in fact have enough cash flow without the investment vehicle in question.

The following three objectives should factor into your planning during the accumulation stage:

1. Focus on growth assets that will help meet purchasing power challenges over a full and extended retirement. Inflation protection matters!

2. Emphasize long-term income assets that provide consistent, reliable cash flow during retirement.

3. Include protection assets that sustain the retirees and their

families during long-term critical care situations. Annuities or universal life insurance with long-term care riders should be integrated into a client's overall financial landscape during the accumulation stage. Variable annuities with living benefits often have income increases built into the contract that offer some protection against inflation, as do some life insurance products that increase benefits over time. Thus, when a client balks at considering investing in such a product, it's important to point out the additional benefits instead of allowing the client to fixate solely on a large lump-sum cash outlay, high annual premiums after a large down payment, or the modest returns many of these products deliver.

Future retirement cash flow, not assets, should be the primary consideration during the accumulation phase. This concept represents the chief deviation in terms of thought processes from the current norm. Focusing attention on the accumulation period ten years prior to retirement should emphasize asset allocations to maximize cash flow when a senior retires. Typically, the emphasis is solely on asset accumulation, which is a big mistake many financial professionals make.

Naturally, consuming principal reduces future cash flow/income for retirees, so every investment should be evaluated based on current and future cash flow/income and on downside risk potential. Some investments have both limited term (life), while others have declining income, making it important to choose wisely for your clients.

Principal investments should be evaluated based upon:

1. Current and future income stream

2. Term or life

3. Liquidation value

4. Risk of loss of income and principal (liquidation value)

Important point: The ideal investment provides cash flow, growth of principal over time, and promises little or no risk of principal loss. Does this sound too good to be true? Well, it might. But there are products out there that come pretty close to delivering the ideal investment package. All you have to do is look, make sure you do your due diligence to weed out the bad apples, and give your clients a sound and reasoned presentation of all the pros and cons of a given product to enable them to make an educated decision that could positively impact their lives during retirement.

Let's take a closer look at some investment products that best position your clients for cash flow during retirement with as little risk of losing principal as possible. Ideally, the investment will also provide inflation and long-term care protection. In fact, if the clients don't have these two important issues taken care of, at least to the extent that is possible, then they may not be in a position to retire even if cash flow seems adequate. We'll discuss these issues in greater detail later. For now, let's look at the various investments that can be brought together to make a brighter future for your clients.

Fixed income

The three most common income assets retirees typically use are certificates of deposit, money market funds, and bonds. During the high-interest-rate environment of the 1980s and 1990s, these vehicles served retirees very well. Unfortunately, since the financial crisis of 2008, the aggressive pro-growth tactics of the US Federal Reserve and foreign governments have virtually eliminated any reasonable return on these three vehicles.

These three traditional income vehicles have classically been viewed as very low risk. However, clients wedded to low-return CDs should be reminded that FDIC insurance only covers the principal if a bank fails.

Any interest accrued will be lost. Long-term CDs these days are also risky because interest rates are rising, so tying up a lump sum for five years at a low interest rate makes no sense at all. Yet, people without the benefit of your sound advice will flock to long-term CDs thinking they're protecting their money, when in fact they're on the losing end of the equation.

Fixed-income investments can help to reduce portfolio volatility, but they do so at the cost of low returns. I often see clients with 60 percent or more of their assets tied up in these low-return investment vehicles, and the first thing I do is explain that they're losing money due to the steady creep of inflation, and they're facing opportunity costs because they're not invested in vehicles that offer higher returns with potentially the same low downside risk. Risk-averse clients, particularly older ones used to the way it was, as opposed to the way it is, are prone to gravitate toward these easily understood low-return investments. While fixed-income vehicles do play a part in a portfolio during the accumulation phase, I'm not a really big fan of them for retirees in this low-interest environment. Of course, if interest rates climb as we expect them to, my views will naturally change to a more favorable outlook on fixed income.

A word on bonds

Bond funds have enjoyed declining interest rates for most of the last thirty years. Thus, bond funds have provided both cash flow and capital gains upon liquidation. However, bond funds incur capital losses during periods of rising interest rates. Given the current low interest rates and almost unanimous agreement that rates will rise over the next few years, bonds are very risky assets for retirees! If interest rates do rise as expected, bonds with maturities greater than five years will likely lose value if sold prior to maturity. Bond mutual funds will suffer even more than individual bonds because they are always sold prior to maturity. Purchasing short-term or medium-term bonds in 2014 reduced the risks associated with rising interest rates, but the return on the investment continued to be very low indeed!

However, the good news is that the enormous investor thirst for higher yields on intermediate term (typically five- to ten-year) investments has led some corporations to issue what are sometimes called baby bonds. Risks are low, and yields of 6 percent on a five-year investment are becoming common.

Important point: I love baby bonds as a viable alternative to CDs and/or fixed annuities. Growth is not the goal, but an "equity sweetener" in the form of warrants sometimes attached to the sale of the bonds makes them a potentially ideal investment, particularly in the last years of accumulation and in retirement.

Growth assets

Apart from fixed income, clients are likely most familiar with stocks and mutual funds as investment vehicles. In fact, that's all most clients know about. They fixate on the Dow Jones or the S&P 500 without really understanding the numbers they hear on the news. Sure, some of your more sophisticated clients know the real score, but in my experience, even the savvy bunch get key concepts wrong more often than not. It's important to remind clients that these traditional investment vehicles, while important, are definitely not the only game in town. The risk and rates of return vary widely in both of these asset categories, as we've all seen in the last decade or so. Clients need to understand that they should only purchase quality investments, and that taking a long position on those investments is the recommended course. The temptation to day trade should be discouraged. Traditionally, sound allocation strategies have yielded the highest returns, not market timing.

Dividend-paying stocks

I believe dividend-paying stocks may currently be greatly undervalued because some investors unduly fear the risk of high-quality corporate stock. Older financial historians see similarities between 2014 and the

1950s or 1970s. During both the 1950s and 1970s, stock dividends were higher than bond or CD interest. History shows both these eras were very good times to be making investments in common stocks and/or real estate. While there are no guarantees that investing today will follow either of those two experiences, clients in need of cash flow should evaluate dividend stocks as a potential source of both cash flow and increasing value. Reinvestment of returns during the accumulation phase will grow principal as share prices increase over time. In 2014, a dividend of 4 percent on a quality stock was not uncommon.

However, chasing dividends is a common mistake. High dividends often come with increased risk. A somewhat conservative approach is recommended, especially if the client has a short-time horizon and increased risk aversion as he or she nears retirement. Capital preservation at that point is just as important as returns, but neither should become the tail that wags the dog. It is best to avoid the danger of over investing in any single market sector, such as tech or financials, despite the temptation of higher returns.

Important point: Dividend-paying stocks from solid blue-chip companies are an excellent investment for retiree cash flow and for workers seeking to accumulate assets. When selling these stocks to clients, it's important that the client knows that companies can and do change dividend rates all the time, and that the company can cancel dividends at any time. The right basket of dividend-paying stocks is a wonderful source of cash flow, but it can't be the sole source of income beyond Social Security. Diversification of cash flow is an essential component of sound planning for clients during accumulation and distribution.

New form of preferred stock

Historically, preferred stock has provided a solid cash flow but with no upside potential and interest rate risk at liquidation because of its theoretically infinite life. However, there is a new breed of preferred stock available that cures both of these problems. The new form of preferred stock typically has a five-year term, making it an intermediate-term investment. It is accompanied by warrants allowing the preferred stock purchaser to buy the company's common stock at a given price for five years. Thus, if the company does well, the warrants will have value, but if the company's results are modest, the investor gets a nice cash flow for five years (5 to7 percent typically) and then receives their principal back.

Important point: As with baby bonds, this new form of preferred stock is a superb investment for retirees or for clients still in the accumulation phase of their financial lives.

A word on taxes

When corporate stock is owned inside a tax-deferred retirement account, it gets taxed as ordinary income at the highest marginal tax rate for that client in the year of distribution. By contrast, when corporate stock in Coca Cola is purchased with after-tax dollars, there are both tax and timing advantages. First, the taxpayer can choose when to sell appreciated corporate stock, and secondly, both the annual dividends and price appreciation since the initial purchase may receive preferential long-term capital gain treatment.

Mutual funds

Stock mutual funds are an attractive investment vehicle for individual investors, but unless they are indexed funds that are not managed, they will incur taxes based upon manager trading. Stock mutual funds were created by the Investment Company Act of 1940. The mutual fund itself is not taxed because it distributes out its realized income and capital gains to the fund owners. Taxation occurs at the level of the individual owners. Those owners do not know their taxable income and capital gain share until after the end of the fund's year. Tax control is very difficult.

A classic illustration is the tax year 2013. It was an extremely good year for US stock markets. Index fund investors incurred little or no taxable capital gains unless the individual investor chose to sell some of their holdings. Managed stock mutual funds typically incurred substantial taxable capital gains from manager decisions to sell within the fund.

Important point: For retirees, I typically prefer index funds that allow us to control the timing of tax recognition of capital gains.

Annuities

Annuities today aren't the same as they were in the past. The changes are not all for the good. In fact, I currently don't like fixed annuities. I'll explain why in a moment. I also find that variable annuities range from absolutely awful to okay to potentially great for my clients. It all depends on the benefits ensconced within the contract. Some variable annuities don't offer the same benefits as others, and so it takes a lot of work to truly evaluate these products on an individual basis. I frequently find that certain financial professionals fail to do the work required to best match a client's needs with the provisions contained in a variable annuity contract. Worse, some financial professionals simply push the product they're told to push without investigating alternatives that could be better.

Annuities deservedly got a bad rap during the period prior to the early 2000s. The negative characteristics included:

a. High costs.

b. Tax deferral was less important because Presidents Reagan and Clinton lowered tax rates.

c. The primary guarantee was return of capital, which was seldom needed in a period of rapidly rising stock values.

d. Income from annuities is taxed as ordinary income when

distributed out from the policy. Thus, investing in stock funds within an annuity had the negative effect of converting capital gains into ordinary income. As I think you've noticed by now, tax considerations are equally important as investments and returns for retirees. The taxman can be tamed, but you'll have to plan around him as you advise your clients in the accumulation and distribution stages.

Let's take a closer look at the world of annuities from a financial professional's point of view.

Fixed annuities

As you know, fixed annuities are the insurance industry's answer to certificates of deposit, and you know how I feel about CDs! Fixed annuities have nearly the same low-risk profile that CDs have, but like CDs, their yield is highly dependent on the interest rates when they are issued. Many fixed annuities issued during the high-interest-rate environment of the 1980s and 1990s had very high rates guaranteed for a long period of time. Way back then, a fixed annuity had a lot going for it, despite the high costs and the high charges for early withdrawal.

Unfortunately, fixed annuities issued over the last ten years have had very low yields for obvious reasons. Another deficiency of fixed annuities is they do not grow the principal. Investors receive their annual interest or the accrued interest if left in the contract plus their original principal minus any withdrawal charges for early withdrawal. I believe astute financial professionals like you can find better alternatives for clients in the current low-interest-rate environment. However, should we return to 8 percent fixed annuity yields, I would once again be a big proponent of these investments.

Important point: In this current low-interest environment, I do not recommend fixed annuities.

Variable annuities

I'm a bigger fan of certain products within this type of annuity for a couple reasons, though they can all be tricky to evaluate, as I noted earlier. The new breed of variable annuities can be a classic example of an investment that can be very useful sources of retirement cash flows and provide growth potential when the stock market gains. The key to the best of variable annuities on the market today lies in the living benefits contained in some of the contracts. If you are unfamiliar with these products, it will no doubt greatly assist some of your clients for you to learn more.

Living benefits: Living benefits guarantee cash flows for the life of the annuitant and sometimes their surviving spouse. The cost of this benefit can be high, but the gains in consistent cash flow and removal of uncertainty make it well worth paying in many cases. The uncertainty I'm talking about derives from unexpected life events like the need for long-term care and from expected economic pressures arising from inflation.

Analyzing variable annuities: Look for the following features in any variable annuity with living benefits that you might consider recommending for a client:

1. Costs for the basic contract and elective riders

2. Withdrawals allowed without compromising surrender value

3. Long-term care protection either in the form of long-term care insurance or increased benefits during a critical care period

4. Guaranteed income growth during the accumulation period

5. Future cash flow increases (automatic or elected) to offset inflation

6. Joint benefits for the annuitant and their spouse

7. Survivor benefits for the spouse

8. Annual no-loss or provisions that limit investment loss

9. Potential for annuity gain based upon the greater of a stock market formula, a bond formula, and a minimal gain guarantee

Cash flow increases: An important part of the contract hinges on future cash flow increases. Are those increases automatic or must they be elected? You'd be amazed at how often elected increases are missed, but if they're in the contract, they're very important. Another important question is whether guaranteed increases in future cash flow ends with the first withdrawal, forcing the client to rely on outstanding market performance to get cash flow increases. Or do guarantees continue during the distribution stage? Naturally, if your client can get guaranteed cash flow increases during the distribution phase, your client will likely pay more for the product. The value received from the higher cost will eventually be realized from the ongoing hedge against inflation.

As noted above, one of the biggest attractions of a variable annuity with living benefits is the provision for long-term care events within the contract. The best products will include cash flow increases if a licensed physician documents in writing that the annuitant is incapable of performing two of the six activities of daily living. I'll get into the long-term care issues later, but suffice it to say here that such a rider is worth its weight in gold in helping clients offset the potential financial disaster that a long-term care event can trigger. Most contracts will double the annual payout in a long-term care event, and they don't require the annuitant to receive care in a skilled-nursing facility. Traditional long-term care insurance policies generally do require placement in a nursing home before benefits are paid, though insurance companies are quite rightly getting a lot of pushback on that requirement. In fact, today the majority of long-term care is received at home, not in skilled-nursing care facilities.

Important point: A fair comparison would suggest that variable annuities with living benefits frequently represent a reasonable bond substitute.

A look back

Prior to the early 2000s, variable annuities provided way too few benefits to justify their cost. However, I caution financial advisors against blindly recommending clients forfeit these contracts because many are worth less than their original purchase price. They are worth less because of market downturns from 2000 to 2003 and again from 2007 to 2009. One of the few benefits variable annuity contracts from this era have is guaranteed of return of principal on the annuitant's death.

Ironically, what I would call the "golden era of variable annuities" is from 2003 to 2008. During this time frame, variable annuities provided many too-good-to-be-true opportunities. Insurance companies became very aggressive trying to out-promise the competition. As noted, contract terms changed rapidly because of both competition and excess demand when a promise was too good to be true. Following the market downturn of 2007 to early 2009, many insurance companies exited the variable annuity market in an attempt to absorb the blow to the insurance company's earnings caused by excess promises. It should be noted that virtually 100 percent of these too-good-to-be-true contracts have been honored by the insurance companies.

Variable annuities issued from 2009 to date are even harder to evaluate. My advice is to recognize that there are no one-size-fits-all solutions. I find that I must analyze a very large number of annuities to determine which, if any, clients will benefit from a particular product.

With decreasing pensions, I do believe guarantees of future cash flow by insurance companies provide an important source of monthly cash flow. Declining government and corporate pensions necessitate filling the gap with what many call a "private pension" from a solid insurance company. The ideal time to discuss variable annuities with living benefits with your clients is during the accumulation stage, preferably earlier rather than later.

Equity indexed annuities

Like most financial advisors, I have gotten very irritated on several occasions in the last ten years when I see a very bad equity-indexed annuity sold by an insurance professional to a client. Most of the early products had very long surrender terms, very high commissions to selling agents, and very limited upside return. However, the appeal of these contracts is that they typically guarantee no down years. Each year the investment return is either zero in a down year for the underlying equity index, or a positive return based upon performance of the index and the limit imposed for upside for that year.

Equity-indexed annuities had little or no appeal when a reasonable rate could be earned on a fixed annuity. However, product changes, including lower commissions paid to agents and lower surrender charges, have combined to give these products some appeal in the current low-interest-rate environment. However, I urge you to exercise extreme caution when evaluating or even suggesting these products to clients. Yet, they may be worth a look in some cases because market forces have acted on this product category to bring it more in line with what's reasonable.

Reductions of both commissions and surrender costs have made equity-indexed fixed annuities a suitable investment for clients that have almost zero tolerance for investment losses. The upside potential annual average return of these investments typically is 5 percent or less in most cases I have examined, but that return compares favorably with CDs, money market instruments, and bonds. Distributions from equity-indexed annuities are taxed as ordinary income, but if used as an alternative to

CDs, money market funds, or bonds, that should not be a disadvantage since they are taxed similarly.

Important point: Equity-indexed annuities can be a viable alternative to traditional fixed-income investment vehicles.

Limited-term variable annuities

Never underestimate the financial service's ability to create new ideas. Limited-term variable annuities are a cross between an equity-indexed annuity and a variable annuity. Limited-term variable annuities limit but do not eliminate client downside in a bad equity market but also generally provide investors with substantially more upside than equity-indexed annuities.

Important point: I like these annuities for younger, risk-averse clients or some of my older clients with longer than average periods before they wish to start withdrawals.

Real estate investment trusts

Real estate investment trusts were designed to follow the mutual fund principles identified in the Investment Company Act of 1940, and true to their name, they're all about real estate, usually commercial properties. REITs exist because real estate is a capital asset, but it typically is not liquid, and cash flow may not be predictable. When sold at a profit, the gain is a capital gain. Due to both liquidity and cash flow issues, many investors prefer to buy REITs. Investing in REITs during 2000–2004 worked well because real estate values were growing. REITs that purchased commercial or residential properties during 2005–2008 generally overpaid based on today's values and yielded mixed results. REITs purchasing since 2009 has tended to have great results and has resulted in strong investor favor.

If 90 percent or more of taxable income is distributed, REITs do not pay tax at the corporate level. Unfortunately, the tax disadvantage is that REIT dividends are by definition not qualified dividends and are therefore taxed as ordinary income at the investor's highest marginal tax rate for that year. Ordinary income is among the basket of income streams used to calculate whether Social Security benefits are taxable. Whenever possible, cash flow should derive from income that is not factored into a retiree's modified adjusted gross income, to shield as much of Social Security as possible from taxation.

Important point: A depreciating REIT can actually be good for retirees.

REITs may have sufficient depreciation to make their annual dividends nontaxable return of capital. In fact, newer REITs often offset all or nearly all of their dividends with depreciation. Note that this is one case where newer investments may have a big tax advantage over established REITs. Older REITs like to promote long track records, but I find that carefully chosen newer REITs may best serve clients. I find these REITs may be very desirable for retirees with substantial Social Security benefits. The REITs provide cash flow over and above the cash flow from the Social Security benefits but don't result in taxable income based upon the depreciation. Ultimately, when a REIT is sold, the gain is treated as capital.

As I said, not all REITs' dividends are return of capital. For example, net-lease REITs require tenants to pay most or all of the operating and maintenance costs, which result in taxable dividends. As is the case with variable annuities, not every REIT is created equal. Take the time to really shop around before suggesting one for a client.

Nontraded REITs

Confusion often exists about the difference between nontraded public REITs and exchange-listed REITs. Nontraded REITs have served as a place for new REITs to incubate prior to listing on an organized exchange in three to seven years. The clean slate when they start allows them to buy attractive properties with their cash that traded REITs might not be able to buy because they are too small for them due to evaluation procedures designed for buying larger properties. Decision makers for traded REITs typically are unable to move as quickly due to their due diligence checks and balances, which means executives at nontraded REITs may make more bad decisions because they act hastily.

Another key difference between the two forms of REIT, aside from size, lies in liquidity.

Nontraded REITs lack current liquidity. Nontraded REITs generally use independent financial advisors to both educate investors and sell the shares. Lack of liquidity causes a number of investors to dismiss nontraded REITS without a reasonable examination, but in my view, this is a mistake.

Here's how it works: Early investors buy a blind pool of commercial properties. The term "blind pool" means investors do not know specifics about investments because they have not yet been purchased. The blind pool makes some investors nervous. Nontraded REITs commonly have a term of three to seven years before closing to new investors and providing liquidity to existing investors if the REIT is successful.

Nontraded REITs provide one of my favorite investments, and for the right client, a REIT can be a fabulous source of cash flow. There are many excellent upsides to these investments. These can include:

    a. Distributions are frequently nontaxable returns of capital due to depreciation.

    b. Cash flow is very attractive (typically 5 to 7 percent annually).

    c. Reinvestment of dividends at 95 percent of investment cost adds to compound return.

    d.   The exit event can produce a capital gain.

    e.   Nontraded REITs offer higher yields than traded REITs.

Disadvantages include:

    a.   Projected lack of liquidity for three to seven years.

    b.   Taxable dividends are nonqualified and therefore taxed as ordinary income.

Public nontraded REITs have received a bloody nose as a result of the history in the early years of the twenty-first century. Several industry icons had structured their companies to operate and manage these REITs and had little or no incentive to provide liquidity. Fortunately, recent history has seen many very successful exit events. Almost every one of these REIT sponsors owes a debt to American Realty Capital for demonstrating that successful quick exits can and should be possible.

My favorite public nontraded REITs utilize a combination of the following:

    a.   An attractive niche, such as self-storage, student housing, office buildings, New York recovery, apartment complexes, data centers, or health care

    b.   Take advantage of the lack of bank financing that would have been provided in previous eras

    c.   Recognition of demographic trends, including reduced home ownership

    d.   Allow compounding of cash flows by providing reinvestment at 95 percent of investment cost

    e.   Deliver consistently high cash flows

f. Enjoy a scale that enables REITs to raise mountains of cash to take full advantage of prime real estate deals

Historically, a major driver of stock market performance has been dividend reinvestment. These nontraded REITs have historically unprecedented distributions and provide opportunity for reinvestment of these distributions at a discount. It makes me want to scream when I read that only 50 percent of REIT dividends are reinvested at these favorable REIT prices. We need to do a better job of educating clients about the opportunity cost they incur when choosing not to reinvest these distributions, thereby allowing clients to take full advantage of favorable compounding and reinvestment discounts.

One final but very important caveat I offer is that traditional accounting earnings per share (EPS) do not measure REIT performance well. Older REITs used most of their depreciation in earlier years, and thus cash flows produce greater EPS. Top analysts for several well-known financial newsletters don't realize that real estate depreciation is frequently not realistic in measuring ongoing costs. Newer properties with greater depreciation often appreciate rather than depreciate. Accounting professionals with real estate backgrounds use fund from operations (FFO) rather than EPS as the key evaluation measure.

Like most experts, I do not like REITs with dividends greater than the cash flow netted from operations (FFO) but do not worry about newer REITs paying dividends great than EPS. Even negative EPS do not concern me because very new properties require far less capital expenditures than older properties and are therefore able to pay most or all of their net cash flow to investors. Investors love high tax-sheltered returns. A 7 percent dividend that is totally tax sheltered by depreciation is very attractive.

Important point: REITs can deliver excellent cash flow that does not contribute to Social Security tax liabilities if distributions are nontaxable returns of capital due to depreciation.

Business development companies

In the early 1980s, Congress established guidelines for the creation of business development companies to help fill a void when mid- to small-sized businesses were unable to find bank financing. These entities function in ways very similar to the traditional venture capitalist model. Their sole mission is to help well-established, growing businesses succeed through accessible financing. At the time, BDCs did not become popular because interest rates were running in the high teens to more than 20 percent, making borrowing prohibitively expensive. The law permitted the establishment of this type of company, but business conditions for creating them were all wrong.

Enter the financial meltdown that began in earnest during the last quarter of 2008. Banks stopped lending, and the credit markets froze. We're still not out of the woods. Credit for thirty-year fixed mortgages is tough for some Americans to secure even as the economy lumbers out of the doldrums. BDCs have come into their own since 2010 because banks have very little incentive to loan to even the perfect loan candidates. After all, banks can borrow at 0.25 percent and invest in US government ten-year bonds at between 2.5 and 3.0 percent. With banks being able to lend nineteen dollars for every dollar of deposits, they can earn close to 50 percent on the differential! No wonder they're tight-fisted with their hordes of cash! The federal government has essentially given them a free license to print money.

BDCs can typically lend at rates 5 to 10 percent above their borrowing costs. If BDCs raise equity capital and use the equity capital to borrow an equal amount, they can turn 7 percent into 14 percent return on capital before expenses. Many people would worry about the loan loss potential. BDCs pick and choose their loans very carefully, resulting in very small default rates. Even defaults often result in a gain because BDCs take protection in the form of collateral for loans.

Paralleling REITs, BDCs exist in both traded and nontraded forms. BDCs can play a very important role in helping seniors match cash inflows with their expenditures. BDCs with consistent intermediate-term yields approaching or greater than 10 percent exist, though the annual return on BDCs is typically between 7 and 10 percent. The return is attractive, but investors should realize the tax rules do not favor BDCs. Most of the income is both taxable and ordinary income. However, BDCs typically allow reinvestment at a 10 percent discount.

Important point: I love the compound return potential clients can realize from investing in a BDC! I suggest using Roth IRAs for BDC investments to take advantage of very favorable returns without negative taxation rules.

Master limited partnerships

Master limited partnerships trade on public security exchanges. They combine tax benefits of a limited partnership with the liquidity of publicly traded securities. Federal tax law limits MLPs to enterprises that engage in certain businesses, such as petroleum and natural gas extraction and transportation. Generally 90 percent or more of the partnership's income must be generated by "qualifying" sources. MLPs pay investors quarterly distributions based upon income and contractual terms. General partners are motivated to maximize distributions to limited partners by increasing fees to the general partner based upon payments to limited partners.

MLPs are taxed as partnerships, avoiding corporate tax at both state and federal levels. Limited partners get a large tax benefit in the form of tax write-offs on their personal share, thus reducing substantially the taxability of distributions. This tax benefit helps shelter cash flow, making MLPs attractive sources of cash flow. There is no tax advantage to holding an MLP interest in a tax-deferred or tax-free retirement account. Thus, MLPs generally belong only in nonretirement accounts. Their use in tax-qualified accounts is generally a mistake.

There are four basic ways to invest in MLPs:

1. Investment in publicly traded stock for a single company

2. Investment in an open-ended mutual fund that accepts purchases and withdrawals daily

3. Investment in a closed-end mutual fund that raises a defined amount and trades like a stock on an exchanges

4. Investment in an exchange traded fund (ETF) of MLPs

I've found that many clients own MLPs but don't understand what they have. MLPs are a favorite investment of Registered Representatives (brokers or registered reps in everyday language). Unfortunately, because brokers frequently don't consider tax consequences when advising clients, I've found that MLPs frequently appear in tax-qualified client accounts, which, as I've indicated, is a mistake that should be avoided. The key advantages of MLPs are:

1. High tax-advantage yield

2. Relatively steady and high cash flow

3. Growth potential

4. Liquidity

Parting words: The importance of proper strategic planning during the accumulation phase of a client's financial life cannot be over emphasized. The traditional investment vehicles that provide fixed and growth income play a major part in amassing sufficient assets to generate cash flow, but these investments are just some of the tools at our fingertips. If we fully assess where our clients stand in terms of their CAMP Score five or ten years before they expect to retire, we can get out in front of issues that could delay their retirement. Investments in variable annuities or life insurance policies with living benefits are becoming increasingly important as workers grapple with the disappearing pension in contemporary America and the looming, potentially catastrophic costs of long-term care that will impact tens of millions of baby boomers in the decades to come.

As a financial professional, it should excite you to dip your proverbial toe into investment vehicles that reside off the typical beaten path. I particularly love opportunities to show clients how to generate cash flow at minimum risk while protecting their Social Security benefits from taxation. The use of a vehicle like a nontraded newer REIT that depreciates, thereby assuring a return of capital instead of a taxable dividend, is a terrific opportunity for some clients. For others, perhaps the REIT is too exotic, as is investment in a business development company, but you'll never know until you investigate the numerous intriguing possibilities that continue to emerge in the yield-oriented investment marketplace of today!

6

The Sequencing Factor
Sequencing Risk and Client Draw Downs

> The question isn't at what age do I want to retire, it's at what income. —George Foreman

AS THE SAYING GOES, timing is everything. I'm not talking about timing the market. We all know trying to do that doesn't usually work. No, I'm talking about sequence risk and about how to properly time drawing down client assets during the distribution stage. Both are linked, and both can exert positive or negative pressure on cash flow for retirees. As you help guide your clients into retirement through the distribution phase of their financial lives, it's important to keep a steady hand on the helm, always thinking with a clear head about potential downside risks and upside reward potential. The jump from working life to retirement is often a profound change for most people, especially men, and at such potentially stressful times, your clients will need you more than ever. Naturally, we can't see into the future to avoid costly mistakes, unexpected downturns, or bum investments we initially thought were good, but we can and should try very hard to do just that even if we don't own a crystal ball.

Balancing income needs with asset accumulation and retention can be very difficult, so before we proceed, I need to simply point out that there are two distinct sets of calculations you'll need to do up front.

Preliminary calculations: 1) Evaluate all cash flows and assets based upon cash needs. This calculation helps determine whether assets need to be converted for income production. Ideally, cash flow will be sufficient to meet day-to-day needs, and assets can be allowed to grow to provide a margin of safety and to combat the erosive effects of inflation. 2) Convert all monthly income sources, including pensions and Social Security, to expected economic value over life expectancy. Only in this way can you project into the future over a life expectancy of twenty years or more to see how much cash flow will actually be required once inflation is factored into the mix.

You'll also need to evaluate your client's individual standing before proceeding with an analysis of sequence risk and sequence of draw down. For example, you might have a client who's lucky enough to have a pension and Social Security. But that same client may not have any or very few assets that could be easily and quickly converted to cash in the event of an emergency. In that scenario, sequence risk and sequence of draw down is almost irrelevant. In a case like that, I'd suggest that the client establish a home equity line of credit prior to retiring. The funds could be used to build up tax-deferred retirement accounts, and the funds could create a cash cushion for emergencies. A reverse mortgage, which we'll discuss later, is another option, though those come with some negatives. Still, a reverse mortgage could work for some of your clients who need a cushion of cash to hedge against unforeseen financial drains.

Other assets such as non-income-producing land could be converted to cash, which could then go into a Roth IRA over time as the client approaches full retirement age. Incidentally, clients with cash flow from pensions and Social Security, but with few assets, are not good candidates for a variable annuity, whereas clients with lots of diverse assets and small Social Security annual payments are much more likely to benefit from a variable annuity.

Important point: As your clients enter the distribution stage, it's best to restrict illiquid assets to roughly one third of their portfolios.

It is very important to balance cash flow needs and the need for liquid assets. All monthly cash flows and assets should be considered in determining an appropriate mix. Thus, some assets may be selected to provide cash flow while others provide long-term security in exchange for less liquidity.

A word about pensions

Corporate/government pensions sometimes offer a choice between cash flow for life in the form of a monthly income or a lump sum. Most corporate pensions do not index for cost of living while most government pensions are indexed for inflation. When given a choice, I frequently advise taking the government pension, but by contrast, I often advise taking the lump sum from corporate pensions. Although each situation has to be analyzed carefully on its own merits, corporate pensions seldom provide cost-of-living protection. You can often do better for your clients if you convert the corporate pension to cash and invest it wisely in a diverse pool of assets selected for the most effective low-risk production of cash flow.

Dollar-Cost averaging

While it's important to choose investments that provide cash flow with as little risk as possible during the distribution phase, during the years prior to retirement, volatility may actually help an investor's return through the phenomenon that mathematicians and investment professionals call dollar-cost averaging. The following example shows the difference between having volatile investments during a ten-year accumulation period and a ten-year withdrawal period.

Table 1

Dollar-Cost Averaging (Accumulation Stage)

Yr	Invest	Invest Return	Beginning Unit Price	Ending Unit Price	Units Beginning	Units Bought	Units Ending	Year End Value
1	10000	-9.10%	$10.00	$9.09	0	1,000.00	1,000.00	$9,090.00
2	10000	-11.89%	9.09	8.01	1,000.00	1,100.11	2,100.11	16,820.20
3	10000	-22.10%	8.01	6.24	2,100.11	1,248.56	3,348.67	20,892.94
4	10000	28.69%	6.24	8.03	3,348.67	1,602.78	4,951.45	39,756.12
5	10000	10.88%	8.03	8.90	4,951.45	1,245.46	6,196.91	55,169.58
6	10000	4.91%	8.90	9.34	6,196.91	1,123.25	7,320.16	68,369.41
7	10000	15.79%	9.34	10.81	7,320.16	1,070.68	8,390.83	90,743.94
8	10000	5.49%	10.81	11.41	8,390.83	924.67	9,315.51	106,274.78
9	10000	-37.00%	11.41	7.19	9,315.51	876.55	10,192.05	73,253.11
10	10000	26.46%	$7.19	$9.09	10,192.05	1,391.35	11,583.40	$105,281.89

Dollar-Cost Averaging (Distribution Stage)

Yr	Invest	Invest Return	Beginning Unit Price	Ending Unit Price	Units Beginning	Units Sold	Units Ending	Year End Value
0								$105,281.89
1	-10000	-9.10%	$10.00	$9.09	11583.4	(1,000.00)	10,583.40	96,203.11
2	-10300	-11.89%	9.09	8.01	10,583.40	(1,133.11)	9,450.29	75,689.23
3	-10609	-22.10%	8.01	6.24	9,450.29	(1,324.60)	8,125.68	50,697.50
4	-10927.27	28.69%	6.24	8.03	8,125.68	(1,751.40)	6,374.29	51,180.30
5	-11255.088	10.88%	8.03	8.90	6,374.29	(1,401.77)	4,972.51	44,269.08
6	-11592.741	4.91%	8.90	9.34	4,972.51	(1,302.15)	3,670.36	34,280.75
7	-11940.523	15.79%	9.34	10.81	3,670.36	(1,278.44)	2,391.92	25,867.75
8	-12298.739	5.49%	10.81	11.41	2,391.92	(1,137.23)	1,254.69	14,313.95
9	-12667.701	-37.00%	11.41	7.19	1,254.69	(1,110.39)	144.30	1,037.13
10	-13047.732	26.46%	$7.19	$9.09	144.30	(1,815.39)	(1,671.09)	$(15,188.60)

Note that in this example, the top part assumes investing $10,000 per year while the bottom part assumes that $10,000 per year with an inflation rate of 3 percent is withdrawn.

My example is intended to demonstrate the mathematical properties of dollar-cost averaging. The top part shows that a worker contributing $10,000 per year to their tax-deferred retirement plan with the investment returns of 2000–2009 would have accumulated $105,281.89 at the end of the ten-year period. By contrast, an investor with an initial investment of $100,000 at the beginning of year 1 and no other activity would have had approximately $90,900. Thus, dollar-cost averaging substantially improved returns. Yale International Center for Finance labeled 2000–2009 the worst decade in US market history. Ironically, the decade was worse than the 1930s.

Dollar-cost averaging protects investors in the stock market during the accumulation stage. It increases investor returns over the reported average rate of return for the period. This occurs because the investment discipline allows the investor to buy more units when the price is low, and less when the price is high. Note that the technique provides the discipline. The investor does not have to decide when to buy. The investor simply invests the same fixed amount each year.

Important point: During the distribution stage of retirement, dollar-cost averaging is generally disastrous for investors. When prices are low, they have to sell more units to get the same distribution. Buy high, sell low doesn't work!

The differences between the accumulation stage and the distribution stage makes the investing approach for retirement counterintuitive for even some of the most sophisticated thinkers. That's why it's so important to approach counseling your clients about retirement cash flow with a more sophisticated strategy that takes the entire picture into account when making financial decisions.

Sequence risk

With pensions disappearing and the savings level among new retirees at historic lows, the deck is stacked against a large number of baby boomers. Those who have been smart and disciplined enough to save and invest wisely, even in spite of the two stock market crashes since 2002, are clearly in a more advantageous position. Chances are your client is banking on supplementing Social Security benefits with income from investments. When investors use the return from investments to meet living expenses, the investment return sequence becomes quite important.

Poor returns in early retirement years force the retiree to utilize a percentage of their investments to meet living expenses. In other words, they're dipping into principal. Once used to meet living expenses, those assets no longer produce future income. Cash flow naturally is reduced. Thus, if at all possible, you want your clients to earn excellent returns early in their retirement, not the opposite. When good investment returns occur during early retirement, they either preserve investment assets or increase retirement assets.

Academics use the term "ceteris paribus" when showing that if one thing happens, the result should be a given if "all other things are equal or constant." Professor Moshe Milevsky of York University in Toronto made a very important contribution to the retirement planning discipline when he discovered that sequence or order of returns becomes important once clients retire and "begin to live off the cash flow from their principal." Note that during the accumulation stage, sequence is unimportant if a lump sum is invested for a given period.

Important point: The timing of negative returns versus positive returns makes a big difference. Starting retirement with positive returns puts a retiree in a better financial position for future cash flow and capital preservation.

As you advise your clients prior to their retirement, keep sequence risk in mind as you evaluate whether retirement makes sense at a given time. For example, if the market is trending downward, it might be smarter for your client to defer retirement until more favorable market conditions prevail. Losses of principal early in retirement reduce future cash flow potential and increase financial and psychological insecurity. Markets always eventually rebound, but damage to expected cash flow from investment principal that had to be spent down can be permanent and devastating to clients.

Consider anyone who retired in early 2002 after the tech bubble burst, or in late 2007 when the Great Recession was just getting started. Both periods were disastrous for millions of retirees. Indeed, by most estimates, the half of Americans that owned 401(k) or individual retirement accounts lost nearly 50 percent of their money, or roughly $2.8 trillion during the most recent economic collapse. I've mentioned these numbers before. I repeat them here to reinforce the points I'm about to make about sequence risk. The issue is that serious.

Obviously, all your clients should have a built-in margin of safety to cover market reversals, health emergencies, or any other unforeseen expenses. It's just best not to have to cut to the bone too early. The margin of safety should be retained for as long as possible. The scenarios below graphically illustrate the importance of accounting for sequence risk. It's one thing to point out that it's probably not too intelligent to pull the plug on working to retire in a down market. Your client will understand the point you're making, but the concept will hover in that intangible realm of the intellect without becoming concrete. If you were to show the client the case examples below, I suspect your point would be made far more tangible, just by taking a hard look at the two scenarios. Note the difference in assets after a mere five years between someone who retired based upon investments of $400,000 with annual income needs of $20,000 between Cases 1 and 2.

In case 1, the retiree got whacked with negative returns in the first three years of retirement. Drawing down principal was required to make up the shortfall between returns and living expenses of $20,000, leaving the retiree with $239,747 left from the initial invested amount of $400,000.

> **Case 1 return**
> Yr 1 -9%
> Yr 2 -11%
> Yr 3 -22%
> Yr 4 +25%
> Yr 5 +11%
> **Remaining assets $239,747**

Financial products have been developed to reduce or ameliorate sequence risk, but it's still very real in traditional fixed- or growth-income types of investments subject to market downturns. As you can see, case 1 shows losses for the first three years and positive returns in the last two years of our scenario. Now, take a look at the big difference the same retiree would experience were you to flip the same positive returns gained in the same five-year period, putting the positives into the mathematics at the start instead of at the end. In case 2, we have positive returns of 25 and 11 percent, followed by the same negative returns we had in case 1. All that differs is the order.

> **Case 2 return**
> Yr 1 +25%
> Yr 2 +11%
> Yr 3 -9%
> Yr 4 -11%
> Yr 5 -22%
> **Remaining assets $274,463**

Thus, the difference between case 1 and case 2 is $34,716 or 14 percent in case 2 where we started off with returns of 25 percent versus 9 percent in case 1. We had the same returns of 11 percent in the second year of retirement, and so on down the line.

When discussing sequence risks with your clients, it's also important to make them aware of just how much it takes to recover from losses of principal due to economic downturns. Refer to table 1 as an excellent illustration.

Table 1

If the Investment Loss Is	It Requires Gains of to Return to the Original Balance
20%	25%
25%	33 1/3%
33 1/3%	50%
50%	100%

There are steps you can take to help clients reduce their exposure to sequence risk. For example, diversification of cash flow sources will spread the risk around. Cash flow from a nontraded REIT, variable annuities, and dividend-paying stocks is better than relying solely on dividend-paying stocks and/or fixed-income sources like bonds and CDs. Of course, it's perfectly fine to lower your client's equity position in favor of more stable investment vehicles, provided that the rate of return is sufficient to generate the needed cash flow, but diversification should be at the core of your financial strategy no matter what because it helps guard against sequence risk. Diversification into low-interest, fixed-income vehicles can also diminish long-term returns, so you'll need to work hard to get the right balance.

Inflation protection is also a major consideration as you develop a pool of assets that will generate cash flow from a variety of sources for your clients in the distribution stage. Table 1 provides some examples of assets that have some degree of inflation protection, while others don't. The end goal is to maximize return for a given level of risk and to build diversity into the mix of cash flow sources.

Table 2

Retirement Vehicle	Cash Flow Increases When This Happens
Social Security	Inflation Occurs and/or Benefits Are Delayed
Stocks	Corporate Revenues Grow Increasing Dividends
Corporate Bonds	Almost Never
Treasury Bonds	Never
Treasury Inflation Protected Bonds (TIPS)	Cash Flow Doesn't Increase, but Principal Grows With Inflation
Federal Pensions	Inflation Occurs and/or Benefits Are Delayed
State Pensions	Inflation Occurs and/or Benefits Are Delayed (No Index in Some States)
Local Pensions	A Very Few Are Inflation Indexed
Corporate Pensions	A Very Few Are Inflation Indexed
Stock Mutual Funds	Corporate Revenues Grow Increasing Dividends
Bond Mutual Funds	Slowly When Interest Rates Rise But Principal May Be Lost
Fixed Annuities/ CDs	Slowly When Interest Rates Rise
Variable Annuities	Cash Flows Rise Based Upon Delayed Receipt and Increasing Mutual Fund Values
Nontraded REITS	Rents Grow and Dividends Are Reinvested Increasing Future Dividends

As table 2 reflects, there are a number of cash flow sources to include. It's all about diversity to guard against sequence risk and a premature drawing down of principal to maintain the client's desired standard of living. Sequence comes into play on other levels as well. For example, it matters when deciding which assets to draw down first and which ones to leave for later.

Draw down after-tax assets first

It may sound obvious, but it bears saying that drawing down low-interest after-tax fixed-income investments first during the beginning of the distribution stage is the most sensible strategy. A money market or CD at maturity triggers tax liabilities when clients must pay taxes on interest as ordinary income, but clients are not taxed on the principal from these assets that is used to pay for retirement expenses. Distributions from tax-deferred retirement accounts do trigger taxation of the entire amount withdrawn, and those distributions also factor into calculations of modified adjusted gross income that can impact taxes on Social Security benefits.

I suggest using liquid assets to meet basic expenses and to help clients defer taking Social Security early, as well as deferring withdrawals from annuities and retirement accounts. Putting off those benefits until full retirement age yields a future return of 25 percent per year for life on the Social Security benefits alone, versus beginning Social Security benefits at age sixty-two, plus an additional 8 percent per year from full retirement age (sixty-six) to the age of seventy if the client waits the maximum period before collecting benefits. I'll talk more about Social Security later, but I cite it here to show that sequence really does matter.

Many clients won't think of doing this. They'll immediately latch onto Social Security at age sixty-two when they might have been able to wait a couple more years by dipping into their after-tax assets. Frankly, if taking distributions from a tax-deferred account would mean successfully deferring Social Security until full retirement age,

I'd wholeheartedly support that strategy as a last resort. As you can see, this new philosophy of retirement cash flow planning is a bit of a jigsaw puzzle. It's almost always a compromise.

Yet, arguing for deferring Social Security in favor of drawing down after-tax fixed-income assets is a perfect example of the new philosophy of retirement cash flow management that I am advocating. It's an integrated approach that takes into account the major elements that go into the big picture, as opposed to focusing merely on what to do with traditional fixed- and growth-income assets alone and leaving it at that.

Important point: Advise your clients to draw down liquid assets first, leaving tax-deferred retirement accounts in reserve. Note that liquid assets are also stable, nonfluctuating assets. Drawing from the pool of nonfluctuating assets ensures that draw-downs don't permanently damage capital during down financial markets. Defer Social Security for as long as possible.

Defer drawing from tax-deferred retirement accounts

There are two schools of thought about when clients should tap into their 401(k) and/or traditional IRA accounts. The first says that the client should draw down a Roth IRA before moving on to these accounts because the client earns money as the assets grow tax-free until withdrawal. In many ways, that sequence makes a lot of sense, and I generally support it. The Roth IRA distributions won't incur any tax liability that could reduce cash flow from Social Security benefits that would possibly be taxed if the client took a distribution from a tax-deferred account. The formula gets complicated, of course, because every retiree's financial landscape is unique. What is good advice for one client isn't necessarily good for another client. Tax brackets and assets vary, as does client risk tolerance and financial sophistication.

Situations change as well, which may require tweaking the sequence of which assets to draw down after the after-tax fixed-income assets are spent. For example, if the client has sufficient cash flow from pensions and Social Security, then deferring draw down of the Roth IRA would not be the most desirable course if the client is thinking about leaving an inheritance to heirs. Heirs would not face a tax event with a Roth IRA inheritance, unless it was huge, but they would if they inherited a tax-deferred retirement account and took the cash instead of rolling it over into their own retirement accounts.

As you discuss sequence of draw down, ask clients about their long-term legacy objectives. Those objectives could determine the course of action that is right for the individual. I generally discourage paying too much attention to leaving an inheritance. After all, the client has worked hard and almost always faces a battery of expenses that will require the use of all assets together to create a welcoming retirement experience, and to protect against a costly long-term care event. However, legacy issues are very important to some clients, so I make sure to factor them into the strategic planning from the very beginning of a relationship. By the way, I always make sure clients have wills, advance health care directives, and powers of attorney.

Important point: Consider the cost of all cash flow sources, including home equity loans and drawing down investments, before deciding which sources to utilize first in meeting cash flow needs.

Mix retiree cash flow sources

Mixing retirement cash flow sources can provide a much better retirement for many reasons. Let's briefly recap here. The points I've been making thus far include:

1. Sequence of draw down can lower retirement taxes.

2. Negative consequences for cash flow can result from incorrect sequencing.

    a. Annuities frequently guarantee a given rate of cash

flow growth until the first withdrawal. After the first withdrawal, cash flow growth is no longer guaranteed, and the underlying investment must exceed withdrawals for the principal to grow.

b. Selling stocks or real estate both eliminate future growth and cause capital gain taxes to be due.

c. Withdrawing from IRAs both eliminates deferral of taxes and may cause net proceeds after taxes to be invested less well.

3. Utilizing retirement cash flow sources wisely makes it much easier for many couples to make better decisions about when to retire and when and how to begin receiving Social Security benefits.

As I've mentioned, recent returns on excess liquid funds have been almost nonexistent. Even more importantly, utilizing liquid funds for part of the needed cash flow minimizes retirement taxes and allows the other retirement baskets to continue to grow. Now that we have the theory, let's take a look at three illustrations to show you how cash flow sequencing and mix can play out in the real world for your clients.

Illustration 1

Harold, age sixty-four, and Jane, age sixty-seven, came in for a review of their situation. Jane had already retired and was drawing $1,600 per month in Social Security. Harold was still working, and he had not begun collecting the $2,000 per month in Social Security benefits he was currently eligible for. They didn't have a mortgage. Plus, Jane inherited a stock portfolio worth $85,000 the previous year. There was no tax liability associated with the inheritance. Harold and Jane wanted to stay in their home, and they wanted to travel.

Jane's medical coverage is Medicare Parts A (hospitals) and B (doctors), and she has Part D drug coverage through her local pharmacy. Harold's medical coverage through his work will end when he turns sixty-five in three months. Harold does not like his job (he earns $50,000 per year) and would like to retire immediately.

So, here's what they had to work with in terms of the financial part of their CAMP Score:

Traditional IRAs $165,000
Roth IRAs $120,000
Liquid savings $60,000
Stock portfolio $85,000
Home value $300,000

My recommendations:

1. Harold would work until he reaches age sixty-six, and then he could begin drawing spousal Social Security benefits from Jane's Social Security at age sixty-six. He would defer taking his own Social Security until age seventy. This would maximize his Social Security cash flow.

2. During the next two years, they would convert at least $80,000 from traditional IRAs to Roth IRAs in anticipation of Harold's full retirement. The conversion would result in long-term tax-free cash flow once the immediate tax liability associated with the conversion was satisfied. Minimizing taxes during retirement is vital, particularly when both spouses are receiving substantial Social Security benefits.

3. Harold would make maximum 401(k) deferrals of $23,000 per year for the last two partial years of his employment. Maximizing these contributions would crimp cash flow in the short-term, but it would result in an additional tax-deferred $46,000 into the 401(k), making up for some

of the tax associated with the money converted from the traditional IRA to the Roth IRA.

4. Jane would add a Medicare Supplement Plan F to protect against higher medical costs in the future. Jane fell short of the health protection component in the CAMP Score analysis. Many retirees scrimp on the supplemental insurance side of Medicare because they don't realize the degree of financial liability they would face were they to need extensive medical care that Medicare doesn't fully cover, or that comes with Medicare benefits that end after a specified period of time.

5. Both Harold and Jane would buy life insurance with a long-term care rider to provide death benefits to the surviving spouse and to build in protection against a possible long-term care event.

6. They would consider a reverse mortgage at some point in the future (they do not wish to leave their house).

7. Harold would try to earn $1,000 per month in the first five years of his retirement doing something he enjoys.

Harold and Jane had no idea they could convert traditional IRAs into a Roth IRA, and they also didn't know about spousal benefits from Social Security (these will be discussed later). Harold was a bit disappointed when I told him he had to keep working, but when we figured out their cash flow together with expenses for health care and the life insurance policies, they had a CAMP Score well over 100 percent! They agreed to defer their immediate gratification in favor of long-term tax breaks and guaranteed increases in Harold's Social Security benefits that would grow by deferring taking his full benefits for an additional six years.

Illustration 2

Olive, a widow at age sixty-four, was panicked about her retirement prospects. She was eligible for survivor benefits of $2,000 a month based on her recently deceased husband, Wilhelm. Her own Social Security benefits would be nearly $1,800 per month if she waited to collect until her full retirement age of sixty-six. Olive's medical coverage would be eliminated when she reaches age sixty-five. Other key variable: Olive does not work. She cared for Wilhelm for several years during his last illness. She did not have a mortgage, and she wants to sell the house. Like Harold and Jane, she wanted to travel during retirement.

So, here's what Olive had to work with in terms of the financial part of her CAMP Score:

Traditional IRAs $60,000
Roth IRAs $40,000
Liquid savings $250,000 (from Wilhelm's life insurance)
Stock portfolio $15,000
Home value $130,000

My recommendations:

1. Olive would work part-time or volunteer for a cause she supports to get her out of the house. Ideally, she would get a paying job to continue paying into her IRA and Roth IRA. Because she currently does not work, she can't pay into retirement accounts like an IRA or a Roth IRA because her income is not earned. I encouraged her to give this idea strong consideration.

2. Olive would select a Medicare Supplement Plan F when she turns sixty-five to protect against higher medical costs in the future.

3. Olive should draw survivor benefits until she reaches age

seventy and plan to defer her own Social Security until then. As with Harold and Jane, deferring Social Security would maximize Social Security cash flow.

4. Olive should buy life insurance with a long-term care rider. The long-term care and the basic health care components of her CAMP Score required attention.

5. She would consider a reverse mortgage at some point in the future.

6. Olive would consider using $150,000 of the liquid savings to buy an annuity for her future that will build her guaranteed future cash flow. I strongly advised her to go with this suggestion. The overall cash flow long-term was mainly from her Social Security and from tax-deferred investments in her retirement accounts. Traditional fixed and growth assets are subject to market downturns resulting in principal and cash flow loss. A variable annuity would guarantee income and virtually eliminate the risk of loss long-term.

7. Olive would convert her traditional IRA to a Roth IRA (the future distributions will not be factored into modified adjusted gross income, which could cause her Social Security to be taxed).

8. Olive has too many memories in her house. She wants to move nearer to her only daughter. She should sell the house.

9. Olive needs income with tax benefits and solid cash flow. There are many REITs and preferred stocks that could provide this cash flow in a tax-advantage way. Invest the proceeds from the sale of the house appropriately.

While Olive was initially frightened about her retirement years subsequent to the death of her husband, she realized that her position was not dire at all from a financial perspective. With the right strategy that took into account her basic health care, long-term care, taxes, and cash flow, she was able to put in place a sound long-term plan based on her CAMP Score.

Illustration 3

Richard, age sixty-five, and Joanne, age sixty-three, were both ready to look seriously at their retirement options. Richard, who was still working, wanted to spend more time with his wife and kids, but he liked his job well enough and wasn't opposed to staying put for a couple more years. Joanne was currently eligible to draw $1,500 per month in Social Security, and Richard was currently eligible to draw $2,000 per month in Social Security.

Richard's medical coverage through his work will end when he turns sixty-five in three months. Joanne is eligible to be covered under his policy until she turns age sixty-five. They were not savvy investors, showing a capital loss carry forward of $183,000. They did not have a mortgage.

So, here's what they had to work with in terms of the financial part of their CAMP Score:

> Traditional IRAs $625,000
> Roth IRAs $0
> Liquid savings $160,000
> Stock portfolio $485,000
> Home value $700,000

My recommendations:

1. Richard would work until he reaches age sixty-six, when he could then draw spousal benefits from Joanne's Social Security, thereby deferring taking his full benefits until he turned seventy. Notice the similarities with illustration

1. Combining Social Security spousal benefits with the strategy to defer full Social Security benefits until age seventy is a superb way to maximize cash flow for most potential retirees who are around the same age.

2. During the next two years, they would convert at least $200,000 from traditional IRAs to Roth IRAs in anticipation of Richard's full retirement. Notice that I don't argue for full conversions of traditional IRAs to Roth IRAs. Of course, a conversion triggers the expected tax event, which factors into how much I suggest including in a conversion. The short-term tax pain from the Roth conversions makes sense because during retirement part of their cash flow will come from Roth income, which is not taxable and not part of the calculation of tax on Social Security. Also, tax-deferred accounts are good because they reap upside rewards by allowing clients to earn benefits from the tax deferral itself and on any growth of assets and returns until withdrawal.

3. Richard would make maximum 401(k) deferrals of $23,000 per year for the last year of his employment. As I said above, tax-deferred retirement accounts like a 401(k) are excellent investment vehicles. In Richard's case, his employer had a matching program, so it made sense to ramp up his contributions instead of reducing them.

4. They both would choose to add a Medicare Supplement Plan F when they reach age sixty-five to protect against higher medical costs in the future. There are a number of options for retirees to consider when it comes to Medicare Supplement coverage. I like Plan F because it's comprehensive. There are many hidden expenses and traps in the Medicare program that seniors are completely unaware of. I'll discuss Medicare at length later.

5. Both Richard and Joanne would buy an annuity with a long-term care rider. They had substantial assets, so buying hefty variable annuities with long-term care riders wouldn't greatly reduce their asset pool. The annuities, as opposed to life insurance, would create a reliable cash flow stream they didn't have from anything but Social Security. I generally calculate cash flow from Social Security and use variable annuity living benefits to get combined cash flow matching at least 60 percent of preferred retirement after-tax cash flow. Plus, it would hedge against the ruinous costs of a long-term care event.

6. They would consider a reverse mortgage at some point in the future. A reverse mortgage isn't for everyone, but for Richard and Joanne, the home represented a huge reservoir of untapped financial resources. In essence, the reverse mortgage or a home equity line of credit would enable them to use those financial resources to pay into a tax-deferred account, add to the Roth IRA, and leverage low-interest yielding illiquid assets to grow principal.

7. Richard would try to earn $2,000 per month in the first five years of his retirement doing something he enjoys. Adding cash flow through work would allow Richard to continue paying into his retirement accounts because the contributions would be from earned income. The cash flow from work would also help defray expenses that would otherwise have been met with cash flow from his Social Security benefits.

Richard and Joanne could probably live well during retirement with little retirement planning because of their substantial asset pool. However, they aren't in the catbird seat. Without planning, they will pay a lot more taxes than they could with good planning, and their substantial capital loss carryovers might go unused without careful attention from an advisor fully cognizant of the various tax laws that could apply.

Parting words: Most clients won't know about sequence risk, nor is it likely that they'll give much advance thought to the sequence of asset draw down. That means it's even more important for you to bring the subject up when you counsel clients about the next move they make as they pass from the accumulation stage to the distribution phase of finances in retirement. The tax liabilities of one course of action and the tax advantages of another aren't going to percolate to the forefront of a client's mind either. It's up to us to look at the big picture, as the above three illustrations show so well! While every individual or couple is unique, there are some overriding commonalities to factor into the grand strategy, that big-picture retiree panorama I've been drawing for you in these pages.

As you can see, I'm a big fan of deferring taxes whenever it's possible to do so. I also believe that deferring Social Security until age seventy is the wisest course of action for any retiree, and it pains me when I hear people who are about to retire at sixty-two say they don't care about the loss of benefits. They truly matter. Social Security is often the lion's share of the cash flow mix, even for relatively affluent clients. The integration of health care, long-term care, taxes, and the diverse baskets of potential investment vehicles needed to produce cash flow is what the new philosophy of financial advising should be as the baby boomers make way for Generation X and the Millennial Generation. Sound planning will brighten the futures of millions of Americans as they enter retirement.

7

Social Security 101
Safety Net Essentials

I don't feel old. I don't feel anything until noon. Then it's time for my nap. —Bob Hope

For a program as ubiquitous as Social Security is in American society, it's astounding how many misconceptions exist about the program. The lay public knows little about it except that payroll taxes are deducted to help pay for the benefits of current retirees, and that one day the monthly checks will roll in during the worker's own time on the golf course. In view of the aftermath of the Great Recession, and in view of the sweeping changes in American demographics as baby boomers age and retire, the belief that Social Security is going the way of the dinosaurs for younger workers gains more traction every day. The perception may be real enough, but the reality is far from what most people think. Workers also know that disability assistance from Social Security exists. However, unless the worker or retiree is disabled or knows someone who is in that aspect of the program, it remains in shadowed obscurity. The idea that Social Security benefits are calculated based on the last ten years of a worker's earnings is widespread and totally incorrect.

Financial professionals know more, or at least they should. However, the fact of the matter is that many *don't* know as much as they should, primarily because the nuances of Social Security don't usually figure into most educational programs for financial advisors and insurance sales associates. Certified public accounts and tax attorneys are often more well-versed in the key accounting issues related to the program. Yet even these professionals generally have not delved deeply into the guts of Social Security, how it works and why, and the various virtually unknown and underutilized parts of it that can make all the difference when it comes to retirement planning.

Financial professionals today are a highly specialized lot. That's just the way it has always been, but what was fine yesterday won't necessarily work now. Sure, focus on what you do best. Just know that when it comes to counseling clients on retirement issues, you'll need to know more to do your very best for the people who are counting on you for the continued viability of their financial lives as they age and hope to enjoy a retirement marked by dignity and comfort.

A central premise of this book is that we as financial professionals must learn to pursue a new philosophy of retirement planning for our clients, one that fixates less on assets and more on cash flow in the context of inflationary safeguards and protection against a wide array of health care pressures that can prove ruinous for clients who aren't prepared. I am arguing for an approach that takes the full picture of taxes, fixed-income investments, growth investments, and alternative investments; Medicare and its gaps; long-term care liabilities; and Social Security into account from an integrated perspective in the formulation of sound strategies focused on cash flow resources and appropriate allocations to guard against inflation.

Social Security needn't be overly complicated. A solid take on its main functions and options will get you started on your way quite nicely while you learn more about the inner realms of the program as you become more of an expert! Let's begin with the basics.

How Social Security is calculated

Social Security provides three types of benefits to qualified individuals—retirement, disability, and survivor's benefits. There is also a lump-sum payment of $255 in 2014 to surviving spouses or children eligible for benefits upon the death of the worker, barely enough to buy a nice arrangement of flowers for the funeral. The retirement benefit can be subdivided into direct payments to the retiree and/or spousal benefits to a spouse based on the client's work record. I'll get more into spousal benefits a bit later. Social Security benefits begin the first day of the month following the enrollee's chosen starting point. If a Social Security check is issued for the month of death, that check must be returned to the Social Security Administration. Thus, the participant doesn't receive a check for either the first month of eligibility or the month of his or her death.

Employees and employers each pay 6.2 percent of covered wages into the system up to each year's old-age, survivors, and disability insurance (OASDI) maximum earnings. The OASDI maximum earnings for 2014 was $117,000. No additional contributions are necessary if your client exceeds that amount in annual earnings. Employees and employers also each pay 1.45 percent into the system each year for Medicare, and there's no cutoff on those contributions. In other words, employers and employees keep paying 1.45 percent into Medicare on all wages earned no matter how much they amount to.

If your client is self-employed, only the employee portion (6.2 percent) of the total contribution counts when calculating Social Security benefits. The employer portion is not included in the Social Security benefit calculation. Many self-employed individuals don't have a clue that only 50 percent of the high self-employment taxes they pay count toward their eventual Social Security annual draw. Make sure to tell them, even if it totally annoys them for a little while. If self-employed clients have employees, the clients will be responsible for the employer portion of their employees' OASDI and Medicare payments.

The Social Security base, or primary insurance amount, is computed over thirty-five of the recipient's best earning years. The calculation is indexed. Here's what the Social Security Administration says about how it calculates PIA: "Social Security benefits are based on your lifetime earnings. Your actual earnings are adjusted or 'indexed' to account for changes in average wages since the year the earnings were received. Then Social Security calculates your average indexed monthly earnings during the thirty-five years in which you earned the most. We apply a formula to these earnings and arrive at your basic benefit, or 'primary insurance amount' (PIA). This is how much you would receive at your full retirement age—sixty-five or older, depending on your date of birth.

"The primary insurance amount is the benefit (before rounding down to the next lower whole dollar) a person would receive if he/she elects to begin receiving benefits at his/her normal retirement age. At this age, the benefit is neither reduced for early retirement nor increased for delayed retirement."

PIA for 2014 includes:

a. 90 percent of the first $816 of his/her average indexed monthly earnings (AIME), plus

b. 32 percent of his/her AIME over $816 through $4,917, plus

c. 15 percent of his/her AIME over 4,917

Important point: A worker needs a work record totaling at least forty quarters to qualify for benefits.

For purposes of our discussion, let's assume your client retired in 2013 at age fifty-five and had maximum OASDI earnings for ten years from 2003 to 2012. They would have the equivalent of between $25,000 and $30,000 per year (remember the base is an index) earned over thirty-five years. Because the Social Security system gives greatest weight to workers earning most of their dollars in the 90 percent and 32 percent levels, they get a lot of benefit from those last ten years. The idea here is you want your highest paying years to go into the computation of your Social Security benefits, and for most of us, those years are at the end of our working life.

Important point: While the last ten years of earnings are usually the most valuable in calculating Social Security benefits, because those are typically the years of the highest quarters, a client with high earning years in the middle of a career is not going to be penalized for lower earnings toward the end of a career. Social Security is *not* calculated like a pension.

Quarters for Social Security are earned on an annual basis. No more than four quarters may be earned in a single year. In 2014, a quarter of eligibility requires $1,200 of qualifying earnings. Thus, qualifying earnings over $4,800 earn four quarters of eligibility. Note that earning quarters each calendar year are based entirely upon qualifying earnings in that calendar year, not days, months, or quarters worked. As noted, you need to have a work record of at least forty quarters of qualifying earnings to receive Social Security benefits.

Although I just noted this above, I'm going to repeat it here because the misconception is so widespread: Contrary to prevailing opinion, Social Security is not a true retirement plan like a corporate or government pension that is typically weighted on the highest earnings at the end of a worker's career. Social Security benefits are based upon layering. In other words, they're indexed. Just what does that mean, and how can you make the distinction clear for your clients?

A closer look at Social Security calculations

In 2014, the first $816 of average monthly earnings, or $9,792 for twelve months, accrued a monthly benefit (when retiring) at 90 percent credit. You are credited 90 percent of these amounts toward your Social Security benefits at full retirement age. That's pretty good if the client doesn't earn or hasn't earned much money! It means what dollars the client did earn were earning a high credit toward eventual benefits.

Between $816 and $4,917 average monthly earnings benefits were accrued at 32 percent (twelve times for annual amount). Now with these parameters, clients are getting less of the funds credited toward their Social Security benefits at full retirement age, but the calculations are based on a higher number, so the client is better off than the guy who's getting 90 percent credit on a lower number. Average monthly earnings over $4,917 mean the client's benefits were accrued at 15 percent. As you can see, Social Security was designed to be as fair as possible for everyone, regardless of income.

However, people who earn higher incomes end up with higher monthly Social Security payments when collecting at full retirement age than those who earned lower wages during their working years. Conversely, very low-income earners get a much higher percentage of their wages subject to Social Security in eventual Social Security benefits. In 2014, the maximum monthly Social Security payment was $2,642.

Look at it this way. Someone averaging roughly $25,000 per year in today's dollars earns over 2.5 times the annual 90 percent level per year in credit toward eventual Social Security benefits. Thus, in their first fourteen (35/2.5) years, they have earned the full 90 percent Social Security layer. Higher earners often go through both the 90 percent layer and the 32 percent layer by age fifty. It almost never pays clients to try to boost Social Security benefits in the last five years of their careers unless they have a very short work history. Workers with substantially less than thirty-five good earning years for Social Security will get a greater increase in their Social Security benefits by continuing to work even after they are eligible to begin drawing benefits. These workers will substitute good earning years for years with either no earnings or very little earnings. Workers with nearly thirty-five years of maximum earnings will gain almost nothing by continuing to work, at least from a Social Security perspective. They may well need to keep working for other reasons, though.

Important point: The Social Security Administration website has a convenient and easy-to-use benefit calculator that you and your clients can use to get a better idea of what they can expect to collect each month after reaching full retirement age. *Never* let your clients put in for Social Security without finding out the benefit amounts and doing a fully integrated analysis of their retirement situation based on their CAMP Score results.

Social Security benefits

Now let's take a close look at what workers actually can get. The program provides benefits in many more ways than a simple monthly check to retirees from Uncle Sam.

Supplemental Security Income

Some persons may qualify for Supplemental Security Income and have Medicaid pay their medical costs. Qualification for Supplemental Security Income is common for very low-income individuals, disabled individuals, and special needs individuals. Supplemental Security Income is a federal needs-based program designed to benefit the following groups of people:

1. Aged, blind, and disabled
2. Benefits are for food, clothing, and shelter
3. Income and assets are very low

Supplemental Security Income (SSI) and Medicaid may pay Medicare costs for qualified individuals. Qualification for SSI are very complex and beyond the scope of this book. I encourage families of potentially qualified individuals to contact someone with appropriate education and experience for assistance with these cases. Indeed, I frequently recommend hiring competent legal assistance to help prepare all Social Security disability applications, which I'll discuss next. However, the earlier assistance is hired, the less likely Social Security administration will subsidize the process, which it will do in some instances.

Now let's move on to Social Security disability coverage.

Social Security disability

Disability for Social Security purposes is defined as for people who "... cannot work because they have a medical condition that is expected to last at least one year, or result in death." The Social Security disability and qualification for Social Security disability have been the subject of much debate and criticism for years. Until recently, disability was historically defined as permanent and total disability. Permanent and total disability was very hard to determine and put doctors, etc. in an untenable position of having to make subjective decisions about recovery possibilities. I had one client that was totally disabled for fourteen years who miraculously recovered, confounding even his doctors. The current definition makes it easier to qualify and exposes the entire Social Security system to increased costs. Nevertheless, the qualification process frequently involves multiple applications and reapplications.

Denial of Social Security disability claims is so common and the application process is so cumbersome that many people choose to hire specialized attorneys to help apply originally and/or reapply after denial. After claims have been denied twice, there may even be government help paying these attorneys. Current qualification for Social Security Disability Income (SSDI) requires a consistent work history. To be currently qualified for Social Security disability requires:

If disabled ...

   a. before age twenty-four, a worker must have six quarters of coverage or half the quarters since age twenty-one.

   b. between age twenty-four and age thirty, a worker needs credit for half the quarters after age twenty-one.

c. after age thirty-one, a worker needs credit for twenty of the most recent forty quarters at the time of the disability onset.

Important point: If you have clients who were never able to work due to a physical or cognitive problem, they are candidates for Supplemental Security Income, not disability!

Social Security disability benefits entitle beneficiaries to Medicare coverage after being entitled to benefits for twenty-four months (42 U.S.C. Section 426(b)(2): 42 CFR, Section 406.12). However, after being entitled to Social Security disability benefits, there must be a minimum of five months' waiting period before Social Security benefits are payable.

To recap: Social Security disability benefits entitle the recipient to Medicare benefits as early as twenty-nine months after the Social Security disability application. Social Security disability may qualify a recipient for Medicare at any age after a five-month waiting period plus twenty-four months of disability. The twenty-four months need not be consecutive. Once Social Security disability benefits recipients become eligible to receive regular Social Security, they are switched to regular Social Security.

Survivor benefits

When one member of a couple dies, the total benefits to the surviving spouse normally are the greater of the deceased spouse's benefits or the surviving spouse's own benefits. The surviving spouse does not get the benefit of both! They do get the greater of their own benefits or their deceased spouse's benefits. Survivor benefits are a valuable part of Social Security that many of your clients won't have thought much about. I'm amazed at how many clients come to my office after already collecting Social Security early, only to find out about the importance of survivor benefits in overall retirement planning. It's usually too late to do anything to help rectify the situation at that point.

To collect the survivor benefits, clients have to be or have been in a valid marriage, and the spouse whose benefits are drawn upon has to have qualified to receive benefits. In other words, the spouse would have to have a minimum of forty quarters of credit with Social Security. Even if a couple has been married only nine months, they qualify as spouses.

There will not be a reduced survivor benefit if the deceased had remarried and was either married at the time of death (nine months for surviving spouses to qualify) or had been married more than once for at least ten years. Survivor benefits are, however, reduced if either the deceased spouse started their benefits early *or* the surviving spouse draws survivor benefits before their own full retirement age. Survivor benefits are not affected by the existence of more than one qualifying spouse. Multiple marriages can and do result in full survivor benefits being paid to multiple qualifying spouses or ex-spouses.

The key is the surviving spouse's age. If the surviving spouse has reached full retirement age (FRA), they will generally receive full survivor benefits. If the surviving spouse has not reached FRA, they will receive a reduced benefit unless they wait until FRA to receive survivor's benefits. Deferred benefits will exceed the nondeferred benefits. Remember, the surviving spouse is entitled to the greater of their benefit or benefits based upon the deceased spouse's record. Again, to get full benefits, a surviving spouse must have reached full retirement age. If the surviving spouse's earned income is not too large, the client can begin drawing reduced survivor benefits as early as age sixty.

Important point: The survivor's benefits reduce when the deceased participant chose early benefits. So there's another argument in favor of not collecting Social Security early! Benefits increase when the deceased participant deferred receipt of benefits beyond FRA. In other words, survivor benefits go up when the spouse defers Social Security until age seventy. In order for your client to receive this spousal benefit and delay receipt of their own benefit, their spouse must be receiving Social Security or suspended their benefit at FRA.

It gives me great pleasure to show clients that both the spousal benefits the worker draws and the increased survivor benefits are essentially a bonus because the worker's increased benefits from delaying receiving benefits typically has a higher lifetime expectancy than the worker drawing benefits at FRA. I place great emphasis on maximizing social security benefits to the survivor. If the worker survives, they collect greater benefits, and if the spouse survives, the spouse enjoys greater benefits.

Spousal benefits

At full retirement age, your clients can draw spousal benefits of 50 percent based upon the spouse's Social Security record while deferring and growing their own benefits at 8 percent per year between the age of sixty-six (or sixty-seven for people born in 1960 or thereafter) and the maximum of age seventy. This is a hugely important benefit that a very large number of financial professionals fail to account for when counseling their clients. But think about it! If a higher earning spouse can defer Social Security until age seventy, earn 8 percent additional benefits through that deferral, and collect spousal benefits in the meantime, then that client and the spouse both win because benefits are greater during the life of the higher wage earner who deferred. Upon the death of the higher earner, survivor benefits are greater.

Important point: I cannot emphasize enough the importance of counseling married clients of roughly the same age on the tactic of deferring the Social Security of the higher earning spouse while having the higher earner draw spousal benefits starting at age sixty-two or the earliest age not earning over the maximum allowed between ages sixty-two and sixty-six. As noted above, the payoff is in higher benefits for the couple and higher survivor benefits for the lower earning spouse upon the death of the higher earning spouse.

To recap: Any clients qualified to receive Social Security benefits at age sixty-six can draw half of their spouse's benefits and increase their own benefit by 32 percent until they reach the maximum at age seventy. At that point, clients would begin collecting greatly increased benefits.

Using spousal benefits to enable the other spouse to defer taking Social Security benefits, thereby increasing the value of those benefits, represents an opportunity so poorly understood that it is estimated that less than 10 percent of Social Security participants choose the option!

A closer look at the numbers for survivors

If your client were to die prematurely but after age seventy, the surviving spouse could draw the now enhanced benefit of 132 percent of the age sixty-six benefit. The actual increase is two-thirds of 1 percent per month. At age sixty-seven, the client would have a benefit of 108 percent of the age sixty-six benefit simply by deferring and taking advantage of spousal benefits. In the event of the client's death, the spouse would do better by 8 percent, provided that the surviving spouse's Social Security benefits were less than those of your deceased client. If they were greater, then the spouse would naturally take those instead.

Important point: When there is an age difference of a few years, and the earnings records are *similar*, it will generally be best for the older member to begin receiving benefits at full retirement age and the younger to defer receiving retirement benefits at full retirement. The younger member should elect to begin spousal benefits at full retirement age and defer their own benefits until age seventy.

Illustration 1

Martin and Linda both have nearly maximum Social Security earning's records. However, there were subtle differences I had to be careful to note. Linda will reach her full retirement age in a few months. Martin is eighteen months younger. My initial thoughts were to advise Martin to continue employment and for Linda to defer her Social Security benefits. If Linda defers her benefits, they will not receive any Social

Security for eighteen months. When Martin reaches full retirement age, he would like to retire. They will lose his current income of $10,000 per month.

If Linda begins her benefits now, they will have her full Social Security benefits for eighteen months, and when Martin reaches sixty-six, they will have Linda's full benefits plus Martin's spousal benefits when he reaches FRA from Martin's age sixty-six to age seventy. Linda begins drawing approximately $2,642 per month (the maximum for workers reaching FRA in 2014 is $2,642). Martin's spousal benefit beginning in eighteen months is approximately $1,300, and when Martin reaches age seventy, his enhanced benefit should be approximately $3,500 per month (132 percent of $2,642). When viewed that way, the tactic I suggested makes perfect sense.

Provisions to consider

Provision 1: Drawing benefits *as a spouse caring for a retired or deceased participant's child* does not reduce future spousal or survivor benefits. The children will qualify for children's benefits since they are both under age eighteen and the parent caring for them as a spouse of a qualifying worker qualifies to receive benefits while they are under age sixteen. Note that the spouse's benefits as a *spouse caring for a participant's child under age sixteen* end when the child reaches sixteen, but the child's benefits continue until the child is eighteen or even nineteen if the child is still a full-time student in elementary or secondary school.

Provision 2: For a client to receive spousal benefits and defer his or her own benefits, he or she *must* have reached full retirement age. Drawing spousal benefits even one month early would negate this opportunity. Note that drawing spousal benefits early does *not* affect survivor benefits. This reduction can be more than 30 percent.

Divorced spouses

Divorced ex-spouses may draw spousal benefits if they were married at least ten consecutive years and the ex-spouse is eligible to draw. Note that the law does not require the ex-spouse to be drawing. By contrast, it does require a current spouse to have applied for Social Security. This seems a reasonable provision to prevent ex-spouses from delaying drawing to delay the availability of ex-spouse benefits. The rules for qualifying ex-spouses are another very poorly understood opportunity that financial professionals often miss, and yet it could really make a difference for some clients.

Let me just say that on more than one occasion, a client who was married for more than ten years, was divorced, and never remarried has come to the office wondering if getting married again would be a big mistake. If the client remarries, ex-spousal benefits disappear! Thus, sometimes it's more practical from a Social Security benefits perspective *not* to get remarried. If you don't ask questions to find out about potential financial pros and cons associated with major life decisions, such as getting remarried, when you're advising clients, you run the risk of exposing them to some very unpleasant surprises.

Spousal benefits and survivor benefits are automatic and *do not require* the approval of the ex-spouse and may not even require the knowledge of the ex-spouse. Remember, divorced ex-spouse status requires ten years of marriage versus almost immediate qualification as a current spouse. Remember too that remarriage terminates divorced ex-spouse status.

Important point: If the second marriage ends as a result of death, divorce, or annulment, eligibility for ex-spouse Social Security benefits based on the first spouse can be reinstated.

A critical exception to the remarriage rules exists if the surviving divorced ex-spouse remarries after age sixty or after age fifty if the surviving ex-spouse remarries after age fifty and is entitled to disability benefits at the time of the disability. In those cases, the Social Security rules disregard the remarriage.

To recap: Qualification as a divorced ex-spouse on a former spouse's record requires that he or she:

*was married to the ex-spouse for at least ten consecutive years;

*is at least sixty-two years old;

*is unmarried; **and**

*is not entitled to a higher Social Security benefit on his or her own record.

Provision 1: When qualified as an ex-spouse, a taxpayer can choose to defer their own benefits and draw spousal benefits. It is *not* necessary that the ex-spouse begin drawing benefits, only that they have reached age sixty-two. This prevents ex-spouses from deferring their own Social Security qualification to spite their ex-spouse. In some cases, the only thing a qualifying ex-spouse needs to begin drawing spousal benefits is their ex-spouse's social security number and date of birth. Spousal benefits will not be affected by multiple ex-spouses, and survivor benefits are also not limited. Family benefit rules only affect spouses if children are receiving benefits.

Provision 2: When one member of a divorced couple dies, the greater benefit goes to the surviving spouse. The benefit received is the greater of the deceased spouse's benefits or the surviving spouse's own benefits. The surviving spouse does not get the benefit of both! They do, as explained earlier, get the greater of their own benefits or their deceased ex-spouse's benefits.

Illustration 2

As you can see, divorce has many implications when it comes to Social

Security benefits for both divorced spouses. For example, a divorce before ten consecutive years of marriage may terminate not only spousal benefits but also eliminate eligibility for no-cost Medicare Part A. This is a real sticky wicket that often eludes financial professionals. It's a sort of out of sight, out of mind thing, but it bears saying that Social Security is essential for client eligibility for no-cost Medicare Part A. Almost nobody is going to think about the nuances of that in the heat of the moment as a divorce is happening!

Check out the following scenario:

Sherrie was married twice, but each time she was married for less than ten years. Sherrie has been a care giver for her parents and in recent years for her brother. Thus, she has never accumulated enough credits (forty quarters or ten years) to qualify for Social Security benefits. Unfortunately, Sherrie has not therefore qualified for Social Security, and she does not have a qualifying relationship that qualifies her for Medicare.

She can purchase Medicare Part A hospitalization benefits, but the cost is very high. If she does not have thirty quarters of Social Security qualification, it will cost up to $426 per month for Part A Medicare. Part A Medicare is free for all qualified Social Security participants and those who are qualifying ex-spouses. Note that if Sherrie had been married ten consecutive years, she would receive both spousal Social Security benefits and free Medicare Part A hospitalization costs.

Family benefits

The most valuable family benefit occurs when a Social Security participant has children under age eighteen. The Social Security participant must apply for Social Security to let their children draw. If the participant's spouse doesn't work, they may also draw benefits based upon the participant's Social Security record. Even though the participant must apply for Social Security, they may actually suspend their own benefits if the participant is at least age sixty-two while enabling their spouse and children to receive benefits. Suspending the participant's benefits is particularly important if he or she is still working. Benefits grow, and contributions to Social Security continue. These strategies are another poorly understood and therefore underutilized means of getting the most from Social Security benefits.

At a recent seminar I gave before an audience of financial planners and certified public accountants, two CPAs said they had a friend who was forty-nine who had just given birth to twins. Their friend's husband was sixty-three and retired. The spouse and children might draw well over $1,000 per month. In this case, I believe the amount was about $1,600 per month. Nobody realized the opportunity. A word of caution: the children's benefits could begin immediately, but spouse caring for a Social Security participant's children begin at age fifty.

Family benefit limits vary, but they generally equal or exceed 150 percent to 180 percent of the worker's benefits. The limit on family benefits allowable on one's social security record may result in both a current spouse's survivor benefits and the former spouse's survivor benefits being limited. Thus, if an ex-spouse draws upon a worker's benefits, it may impact the benefits available to the current family. The benefits are split evenly between family members receiving benefits but limited to a maximum of 180 percent. It is, however, unlikely that spousal benefits are being limited.

Family benefits are computed based upon a very complicated formula:

Benefits payable in 2014 are:

a. 150 percent of the first $1,042 of the worker's primary insurance amount, plus

b. 272 percent of the worker's PIA over $1,042 through $1,505, plus

c. 134 percent of the worker's PIA over $1,505 through $1,962, plus

d. 175 percent of the worker's PIA over $1,962.

The actual family maximum for 2014 maximizes at nearly 188 percent at a PIA of $1,505 and generally averages approximately 175 percent of PIA at levels over half the maximum PIA for 2014 of $2,642, as shown in the following calculations.

Table 1

	PIA in $			Maximum Family Benefit	PIA in %
First	$1,042.00	times	1.5	$1,563.00	
Cumulative	$1,042.00			$1,563.00	150%
Next	$463.00	times	2.72	$1,259.36	
Cumulative	$1,505.00			$2,822.36	188%
Next	$457.00	times	1.34	$612.38	
Cumulative	$1,962.00			$3,434.74	175%
Next	$680.00	times	1.75	$1,190.00	
Cumulative	$2,642.00			$4,642.74	175%

Note that the family benefits are based upon the worker's PIA, not the worker's benefit. Family benefits remain in effect when a worker has applied for Social Security benefits but earns too much to receive benefits. Thus, many people should apply at age sixty-two even if they expect to earn too much.

Family members who may receive benefits include:

- Worker
- Worker's spouse (married to the worker for at least one year immediately preceding the application for spouse's benefits)
- Worker's qualifying divorced spouse (married ten years)
- Worker's surviving spouse (married nine months immediately prior to death)

- Worker's surviving divorced spouse (married ten years)
- Worker's child (under eighteen or full-time elementary or secondary student under nineteen or disabled before age twenty-two)
- Worker's parent

When a worker's spouse is caring for their young child under age sixteen, the worker's spouse is entitled to Social Security benefits if the worker is qualified and applied for Social Security, the worker is disabled, or the worker is deceased. Therefore, it may be very important for the worker to begin Social Security benefits. This can entitle the spouse to receive benefits based upon caring for the child or children under age sixteen and the children eighteen and under or age nineteen and still a full-time student in elementary or secondary to receive child's benefits.

The requirements to be "a spouse of a retired worker" are met by meeting any of the following conditions:

a. By having a child under age sixteen or a qualifying disabled child of any age under his or her care; or

b. By qualifying as a current spouse and being at least sixty-two years old (Note spousal benefits do not require qualifying children. They do require that the worker has applied for Social Security benefits and that the spouse be age sixty-two or greater.); or

c. By being qualified a divorced ex-spouse. This condition is met if they were married ten years and they are currently married. The worker may have remarried.

Important point: Drawing benefits as a spouse caring for a retired or deceased participant's child does not reduce future spousal or survivor benefits.

WEP and GPO Social Security reductions

Very few clients are going to know about the Windfall Elimination Provision that's built into Social Security, mostly because it doesn't apply to all that many people. But it may have an impact on some retirees, so it's worth a brief discussion. For example, some affected clients might be federal, state, or local government employees who were not required to pay into Social Security.

Prior to the Windfall Elimination Provision, government workers could retire as early as fifty or fifty-five and seek a second career in private employment. Ten really good years of private employment could entitle the worker to the entire 90 percent layer used to calculate the primary insurance amount for Social Security, and most of the entire 32 percent layer. Government workers not covered under Social Security for part of their working careers but with forty quarters of Social Security qualification receive a reduced Social Security due to a **reduction** resulting from an adjustment made to compensate for their years of work not subject to OASDI and Medicare payments into the system.

Many people have a mix of government and private employment. These workers will be entitled to Social Security if they become fully insured (forty qualifying quarters) for Social Security purposes. There will be an adjustment to their Social Security benefits for the Windfall Elimination Provision unless they attain thirty years of "substantial earnings" for Social Security purposes.

WEP would apply for workers with at least ten years of Social Security coverage (fully insured), but less than thirty years of "substantial earnings." Substantial earnings are approximately 500 percent of the amount required each year to earn four full quarters of Social Security coverage. For example, in 2014, it required $4,800 of qualifying earnings to get four quarters of Social Security coverage and $21,750 to have substantial earnings. The maximum adjustment for the Windfall Elimination Provision in 2014 for workers reaching sixty-two and beginning benefits at full retirement age is $408.00 per month. The reduction in Social Security benefits may be greater for workers who delay receiving benefits beyond full retirement age because the benefit base is larger due to deferring benefits.

Once a government worker subject to the WEP reaches ten years of Social Security coverage, they can increase their net Social Security received in two primary ways:

1. They increase their average monthly indexed earnings *and*

2. If they increase their years of substantial earnings for Social Security purposes to between twenty and thirty years. They can decrease their deductions. There is no further WEP reduction for workers with over thirty years of substantial earnings.

It is important for government workers to recognize that their Social Security eligibility can be improved dramatically by working in private employment after retiring from their government work. It is worth the effort to carefully consider both the timing of government retirement and whether they choose to work in private employment after government retirement. Spouses of government workers that do not pay into Social Security should not expect to receive either spousal or survivor benefits from Social Security. These persons should therefore attempt to maximize their own benefits.

In addition to the WEP, there is also a Government Pension Offset (GPO) that reduces spousal or surviving spouse benefits to workers that are adversely affected by the WEP. The GPO reduces spousal or survivor benefits by two-thirds of a government pension. The GPO offset is seldom understood by those affected, and further, I believe it is far less fair and equitable and far more damaging than the WEP.

Spouses of government workers that do not pay into Social Security should not expect to receive either spousal or survivor benefits from Social Security. These persons should therefore attempt to maximize their own benefits. If the surviving spouse was a government worker, their benefits are the greater of the deceased spouse's benefits reduced by two-thirds of their government pension offset (GPO) due to their government employment, or their own benefits are reduced by the WEP offset.

Parting words: Social Security is complicated, but it almost has to be if it is to take all the variables of American life into account and still remain as fair as possible to earners at all levels. Familial relationships, levels and types of benefits, timing of benefits, it all matters to your clients, and it should matter to you as you help clients navigate the often unfamiliar terrain of Social Security's fine points.

Now that we have a good working knowledge of how Social Security works, let's take a look at one of the most vexing issues related to the program today. What exactly is that issue? In a word or three, it's Social Security timing.

8

The Wizard behind the Curtain Social Security Timing

> Cessation of work is not accompanied by cessation of expenses.
> —Cato

It should be very clear by now that Social Security has become the most important source of cash flow for most current and future retirees. Of course, that wasn't always the case. Pensions and personal savings were supposed to constitute the other two legs of the supposed three-legged stool, but the stool doesn't exist anymore for most people, and it hasn't for well over two decades. As noted several times in earlier pages, only 20 percent of Americans have a pension, and that number is dropping every year as corporations opt out and transfer pensions into much cheaper 401(k) plans. In conjunction, baby boomers and Gen-Xers simply haven't saved much as they've bought big homes they couldn't afford in the first place, foolishly used their homes as piggybanks to buy boats and second homes, racked up huge credit card debts that they didn't pay down in a timely manner, and indulged in expensive vacations without having the ready cash to pay for them.

Then the party abruptly ended in 2000–2002 with the first of two twenty-first-century stock market crashes. Middle-class manufacturing jobs went overseas. The power of unions greatly diminished, thereby rippling across to contribute to the demise of the pension. Wages stagnated, and unemployment soared, forcing millions to raid their meager 401(k) and traditional IRA accounts, if they even had one. Health care skyrocketed. College tuitions blew through the roof. The Great Recession came along and made the tech bubble disaster look like a cakewalk. Retirees lost trillions of dollars. In a panic, many sold assets at historic stock market lows and plunked what capital they had left into fixed-interest investments that didn't even keep up with inflation, much less yield sane returns. Blunder after blunder combined with the stark realities of a terrifyingly harsh economic environment in the United States crushed tens of millions of current and future retirees like bugs on a rug.

Of course, I'm preaching to the choir here, and I know it! As financial professionals, we see the carnage every day. But sometimes it's good to recap where we've been to better understand where we are. Now this may strike some as a very insensitive thing to say, but the baby boomers and many in Generation X set themselves up for a big fall by failing to take a highly conservative stance in terms of savings percentage rates compared to gross income, income-to-debt ratios, preservation of home equity, and sound investing in boring but solid securities as opposed to the sexy high fliers that they thought would make them get rich quick. It's really no surprise, then, or at least it shouldn't be, that a substantial number of Americans who want to retire just can't do it, or shouldn't do it. And, sadly, it's no surprise that many millions of Americans who should not retire do it anyway because they hate their jobs and feel entitled to the good life when they've already blown their chances.

Enter Social Security! In light of the tremendous shifts that have occurred in American society in recent decades, it also should not be a surprise that Social Security accounts for most, if not all, of the cash some couples have to work with during retirement. That's a real problem when you consider that the Social Security Administrations says that Social Security benefits are meant to only make up about 40 percent of the overall cash flow seniors need to live comfortably. There's a lot your clients don't know about Social Security, and perhaps there are some things you thought you knew but were just a tad off base because studying the program wasn't your main focus in your continuing education as a financial professional. We'll take a comprehensive look at Social Security timing as it relates to your clients in the coming pages. Let's debunk some common myths about the program first. As in the *Wizard of Oz*, there's more behind the curtain than you might think!

The three myths of Social Security

Myth 1: Social Security was designed to pay benefits for a short period of time after retirement because life expectancies were much lower when the program started in 1935. In other words, Uncle Sam figured we'd all kick the bucket before he had to pay us much. I know we hear that all the time, and I believed it myself for many years until I started to dig a little deeper. Yes, life expectancies were much shorter back when Social Security first started, but there's more to it than that. For example, have you ever wondered how the high infant-mortality rate of the first three decades of the twentieth century skewed the statistics? I'd guess you probably never even thought about that. I know I hadn't. The bottom line is that high infant-mortality rates did shorten the actuarial figures for life expectancy during this period. Just the littlest thing can throw off the numbers and give you erroneous data that is subsequently used to make the wrong conclusions. It happens all the time.

Truth: When Franklin Delano Roosevelt signed the Social Security Act into law in 1935, life expectancies were lower than they are today—age fifty-eight for men and sixty-two for women, versus 78.7 in 2011 for men and women, according to the US Centers for Disease Control and Prevention. However, if you lived to age sixty-five in 1940, statistically speaking you'd collect Social Security for thirteen years if you were male and fifteen years if you were female, so says the Social Security Administration. That's pretty amazing when you consider that most Americans think Social Security was designed for the last years of life.

The common figure holds that we were only supposed to collect for five years or so after we turned sixty-five.

So, if you didn't die before retirement, you had a good chance of collecting Social Security for a decade or more. If you were female and lived to age sixty-five in 1940, you'd have about the same life expectancy then as you do now, something most people don't realize. We all think that the advances in medical technologies and drugs have prolonged life in recent decades. That's true. It means more people are reaching age sixty-five today than did in the 1940s, but that doesn't mean Social Security was designed solely on life expectancy projections based on statistics from birth to death. In fact, it was primarily designed around projected life expectancy beyond age sixty-five.

Myth 2: Social Security is in trouble because fewer workers are paying into it as the 78 million baby boomers retire.

Some truth in that: Social Security does face challenges as more baby boomers draw benefits, and more reach age sixty-five than did in 1935. Advances in medical care are prolonging life, which in turn is prolonging the length of retirement for millions of Americans. Ultimately, the Social Security program will be increasingly strained, but is that because of longer life expectancies?

Not according to a 2010 report on the future sustainability of Social Security from Stephen C. Goss, chief actuary of the Social Security Administration (Social Security Bulletin, Vol. 70, No. 3). The diminishing birth rate from three children per woman to two in the United States in recent decades has decreased the pool of future workers, and that's the crux of the problem. It's dropping birth rates *combined* with aging boomers drawing benefits that continues to boost the costs associated with Social Security. The report says that without reforms, costs will keep rising so that by 2035 the program will only be able to pay 75 percent of the promised benefits. Your clients probably have heard something about this. If they're older, they probably don't care. Your younger clients should definitely care, and so should you!

Don't Let Your Clients Eat Dog Food When They're Old!

Interestingly, the same report says that lower birth rates in the United States are expected to remain stable after 2035 (most of the boomers will be dead by then), meaning that if Congress and the Executive Branch in Washington are able to come up with a sound and fair readjusting of the program's fundamentals to bring the accounting in line with reality, Social Security will live on indefinitely. The report states that the Social Security Administration projects that "an immediate reduction of benefits of about 13 percent, or an immediate increase in the combined payroll tax rate of 12.4 percent to 14.4 percent, or some combination of these changes, would be sufficient to allow full payment of scheduled benefits for the next seventy-five years." The most important word in the above quote is "immediate."

As a guy with a doctorate in accounting, it seems pretty obvious that there's really nothing stopping the implementation of a few tweaks of the program to assure Americans full benefits for the foreseeable future, except for one thing. The problem isn't with the numbers, which can always be logically brought in line to meet prevailing economics. It's politics. And that's a very scary proposition indeed because it probably means nothing is going to get done until it's too late for sensible corrective action!

A few other things get left out of the equation too. First, the majority of baby boomers can't afford to fully retire, so the smart ones are not taking Social Security early and continue to work even after reaching full retirement age. That has led the number of seniors over sixty-five who are still working to rise 67 percent between 2002 and 2012, bringing the number to 7 million. Other seniors retire when they shouldn't, realize they lack the cash flow to pay basic expenses, and go back to work after they started collecting Social Security. They've usually jumped the gun on Social Security and begun collecting at sixty-two, and then they find themselves in the really silly position of working while paying back into the Social Security system even as they collect benefits. Both of these factors are decreasing the overall strain on the program, but the overall trend remains in place in part because of the enormous scale involved with the declining birth rate and the aging of America. Both are major national demographic trends, Titans, if you will, in the discerning of the American economic landscape.

The so-called echo boom or the Millennial Generation (age eighteen to thirty-seven), currently 87 million people, never seems to get any press in relation to the continued viability of Social Security. I think the Millennials should get more press because this young and vibrant generation of tech-savvy individuals accounts for 27 percent of the US population and outnumbers baby boomers by at least 10 million. Further, studies indicate that the number of Gen-M, if I may coin a term, is expected to steadily increase as immigration rates rise in coming decades. Another interesting fact is that Gen-M will be the most racially and ethnically diverse population in American history, which may blaze a path to a more cooperative federal and state partnership in government, characterized by far less gridlock and partisan antipathy in Washington and at the state houses across the nation.

Perhaps we older Americans can count on Gen-M to create the new technologies we need to stay globally competitive. Whether that's true or not, the least we baby boomers and Gen-Xers can do is to leave Gen-M something to work with instead of a lump of coal. At any rate, the pool of workers capable of contributing to Social Security is definitely not drying up as some people proclaim, but it is diminishing in size to the point where costs for Social Security benefits aren't keeping up with inflow from workers. The prevailing wisdom that the program needs modest reforms is right on the money.

Myth 3: Taking Social Security early at age sixty-two is no big deal.

Truth: It's a very big deal. Here's a detailed look at the issue and how you might convince clients not to shoot themselves in the foot in terms of maximizing their Social Security benefits.

Let's just start with who should collect Social Security early. My contention is that nobody should, if at all possible. However, there are some instances where it could make sense. Perhaps the best candidate for early benefits is a single individual who has never been married and is in poor health. In this case, the client is banking on the fact that death will occur sooner than average life expectancy. Another instance where collecting early may not be as disastrous is if the client is not working, does not expect to work in anything but a low-wage job in the future, and has few if any other financial resources to draw upon.

However, for the most part, the vast majority of clients should wait until they reach full retirement age before collecting Social Security benefits. The fact is that if your clients elect to collect Social Security at age sixty-two, they can expect to lose up to 25 percent of their calculated benefits for life. People in this pool have a full retirement age of sixty-six, and those born in 1960 or thereafter will reach full retirement age at sixty-seven. Anyone who collects early will lose benefits. The maximum loss occurs if the client takes Social Security right at age sixty-two. The loss decreases on a graduated scale the longer the person waits between age sixty-two and full retirement age.

That's another myth of Social Security, by the way. Most individuals in the lay public figure they'll automatically lose the full 25 percent of their benefits if they don't wait to collect until full retirement age, assuming they know the figure in the first place. The graduated scale is readily available on the Social Security Administration website, and I suggest that you consult it if you've got a client who is determined to retire early no matter what. You might be able to convince the individual to wait at least a little longer and take less of a loss, even if it's just 10 percent of benefits versus the full 25 percent.

Important point: Retirees lose up to 25 percent of their retirement cash flow from Social Security if they start collecting exactly at age sixty-two. They lose less if they wait even a year or two longer.

You're going to get flack from clients for suggesting that they defer taking Social Security benefits until they reach full retirement age. Believe me! I know! The pushback is incredible because most people *really* want to retire. There are many reasons for their ardent desire to leave the workplace. Many are obvious. Few of us love the cube farm or the factory floor. Many Americans hate their jobs and simply want to leave.

There are other less obvious reasons for wanting to retire, though, such as having to take care of an aging parent or a spouse with a chronic illness. This is occurring with greater frequency these days as the baby boomers continue to age, and it is having a major impact on some Americans who feel they must retire out of a sense of love and duty. Ask probing questions. There may be imperative reasons behind a client's wish to retire, but I'd hazard to say that in most cases the client just wants to live the good life, and he or she isn't looking at the big picture. Emotions are leading the way when sound logic should prevail.

Illustration 1

Let's say Jack gets $10,000 of annual Social Security benefits just after he turns sixty-two. If he'd waited to collect until full retirement age of sixty-six, his benefits would be 25 percent higher, or $12,500 per year instead of $10,000 per year. Jack does the math. He figures that the added $2,500 per year at full retirement age of sixty-six won't equal the $40,000 he'd get by taking Social Security early. In short, he looks at the forty grand he'd get up front in those first four years between age sixty-two and sixty-six. He notes that he wouldn't earn back that money for sixteen years, or until age seventy-eight. He says, "What the hell! I may not even live to be seventy-eight. I'll take the forty grand now!"

That's going to be a hard objection to overcome. Most clients want their money now, and that's it. And for some of them, it might make sense, though I personally would not support early collection unless there was a very, very good reason for it.

Considering that life expectancies are steadily increasing, it's a good bet that Jack will live long past his break-even point at seventy-eight, even though the CDC puts the official death knell for men and women at around that age. If we could all be sure of when we were going to die, life would be easier! The fact is more and more of us are on track to outlive our assets, so it's a fool's wager to bet against the Grim Reaper. Jack will probably live until his mideighties, or even longer if he stays healthy. If he waits until he's sixty-six to collect his full Social Security benefits, the prevailing wisdom states that he'll collect a much larger sum. But will he really?

The answer? You'd have to say, "Well, that depends." And you'd be right!

Jack does the math again based on what you just said. He says, "Okay, so if I get an additional $2,500 in Social Security benefits per year for twenty years after I turn sixty-six, assuming I really do live to eighty-six, that's only an additional ten grand in my pocket. That's $240,000 paid to age eighty-six if I take Social Security early at age sixty-two versus $250,000 if I wait to collect until I reach full retirement age, and then I live to eighty-six. Waiting still sounds pretty dumb to me."

You may want to say, "Uh, well, it does sound like it's a no-brainer to take Social Security early if you put it that way."

Resist the urge!

Just remember that you have a bead on the entire financial retirement picture, whereas the client probably doesn't. There are indeed scenarios where taking Social Security early based on the figures above can be less of a disaster than some experts, including me, make out. But recall some of the economic realities we've been discussing. Think twice before bowing out of the discussion on Social Security timing.

Let me just drop a bone here. What you and your client may not know is that a study released in the spring of 2014 indicates that couples retiring in 2015 were projected to spend as much as 69 percent of their current combined Social Security benefits to fill in gaps in Medicare. Costs included premiums for Medicare Part B and Part D, and for

Medicare Supplement coverage, as well as co-pays that Medicare didn't presently cover. Further, expectations were that the percentage of Social Security benefits spent to fill gaps in Medicare would rise to 98 percent for couples retiring in 2024. As it is, experts in our field already agree a couple retired for twenty years or so needs to set aside at least $250,000 to pay for health care costs that Medicare doesn't cover!

Important point: So, what Jack doesn't know is that the $250,000 he thinks he'll get from Social Security is already pretty much spent on health care, especially if he's married!

I'll talk more about Medicare and these associated issues later, but the point I'm making here is that if you think it's tough on retirees now when it comes to Social Security and other sources of cash flow, you haven't seen anything yet! Clients need to make informed decisions based on the entire picture of the present state of retirement today, and what it is likely to look like in the next twenty to thirty years from the perspective of inflation, rising health care costs, long-term care, and increased taxes. Jack is right to say he'll only get an additional ten grand if he waits to collect until he's sixty-six, but the ten grand isn't the point. The point is there is very good reason to maximize every available source of cash flow because the big picture is far more complicated than the amount Uncle Sam sends retirees every month in Social Security benefits.

Illustration 2

Now let's say that Jack is married, and he and his wife, Jill, are typical of most middle-class Americans in that they have little money saved for retirement and no pensions. Annual Social Security benefits average $15,000 for individuals and $22,000 for a couple, according to the Social Security Administration. Let's assume that Jack and Jill have the same birthday and that they'll both reach full retirement age at sixty-six. If they each took Social Security at exactly sixty-two, they'd lose 25 percent of their benefits for life, or $5,500 per year, reducing the combined $22,000 they could have had to just $16,500! That's a lot less to live on, not that twenty-two grand is much more.

Important point: When married clients both take Social Security early, the full impact of lost benefits increases in scale. Survivor and spousal benefits come into play as well. If one spouse must take Social Security early, it should be the spouse who will earn the least amount in benefits, not the greater amount. That way you help the client reduce overall losses for both spouses over the long haul.

For a couple both age sixty-five, there is approximately thirty years remaining life expectancy, based on some actuarial tables. Life expectancy is defined as the age that there is a 50 percent of being alive. Thus, for a couple, the high remaining life expectancy means the point at which there is a 50 percent chance one will be alive. If the higher earning spouse defers receiving their Social Security benefits, the likelihood is therefore that one or both will receive the increased benefits for thirty years.

Most financial experts say clients need retirement cash flow equal to roughly 70 or 80 percent of the household income earned while clients were working to enjoy a comfortable retirement. I actually argue that those figures are way too low because they often don't account for the hidden costs of Medicare and Medicare Supplement coverage, long-term care protection in the form of life insurance with long-term care riders (these require premium payments if the policy isn't purchased with a lump-sum payment), unforeseen emergencies, and the increases in basic expenses as retirees travel, play golf, dine out, see plays, and otherwise enjoy the leisure activities they should be enjoying if they can afford to pay for them. I've already discussed the concept of the CAMP Score, but keep it in mind as we continue our discussion. The point here is that most married Americans don't have much more to live on than their Social Security. That means the clients must resist the urge to squander any of it.

According to the US Census Bureau, the median income of senior households comprised of a couple is only $35,000. Thus, $13,000 of the median income must come from investments, consumption of principal, or some other source. That leaves the average combined Social Security benefit of $22,000 for a couple to make up the difference. If Jack and Jill insist on both taking Social Security when they're sixty-two, their income would drop from $35,000 to $29,500, assuming they even had investments or principal to use to supplement their Social Security income. As I've said, most Americans don't. As noted, the majority of even sophisticated clients don't have a clue about the financial costs of Medicare! It's a rude surprise when they find out!

Important point: When you encounter client resistance to your counsel to defer Social Security, bringing up the often overlooked costs of Medicare might convince the client to listen. Most don't understand that more than half of their Social Security could already be spent on health care! Of course, whether that's true or not depends on the combined benefits for a couple and on the health of the couple. This may be less true for affluent couples, but it's definitely the case for those in the middle and working class.

The thrift factor for the affluent: Naturally, as a successful financial professional, you're probably dealing with affluent clients with far more resources to work with. However, that happy reality for these clients should bolster your argument for Social Security deferment. After all, it is often said that the rich are the worst tippers because they hold onto every penny, so appeal to the thrift factor as the discussion progresses with these clients.

You say, "Hey, where else are we going to get a guaranteed return of 25 percent that pays out as long as you live? I'm good, but I'm not that good! Why not take a sure bet?"

Chances are the client's eyes will light up. The client says, "Hey, we don't need the money right now. Why not get more down the road?"

You say, "Now that's the right way to think of this issue! You worked and paid for your Social Security benefits. You might as well collect as much as you can get from the program."

Sometimes numbers really help. Clients may change their minds about collecting early if they see the following table.

Table 1

Social Security Benefit for Retirees Born Between 1943 and 1954
Assume Age 66 Benefits Are $2,000 Per Month

Begin Benefits At:		One Year Adds	Total Addition	
62	$1,500			
63	$1,600	6.7%	$100	
64	$1,733	8.3%	$233	
65	$1,867	7.7%	$367	
66	$2,000	7.1%	$500	
67	$2,160	8.0%	$660	
68	$2,333	8.0%	$833	
69	$2,519	8.0%	$1,019	
70	$2,721	8.0%	$1,221	81%

The seventy bonus: So, as you're dancing through the psychological minefield that accompanies nearly every discussion about when to retire, especially when it comes to the timing of Social Security benefits, trot out yet another figure that might help make the client see some reason. If clients defer taking Social Security until age seventy, they can earn an increase of 8 percent on their calculated benefits from the time of their full retirement age to age seventy. If they defer even for one or two years after full retirement, they'll still win. It's important to make clients understand that the Social Security program is very complicated in part because it was designed to be as fair as possible to its contributors, namely the majority of Americans that pay into the system (some government workers don't). They can split the difference and still come out ahead. The program is seldom black and white. It's not either or, but instead it's what if and here's what happens if you do.

Important point: Clients can earn an additional 8 percent on their Social Security benefits from full retirement age to age seventy if they defer collecting until age seventy. If a worker defers receiving Social Security benefits until age seventy, the worker can expects to draw over 80 percent more per month than was available at age sixty-two.

Illustration 3

Let's say Jack is within six months of his full retirement at age of sixty-six. He received projections showing an expected benefit at sixty-six of $1,500 per month. If he defers receiving benefits until age seventy, his benefit will be approximately $2,000 per month. His CPA did the following analysis for him:

- Lost benefits for forty-eight months of $1,500 per month: $72,000
- Incremental benefits of $500 per month ($2,000 less $1,500)
- Conclusion: break-even time is 144 months or twelve years

The break-even period for deferring retirement benefits until age seventy will be substantially less for individuals eligible for spousal benefits as a current or ex-spouse married for more than ten years to a Social Security wage earner with a good earning record. The combination of the Social Security benefits drawn as a qualifying ex-spouse (between their own age sixty-six and age seventy) and the dramatically higher benefits their own record pays after age seventy make this decision a very important step in preparing for retirement.

Here's a recap of what it costs if your clients take Social Security early.

- More than three years early: (62–63) 5/12 of 1 percent per month

- The three years prior to full retirement age (63–66): 5/9 of 1 percent per month
- After full retirement age (sixty-six), there is an increase of 2/3 of 1 percent for each month of deferral.

Illustration 4

Two of my clients, Andy and Lisa, faced some complicated planning decisions related to deferring Social Security benefits. I suggested that Andy needed to defer drawing his Social Security until age seventy. The extra $700 per month Social Security projected at age seventy seemed critical to their retirement quality.

Andy and Lisa quickly embraced this suggestion. Lisa asked about the risk that Andy might not live long enough to "make up" the difference. She calculated $25,200 per year foregone Social Security for each of four years Andy waited to collect after reaching full retirement age of sixty-six. The $100,800 total seemed hard to replicate. She wondered, how could they be sure that the long-run benefit of $700 per month more cash flow starting when Andy reached age seventy would exceed the lost benefits of $100,800? I answered that there was no guarantee that it would, but that the odds overwhelmingly favored this strategy.

I detailed the following information:

1. Break-even time based upon Andy's life alone was twelve years. ($100,800/$700 = 144 months or twelve years)

2. Lisa's survivor benefit essentially means if **either of them** lived more than twelve years, they would be ahead!

3. Insurance industry averages show the combined life expectancy for a seventy-year-old couple is approximately twenty-five years! While the CDC puts the average life

expectancy for men and women at seventy-eight years of age, a variety of statistical factors can skew the results. Remember the high infant-mortality rates I mentioned earlier that help lower overall life expectancies when Social Security got started in the 1930s? The point is that the life insurance industry has skin in the game in factoring in every possible angle when it comes to actuarial tables. No statistical analysis is perfect, but it's something to keep in mind when you discuss life expectancies. Andy really could live into his nineties. As I said, it's a fool's wager to bet on the Grim Reaper coming when you think he might.

4. If Lisa's Social Security benefits are $1,800, Andy may draw spousal benefits of $900 plus per month for the four years between Andy's age sixty-six and Andy's age seventy. The monthly "give-up" for Andy will be not $2,100 per month but only $1,200 per month. Therefore the break-even time for Andy and Lisa should be calculated based upon forty-eight months of losing $1,200 per month. Losing $57,600 will be made up in eighty-three months! Andy was ecstatic. He realized that when he was seventy-seven (his age seventy plus seven years), they would be ahead for the rest of time either of them lived.

To recap, Social Security wage earners can apply for Social Security benefits at age sixty-two. However, they will find their benefits reduced by several factors. The factors are:

1. The early drawing reduction of 5/9 of 1 percent for every month prior to full retirement age of sixty-six if benefits begin thirty-six or less months prior to full retirement age. However, for an eligible person drawing more than thirty-six months early, the reduction is 5/12 of 1 percent for each month over thirty-six.

2. Excess earnings over the allowed earnings for that year reduce Social Security benefits by one half the excess.

3. However, the Social Security benefits not currently received are not truly lost. The worker's benefits will be increased at full retirement age to account for benefits withheld due to earlier earnings.

Social Security and retiree cash flow

I must emphasize here that in those good old days of the past when interest rates were higher, Social Security was a much more powerful retirement tool because it played less of a part of an overall cash flow role in retirement. Now, of course, it plays the key role. So, the sad irony is that as economics in America continue to become harsher and more people are forced to rely solely on Social Security, the actual power of the program has been substantially weakened from a practical standpoint in terms of allowing Americans to live more comfortably in retirement.

Let me explain what I mean. The best way to go is to take a historic look, a sort of then and now illustration to show you how you can convey the importance of deferring Social Security to your clients in a way that may convince them when nothing else will.

As previously noted, I find any retirement approach based primarily on asset accumulation to be seriously flawed because of the problems of mixing cash flows and assets versus what assets produce and because returns on assets have varied so dramatically over time. The diagram below is intended to demonstrate how flawed an asset-based approach is and to put the big-picture issue of Social Security today into a more refined perspective using numbers to make the point.

The maximum Social Security in 1990 was approximately $975 for a worker reaching age sixty-five. The earning rate on a six-month certificate of deposit (CD) was 7.5 percent and a ten-year US Treasury Bond yielded 7.94 percent. Thus, if you retired in 1990 with maximum Social Security and $100,000 invested in a six-month CD and another $100,000 invested in ten-year US Treasury Bonds, you would have had an annual cash flow of $27,140 initially.

The calculations are:

Social Security	$975 times 12	$11,700 (43.11%)
CD	$100,000 times 7.5%	7,500 (27.63%)
Ten-Year Treasury Bond	$100,000 times 7.94%	7,940 (29.26%)
		$27,140 (100.0%)

Assuming you spent each year's Social Security and investment income, your cash flow in 2014 would be as follows:

Social Security	$1800 times 12	$21,600 (89.26%)
CD	$100,000 times 0.63%	630 (2.60%)
Ten-Year Treasury Bond	$100,000 times 7.94%	1,970 (8.14%)
		$24,200 (100.0%)

The growth in your Social Security check has not kept up with inflation, but diminished investment returns have forced you to rely more every year on your Social Security check. Social Security represented 43.11 percent of your cash flow in 1990 but would represent 89.26 percent of your cash flow in 2014. This bears out my earlier assertions that Social Security comprises the bulk of retiree cash flow in most cases. Of course, there are exceptions, and I hope some of them are on your client list! If you put your clients in these numbers, making them personal, your clients may well find them startling even if they have money in the bank. The figures dramatically show how what clients thought was once a good and relatively risk-free retirement plan got turned upside down over time.

Show clients the following breakdown.

How Valuable Is Social Security?

	1990	2000	2010	2014
Maximum Social Security (Age 65)	$975	$1,435	$2,191	$2,465
Receiving 2013	$1,792	$1,986	$2,309	$2,465
6-month Certificate of Deposit (CD)	7.50%	6.75%	0.75%	0.63%
Assets Required to Match Social Security	$156,000	$255,111	$3,505,600	$4,692,238
10-Year US Treasury Bond	7.94%	6.58%	3.85%	2.40%
Assets Required to Match Social Security	$147,355	$261,702	$682,909	$1,232,500
Return on S&P 500 Index for Last 10 Years	Approx. 18%	Approx. 18%	Approx. 1%	Approx. 10%

Key Conclusions:

1. It takes over thirty times the assets invested in CDs in 2014 (versus 1990) to produce less than three times the monthly Social Security income (versus 1990).

2. It takes over ten times the assets invested in ten-year US Treasury Bonds in 2014 (versus 1990) to produce less than

three times the monthly Social Security income (versus 1990).

3. The S&P 500 Index return varies wildly between decades.

4. A worker who retired at age sixty-five in 1990 with maximum benefits would receive just less than $1,800 in benefits in 2014. The increases have occurred due to Social Security cost-of-living indexes (COLAs).

Theories about the appropriate time to begin Social Security benefits have changed dramatically over the last twenty-five years. The primary reasons are:

1. Earning rates on short-term bank deposits have declined over 90 percent!

2. Stock market results during the two decades from 1980 to 2000 averaged well over 15 percent per year.

3. Since market highs in March of 2000, the average annual real return after inflation for the S&P 500 Index had been less than 1 percent per year in 2010.

4. Life expectancies have increased.

5. Social Security benefits from deferring benefits between full retirement age (FRA) and age seventy have been dramatically increased.

6. Survivor benefits influence more retirees because more retirees have a living spouse.

Paying back Social Security benefits

You may find a new client has already taken Social Security early and now regrets doing so after your discussion of spousal and survivor benefits and how much is lost by taking Social Security early. But there's hope!

Since January 1, 2011, during the first twelve months of receiving Social Security benefits, the taxpayer may repay the amount received *without* interest. This allows the taxpayer the option of choosing a new plan that may better suit his/her future needs. Only one withdrawal from Social Security is allowed per lifetime. This one-year limit superseded the earlier ruling allowing Social Security benefits to be repaid any time until reaching the age of seventy.

Important point: Repaying Social Security benefits can be a very good deal for some clients because it can allow for a higher return on future benefits.

Illustration 5

Frank was able repay his Social Security benefits of $2,200 per month without interest just prior to the one-year (twelve-month) deadline. Frank's current plan is to defer drawing his Social Security benefits until he reaches age seventy. We expect Frank's Social Security, beginning in late 2016 when he turns seventy, to be approximately $3,400 per month.

Frank is married to Sally. If Frank dies first, Sally's survivor benefit will be the higher of either her Social Security or Frank's, in this case the $3,400. Once Frank reaches the full retirement age of sixty-six, he will be able to draw spousal benefits based upon Sally's Social Security benefits' record. Sally must be drawing her own Social Security benefits in order to allow Frank to receive spousal benefits. The bottom line is Frank is not only maximizing his own future benefits by paying back the benefits he took early. He is also building in extra protection for Sally in the event that he dies first.

Parting words: As a financial professional, you can expect to get significant pushback when you advise clients to defer Social Security benefits for as long as possible. The advantage of higher benefits outweighs the short-term gain of taking benefits early, but you'll need to make a solid case for deferral before your clients will accept the wisdom of your counsel. If you include comparative analysis, as we've seen in this chapter, simple logic, an appeal to thrift, and a reasoned look at how Social Security benefits will be increasingly allocated to pay for gaps in Medicare, most clients should agree that grabbing the benefits early may not be such a terrific idea after all.

Don't forget the added bonus of higher survivor benefits for spouses if the higher earning spouse defers taking benefits for as long as possible. Survivor benefits can also come into play if a potential retiree was divorced after more than ten years of marriage and then never remarried. The tactic of deferring one spouse's Social Security by taking spousal benefits, if the couple is of the right age to reap these rewards, is often overlooked. Yet it can play a highly significant role in timing when each person in the couple begins to collect Social Security benefits. You have fewer tricks up your sleeve with single taxpayers who are about to retire, so advocating for deferral of Social Security benefits even if the individual must defer retiring for a few years becomes even more important.

Social Security is now the most important source of retirement cash flow. A solid knowledge of how the program works and how it can benefit your clients is absolutely essential in these currently difficult economic times.

9

No More House Calls
Medicare and Retirees

LIKE SOCIAL SECURITY, MEDICARE is one of the most misunderstood entitlement programs in the United States. People think they know all about it, but they don't, except that they know they are eligible for it once they hit age sixty-five. There the knowledge ends and the misconceptions begin, often including when clients approach enrollment time and are forced to quickly learn as much as they can. Everything from befuddlement about the so-called doughnut hole in the prescription drug plan (Part D) to the highly mistaken belief that Medicare covers long-term care saunters into public perception and lives on until clients discover that what they thought was true absolutely wasn't. They usually find out the hard way too.

Even erroneous ideas about hospital coverage abound. I'd wager that if you asked clients age sixty-four or younger if Medicare pays for hospitalization, they'd all say yes, and they'd be right, sort of. The fact is while the program does pay for some hospitalization costs, it will definitely leave your clients stuck with big bills if their hospital stay is extended and they didn't buy comprehensive and more costly Medicare Supplement plans, as opposed to a Medicare Advantage plan, or no additional coverage at all. The program is full of hidden traps, or at least traps that you've got to look for when making decisions with clients about how they should proceed with Medicare.

Confused yet? Chances are even as a financial professional you don't know all that much about the program either. There's no shame in that whatsoever. Medicare structures and procedures aren't taught as a general rule. Medicare is often viewed as just one of those things retirees have to deal with as part of their health maintenance. It is not something we generally get into in detail as financial professionals. Yet failure to allocate enough cash flow to cover as much health care as possible through Medicare and supplemental programs like Medicare Advantage or Medicare Supplement plans is the second biggest mistake retirees make in terms of overall planning. The other one is not taking steps to protect against the costs of long-term custodial or skilled-nursing care resulting from simple old age, illness, or cognitive degeneration, but that's a story I will get into in the next chapter.

To recap: As a general rule, most experts agree that a couple will spend a minimum of $250,000 in extra expenses for Medicare and other related health care services during the course of a retirement that lasts twenty years or more. In my opinion, that's a very conservative estimate. A Retirement Health Care Cost Index released in 2014 by HealthView Services, a retirement and health care consulting company, contends that clients retiring in 2015 will pay 69 percent of their combined Social Security benefits to cover costs like co-pays, deductibles, prescriptions, and premiums for Medicare Part B, Part D, and for additional coverage to insure against potential expenses that Medicare won't cover. According to the data in the index, that 69 percent translates into extra health care costs for a retired couple of more than $366,000 during the course of their retirement!

If you tell your clients this during your retirement planning meetings, I guarantee you that it'll come as a lightning bolt from the blue. It'll also depress all but the most affluent of your clients, and yet I think it's important for everyone in the conversation to understand exactly what role health care costs will play in how you determine the best way to position the client for maximized cash flow achieved with as little risk of losing principal as possible. If you get right down to it, failure to protect against expenses arising from inadequate purchases of the extra coverage needed to supplement Medicare can result in the demolition of an entire retirement strategy. If the lion's share of cash flow has to go to pay debts that occurred because clients did not buy all the coverage they could afford, then what good was the planning in the first place? The answer would be that the planning was deeply flawed and that clients were done a major disservice, a disservice most will never recover from.

Medicare basics

Back in 1965, Congress passed Title XVIII of the Social Security Act to make health care insurance available to Americans over the age of sixty-five, and to make it available for certain groups of younger people under specified conditions. It was a grand plan designed to combat the expenses of medical coverage that were rising even at that time, and in the intervening years, Medicare has become a hugely popular entitlement program. Taken together with its older but still closely related sister, Social Security, both programs form the backbone of the safety net for retirees.

The four key parts of the program are briefly detailed below. Medicare Supplement insurance coverage is included as well. I'll get into much greater depth in the following pages.

- **Part A covers hospital services**
  This is free for everyone with more than forty quarters of Social Security, but in 2014, clients would pay a $1,216 deductible for every benefit period. Medicare Part A does not restrict benefits paid from a dollar standpoint, but it does limit the time it will pay benefits. This is a crucial distinction.

- **Part B covers doctor services**
  In 2014, clients would pay an annual premium of $104.90 and a deductible of $147.00.

- **Part C covers Medicare Advantage plans**
  These are low- or no-cost plans that replace Part A and Part B, and some plans provide prescription drug coverage (30 percent don't). Costs vary. These plans can be highly restrictive in services and doctor choice. We don't recommend them. We prefer that clients pay for Medicare Supplement Coverage.

- **Part D covers prescription drugs**
  Premiums vary with the plan. Clients should never skimp with prescription drug coverage.

- **Medicare Supplement** insurance (Plan F is my current favorite) fills in the gaps in Medicare Part A, Part B, and Part D, if applicable. For example, without Medicare Advantage or a more comprehensive Medicare Supplement plan, clients would be billed for 20 percent of all hospital costs under Part A. These plans are generally the best in our view because they cover most contingencies. They're also the most expensive.

A word on eligibility

Eligibility for free full Medicare coverage under Part A requires a worker Social Security record of forty or more quarters. Eligibility may be earned based upon a client's own Social Security record, qualification as a spouse of a qualifying worker, a spouse of a deceased worker, or as a qualifying divorced ex-spouse of a worker. In rare cases, qualification may be received by being a surviving parent of a qualified Social Security participant.

Everyone meeting the eligibility rules qualifies for any of Medicare Parts A, B, C, and D.

The initial eligibility period for Medicare Part A and Part B enrollment is within a seven-month period that starts three months prior to the person's sixty-fifth birthday month and ends three months after the enrollee's sixty-fifth birthday. For a person who turns sixty-five on September 10 of this year, their eligibility period is:

> 3 months before (June, July, and August)
> 1 month of birthday (September)
> 3 months after (Oct, November, and December)

Eligibility typically also accrues when coverage is established within sixty-three days of losing or ending certain types of coverage including private health insurance supplemental to Medicare coverage.

Important point: Clients need to enroll in Medicare Part A and Part B within the initial eligibility period. After the initial enrollment year, changes can be made each year during the Open Enrollment Period. For example, the Open Enrollment Period for 2014 changes and was October 15, 2013 to December 7, 2013. Changes became effective January 1, 2014.

Ineligibility: Workers without eligibility for Social Security should strive to obtain qualifications for benefits. Doing so is critical in establishing Medicare eligibility. Persons with fewer than forty quarters of Social Security eligibility should try to earn more quarters by working enough to earn four quarters each year if they cannot qualify for Medicare coverage as a spouse or divorced ex-spouse of a qualifying worker. Partial Social Security coverage (but not enough for eligibility) reduces the cost of Medicare Part A for individuals with less than forty quarters of credit with Social Security, but it's still best for clients to go in with forty quarters or more.

In 2014, individuals with thirty to thirty-nine quarters of Social

Security coverage paid $234 per month for Medicare Part A coverage. That represented a savings of $192 per month versus individuals with zero to twenty-nine quarters of coverage who had to pay a premium of $426 per month. Earning as little as $4,800 in 2014 will allow clients to earn four quarters of Social Security coverage. Buying Part A is vital for protection from full exposure to hospitalization bills if clients haven't fully met Part A eligibility requirements. Besides, clients have to have Part B coverage to be eligible to enroll in and buy Part B.

Important point: Very few financial advisors realize the advantage clients receive from adding to partial Social Security coverage. Note that a client with twenty-eight quarters of coverage could save $192 per month on Part A coverage by adding a mere $400 or more of Social Security earnings in 2014. Clearly adding to partial Social Security coverage can be one of life's great bargains.

Low-income retirees: Persons receiving very small Social Security checks will receive free Medicare Part A, which is worth $426 per month. Medicare eligible participants with limited income should contact their local Social Security Administration office to inquire about programs that may offer help with health care needs covered under Medicare Part B and Part D. The extra help programs may pay 100 percent of prescription costs! These limited- or no-income persons frequently qualify for enriched benefits provided by a combination of Medicare and Medicaid. These enriched benefits may be called a "Shared Plan." At present, there is something of a safety net for seniors with very low income. Whether that safety net lasts remains to be seen.

Exclusions: There is no exclusion for preexisting conditions for any of Medicare Parts A, B, or D if implemented within the seven-month enrollment period based on the date your client reaches sixty-five, or within sixty-three days of losing equivalent employer coverage, whichever is later. However, there is an exclusion for end-stage renal failure. No one is required to pay higher premiums because of existing medical conditions, which is a good thing. Under the Affordable Health

Care Act, exclusions from private insurance for preexisting conditions is now illegal.

Preauthorization: Typical health care insurance providers require authorization for procedures, often through a referral from a primary care physician to a specialist. No preauthorization is either available or required for reimbursement of physicians, hospitals, and other entities under Medicare Parts A and B. The primary requirement is that the procedure or treatment is medically necessary. Bear in mind that preauthorization is typically required for Medicare Advantage plans (Part C) and Medicare Supplement plans.

Medicare Part A

Medicare Part A is hospital insurance for hospital expenses, though as I said, it's not a blank check. Part A is free if your clients have a work record of forty or more quarters with Social Security. Part A pays inpatient care in hospitals for the first sixty days of hospitalization (subject to a $1,216 deductible), skilled-nursing facilities, hospice, and home health care, but not long-term custodial care in the home.

Hospital services under Medicare Part A include:

- Care in semiprivate room, meals, general nursing and other hospital services and supplies
- Care in critical access hospitals
- Inpatient mental health care
- For days one to sixty, there is an initial deductible (the patient pays the first $1,216).
- Days sixty-one to ninety, the patient pays an additional $304 per day.
- After day ninety, the patient has a lifetime reserve of $608 per day for sixty additional days.

Clearly, the above bullet points show that Medicare Part A is based on time. Your clients can actually use up their Part A coverage during a critical event! Most clients won't know that, though the ones about to turn sixty-five should. The value of knowing about these things in advance is that you can figure out how much it's going to cost to protect against the eventuality of running out of Medicare during a certain prolonged medical event. Let me explain in more detail.

For days one to ninety, the deductibles are per qualifying hospital stay (a qualified stay occurs when the patient is in the hospital officially as an in-patient, generally more than twenty-three hours). Once the patient has gone sixty days between stays, they can start a new hospital stay. The lifetime reserve is a one per lifetime. Once the lifetime reserve is used, there is no Medicare coverage for stays beyond ninety days. Medicare enrollees are fully responsible for medical costs once the Medicare eligibility time frame per hospital stay is exceeded. Even if the family is able to negotiate a reduced rate once eligibility is exhausted, the risk of exhausting the personal resources of the Medicare enrollee is very substantial! Medicare enrollees and their families should be very aware of the time between hospital stays. If at least sixty days pass between hospital stays, the second stay is considered a new hospital stay as opposed to an extension of the previous hospital stay!

Important point: Medicare Advantage plans under Medicare Part C typically do little or nothing to resolve the problems of low-cost hospital coverage being limited to sixty days, and high co-pays between day sixty-one and day ninety. The cost goes even higher for those forced to use the sixty-day lifetime reserve for hospital stays over ninety days.

Individual and business health care insurance policies typically establish a dollar limit on benefits, but not a time limit. Some people call these limits "major medical" (an outdated term). Medicare Part A (hospital coverage) and Medicare Advantage plans do not have a dollar limit for benefits, but there is both a reduced payment limit beginning at day sixty-one for each hospital stay and a time limit for extended hospital stays. Keep this important distinction in mind when thinking about balancing costs with coverage.

Medicare Part B

Although Medicare Part A is generally free, an eligible participant must enroll in and pay for Medicare Part B to receive Medicare Part A coverage. Clients can't purchase Medicare Part B unless they either qualified to receive Medicare Part A for free, or unless they bought Medicare Part A. They'd only have to buy some or all of Part A if they'd failed to pay enough into Social Security to fully qualify for full benefits (forty or fewer quarters).

Important point: Coverage under Parts A and B are required for coverage under Medicare Advantage plans in Part C and for prescription drug coverage, Part D.

Medicare Part B pays eligible medically necessary services including doctors' services, outpatient care, home health services (but not long-term care), and other medical services. Durable medical equipment costs are also covered. Under Medicare Part B, patients must pay 20 percent of these costs under coinsurance provisions. Some preventive services are covered.

So, now your clients know that under the basics of Part A, they're on the hook for 20 percent payouts for services to fill the gaps in Medicare. They also know they have to pay premiums for Part B and that co-pays and deductibles kick in. If they want prescription drug coverage, they'll need Part D, a Medicare Advantage plan, or a more comprehensive and expensive Medicare Supplement plan. When you get right down to it, though, how many of your clients really know this? Again, those who are closing in on Medicare have probably been up late at night wondering about how they're going to pay for all the coverage they'll need. Younger clients won't have a clue, and yet you and they should keep all of these details in mind as you plan for their retirement. All of these drains on cash flow factor into the overall CAMP Score. Even younger clients need to be in the know about the current sorry state of retirement in America today.

And there's more! Don't forget! There is a cost for Part B coverage that is standard for individuals who have a modified adjusted gross income under $85,000 per year and for couples who have a MAGI under $170,000 per year. The general rule is that Medicare premiums are based upon the client's MAGI on the last tax return available from the IRS. Because Medicare premiums reset January 1 of each year, that will generally be the return for two years previous.

Provision 1: When income has dropped substantially in the last two years or new marital status would reduce Medicare premiums, participants should appeal to Medicare for premium reduction. Medicare will review cases where income drops or marital status changes.

Provision 2: Individuals still working and receiving employer health insurance deemed to be as good as Medicare benefits will **not** be penalized if they enroll on a timely basis after ending employer coverage (sixty-three days). The employer should provide an annual statement that the worker is covered by a plan equivalent to or better than Medicare. If your clients don't get this documentation, it could cost them big bucks later. For example, as you'll see when we talk about Part D, surcharges can apply, or clients may not even be eligible for certain Medicare Supplement plans because of underwriting restrictions put in place to weed out enrollees in poor health.

Your clients can opt out of Medicare Part B in the initial seven-month Medicare enrollment period, but clients could face a 10 percent per year cost increase in the coverage for every year clients weren't signed up for Part B if they go for coverage later. I recommend signing up for Part B in the initial Medicare enrollment period. It simply makes good business sense.

Medicare Part C

Medicare Part C is now known under the catchall name of Medicare Advantage. The old name for Part C was simply Medicare + Choice. It should not be confused with Medigap, which is another name for Medicare Supplement programs. The important thing to know about Medicare Advantage is that it *replaces* Part A and Part B. The Part B premium is paid to the government, which pays the Medicare Advantage provider. Part B premiums are either deducted from Social Security checks or paid quarterly to the appropriate government agency.

Important point: Medicare Advantage plans replace Part A and Part B, but clients are limited to the benefits of the plan provider, plus other restrictions. Each plan has its own specific costs for a given service. The plans generally provide Part D coverage (drug coverage) at no additional cost.

The average Medicare Advantage plan cost under $40 per month in 2014, but plans vary, and so do costs. Over half the plans are no-cost plans, which means clients may not receive any benefits for prescriptions drugs. In fact, over 70 percent of Medicare Advantage plans provide all or some Part D coverage, so it goes to reason that 30 percent of the plans don't provide that coverage. If this sounds confusing to you, then think about your client who is approaching Medicare enrollment and having to sort through piles of unsolicited offers from a zillion companies!

About 25 percent of Medicare participants go for Part C Medicare Advantage plans because they're trying to keep costs down. Costs are lower because participants in Medicare Advantage receive health care through a provider organization like a health maintenance organization HMO or a primary provider organization (PPO). The idea is certain plans will lower costs, and the plans can increase benefits for an additional monthly premium. I am admittedly no big fan of Medicare Advantage because you get what you pay for, and most of these plans have big potential downside in terms of risk exposure.

Careful consideration should be given before making any decisions about whether to buy a Medicare Advantage plan, or to buy Part D for prescriptions accompanied with a more comprehensive (and more costly) Medicare Supplement plan instead of Medicare Advantage. In addition, Advantage plans can differ by region, so your clients will have to find out what is offered in the area where they're retiring. For example, some Medicare Advantage plans restrict participants to doctors within a specified network or levy extra charges for out-of-network services. Others limit which drugs are on the "covered" list of a specific program.

Medicare Part D

Medicare Part D drug coverage resulted from the Medicare Prescription Drug, Improvement, and Modernization Act of 2003. Part D coverage became available in 2006. Coverage is available only through insurance companies and Health Maintenance Organizations (HMOs). Part D coverage may be purchased in the initial Medicare eligibility period by anyone covered under Parts A and B. If your clients can afford it, Part D is a good way to go in covering some, but not all, of the expenses for prescription drugs. Medicare Advantage plans do pay for prescription drugs, but that's not the main reason people buy those plans. They purchase Medicare Advantage plans because of the promise of lower overall costs for all the coverage needed to fill in for what Medicare doesn't cover. The problem is that these plans are a bare-bones option. Part D has its share of disadvantages as well.

Alternatively, some people choose to get Medicare Parts A and B through a private insurer under a Medicare Advantage plan. As I've mentioned, I'll tell you more about these plans in a minute. Suffice it to say here that Medicare Advantage plans may offer Part D drug coverage for free or require enrollees to pay for the coverage. However, it is important to note that Medicare Advantage plan members are not allowed by Medicare authorities to have separate Part D coverage. The reason separate Part D coverage is not allowed is that naïve seniors might buy duplicate coverage since coverage is included in Medicare Advantage plans.

Important point: Medicare Part D coverage is *voluntary*. Clients have to opt in if they want it when signing up for Medicare. There is a relatively small cost per month, totaling approximately $500 per year. There are co-pays that vary with the cost category of the drug.

The infamous doughnut hole

At present, Medicare Part D standard costs are structured in such a way that some retirees find they fall into a gap where coverage temporarily ends. Prescription drugs are expensive, especially if clients take a lot of them. For seniors with little extra cash flow, a medical event that triggers unforeseen expenditures for costly medications can create a tremendous strain in terms of finances and quality of life. If clients fall into the doughnut hole, the pain gets even worse. Fortunately, Medicare Advantage plans frequently pay part of the costs below, which is better than having no help at all. Medicare Supplement plans are an even better way to hedge against unforeseen expenditures for health care.

Here are the standard costs for Medicare Part D coverage in 2014:

Stage 1: Participant first pays a $310 deductible. When costs are between $2,850 and $4,550, the participant pays the full cost. This is called the doughnut hole. Once the participant's costs exceed $4,550, the participant is only responsible for 5 percent of their prescription drug costs in 2014.

So, you see that Part D definitely has its disadvantages. Yet, it does represent an option millions of retirees take, in spite of the high deductibles and partial payments for the drugs. As you sort through the cash flow issues associated with a CAMP Score, it's important to get some idea of how the client wants to cover prescriptions drugs. Costs for Part D compared to Medicare Advantage plans are sometimes hard to quantify because the variables involved—costs for the plans or Part D, costs for drugs—are so numerous. The prices constantly shift as well, so it's a good idea to build a big safety margin into your figures when estimating for client retirement purposes.

Part D tier system

Prescription drugs are grouped into five tiers. Each tier becomes progressively more expensive for the Medicare enrollee. The tiers are:

Tier 1 (Preferred Generic): Lowest co-pay. Lower cost, commonly used drugs.

Tier2 (Nonpreferred Generic): Low co-pay. Category includes most generic drugs.

Tier 3 (Preferred Brand): Medium co-pay. Many common brand-name drugs, called preferred brands, and some higher-cost generic drugs.

Tier 4 (Nonpreferred Brand): Highest co-pay. Nonpreferred generic and nonpreferred brand-name drugs.

Tier 5 (Specialty Tier): Coinsurance. Unique and/or very high-cost drugs.

Note: The co-pay for Medicare enrollees is a function of both the Medicare Part D drug payment stage and the drug tier. During Stage 3 (the so-called doughnut hole between $2,850 and $4,550 in total drug costs), the Medicare enrollee will be responsible for 100 percent of the high drug costs. Even in Stage 4, the stage Medicare calls the "catastrophic coverage stage," the Medicare enrollee may be responsible for 33 percent of costs of Tier 4 and Tier 5 drugs. If a single drug costs $1,500 per month, the Medicare enrollee's cost is $500 per month. Although the "donut-hole" costs are reducing, this will happen over an extended period of time.

Clients have other options: Medicare Part D has some real financial drawbacks, as do Medicare Advantage plans, but there are ways to get better coverage. The fact is those options will cost clients money as well. There is no free ride for most retirees, which is why costs tend to drive decisions. With a limited fixed income, clients might feel pushed to make unwise choices. I'm here to say that if clients feel this way, just reassure them that options do exist. Chances are there is one that will work out to the best advantage of your clients given their particular level of financial wherewithal.

As noted, there is a 10 percent per year surcharge for years where no Part D coverage is elected by the taxpayer after the initial enrollment period. A taxpayer who does not choose Part D coverage until age seventy-two would pay a monthly premium of 170 percent more than the amount paid by a comparable-age person who chose coverage at age sixty-five and continued the coverage every year. Seniors who live a normal or longer life expectancy will generally rue the decision not to start Part D coverage when first eligible. I generally estimate life expectancy of age eighty for men and eighty-five for women to approximate life expectancy for clients with an attained age of sixty-five to seventy. I then add half a year for every year over age seventy. Eligibility generally begins with age sixty-five.

Important point: Workers employed and covered by their employer health insurance plans may delay the start of eligibility for Part D *without* the 10 percent per year surcharge. They must decide to enroll or not enroll within two months of leaving their position.

Medicare Supplement plans

Medicare Supplement plans are bought to "supplement" Medicare coverage with additional coverage to make up for the gaps. The benefits include:

Hospitalization: In addition to paying deductibles and co-pays for short-duration hospital stays and doctor visits, Medicare Supplement plans offer the following benefits:

- Payment of additional deductibles in days sixty-one to ninety.
- Payments of additional deductibles during use of the lifetime extended stay coverage of sixty days per lifetime. Remember that the deductible is $608 per day!
- As much as one full year of extended stay coverage after the lifetime extended stay coverage is exhausted.

Important point: Medicare Supplement plans provide payment of excess deductible costs of hospital stays between sixty and 150 days, plus coverage for 365 additional days after Medicare hospital benefits end. As I've already said, this coverage could mean the difference between financial ruin for clients and allowing them to get through a very difficult time without going broke.

Medical expenses: Unforeseen medical costs will inevitably come up, and seniors on fixed incomes generally haven't planned for them. The margin of safety, if it exists at all, can easily evaporate, especially if multiple medical events occur with one or both spouses. Still, the impulse of clients will be to go cheap. It will take sound reasoning and a clear presentation of the facts on your part to steer clients away from making potentially ruinous financial errors as they decide what to do when it comes time to enroll in Medicare.

Some Medicare Supplement plans require Medicare participants pay a portion of Part B coinsurance or co-payments. Even then, the supplemental insurance pays more than Medicare Advantage plans. Logically, lower-cost Medicare Supplement plans pay less of the deductibles and co-pays than the most expensive monthly charge for Medicare Supplement plan Type F. Some Medicare Supplement plans pay all deductibles and co-payments, reducing or eliminating the Medicare recipient's exposure to potential large costs for deductibles, co-payments, and extended stay costs. This is critical! If your clients understand what they're getting and the risks they're avoiding, then many will say, "Hey, sign me up!"

In addition, Medicare Supplement plans provide:

- First three pints of blood each year. Medicare Advantage plans may or may not pay for the first three pints of blood per year.
- Hospice: Part A deductibles.

Other benefits of Medicare Supplement plans that are available include:

- Payment of coinsurance for skilled-nursing facilities
- Payment of Part A deductibles
- Payment of Part B deductibles
- Payment of Part B excess (doctors, etc.)
- Payment for a limited portion of health costs during foreign travel
- Payment for some medical protection while away from home within the United States. Medicare Advantage plans pay for emergency service while away from home, but they do not pay for routine medical care.
- Payment for services from virtually any doctor that accepts Medicare. Medicare Advantage plans limit geographical area, doctors, and hospitals to affiliated groups.

Most seniors of modest means or better give a good, hard look at the various Medicare Supplement plans available on the market today. Doing so just makes good sense.

If clients go cheap

As noted, it's human nature for seniors to go cheap on extra costs for health care under Medicare. Perhaps if clients saw the numbers, they might reconsider arguing against paying for those extra costs. For example, if a client thinks investing money saved in health care costs is well spent, it behooves you to point out that such thinking exposes the client to market *and* illness expense risk!

Check out the illustrations below.

Illustration 1

Medicare Supplement plans substantially reduce exposure to large unexpected medical costs. Large unexpected medical costs deplete savings and therefore damage future cash flows for both the Medicare enrollee's lifetime and their spouse and other loved ones.

Assume a Medicare enrollee pays $150 per month ($1,800 per year) for the best Medicare Supplement coverage. Five years in extra cost (absolutely no usage) would have a net cost of $9,000 (five times $1,800). If in year six the Medicare participant has a medical need that results in eighty days of hospital stay and $40,000 of doctor costs, note the extremely negative effect of saving $1,800 per year for five years and *then* having a medical need for eighty days of hospital stay.

Year	Savings	Earnings on Savings	Cumulative Savings
1	$1,800	$36.00	$1,836.00
2	$1,800	$109.44	$3,745.44
3	$1,800	$185.82	$5,731.26
4	$1,800	$265.25	$7,796.51
5	$1,800	$347.86	$9,944.37
6	$1,800	$433.77	$12,178.14

Less:
Hospital Costs	$5,780.00
Doctor Costs	$8,000.00
Net Savings/Cost	$(1,601.86)

Note that over six years, the frugal "why pay the extra cost of a *premium* Medicare Supplement plan Medicare enrollee" has cost himself or herself $1,601.86.

Illustration 2

Medicare Supplement plans reduce deductibles and doctor co-pays more than even the best no-cost Medicare Advantage plan. This is another critical reason why I argue for client purchases of the best Medicare Supplement plan they can afford. Explain to your clients that the adverse impact on retirement cash flow can be much like a death from a thousand cuts. The big expenses can wipe them out if they're not prepared, but the cumulative smaller expenses can be nearly as harmful to cash flow over time.

Let's go back to our Medicare enrollee paying $150 per month ($1,800 per year) for the best Medicare Supplement coverage, five years in extra cost (absolutely no usage), and in year six has a medical need that results in eighty days of hospital stay and $40,000 of doctor costs.

Year	Savings	Earnings on Savings	Cumulative Savings	Plan Pays	Net Savings
1	$1,800	$36.00	$1,836.00	$1,000	$836.00
2	$1,800	$69.44	$2,705.44	$1,000	$1,705.44
3	$1,800	$104.22	$3,609.66	$1,000	$2,609.66
4	$1,800	$140.39	$4,550.04	$1,000	$3,550.04
5	$1,800	$178.00	$5,528.05	$1,000	$4,528.05
6	$1,800	$217.12	$6,545.17	$1,000	$5,545.17

Less:
Hospital Costs $5,780.00
Doctor Costs $8,000.00

Net Savings/Cost $(7,234.83)

Note that over six years, the frugal "why pay the extra cost of a *premium* Medicare Supplement plan Medicare enrollee" has cost himself or herself $7,234.93 even if they receive only $1,000 in greater annual benefits from the Medicare Supplement plan in years 1–5 than would be available under the best no-cost Medicare Advantage plan.

Medicare strategies

There are three alternative Medicare strategies that each fit different Medicare eligible people. They are:

1. Medicare Part A and B with or without Part D drug coverage
2. Medicare Advantage plans
3. Medicare Supplement plans with or without Part D drug coverage

The following illustrations correspond to each of the above strategies.

Illustration 3

Choosing Medicare Part A and B alone

Let's take two hypothetical clients as a brief case in point. Alex and Elizabeth are highly intelligent and very well-educated people, but they confessed to be completely confused by the complexities of Medicare and the many choices. They said that the more and varied literature they read, the more confused they became. Sound familiar?

I explained that a very high percentage of Medicare eligible people have just Medicare Parts A and B because they either:

1. Believe that the combination of Medicare Parts A and B provides the same coverage they had prior to retiring; or

2. Do not feel they can afford additional coverage; or

3. Do not believe they need Part D coverage.

The insurance industry distinguishes between risk assumption and risk avoidance. Clients choosing not to insure for drug costs are assuming the risk, which I think is just simply nuts. Naturally, when people like Alex and Liz take the ostrich position, that of burying heads in sand, it makes me very uncomfortable. It should make you uncomfortable too. Risk assumption decisions should be made on a cost versus benefits basis, not on a knee-jerk response to what up front seems to be a big bill that doesn't require payment. I strongly believe that the low costs of a Part D plan are greatly outweighed by the large potential benefits of a Part D plan. The cost of Part D drug coverage for Alex and Elizabeth would be between $40 and $100 each per month.

The retiree's mistake in failing to adequately insure against all kinds of health care risks, not just drug coverage, is far more likely to result in financial ruin for two primary reasons. The reasons are:

1. Retirees don't have future income to recover from medical disasters; and

2. The medical costs of health concerns for seniors are typically much higher than the medical needs of twenty-somethings.

Alex and Liz expressed the rationale for choosing part A and B alone as follows: "If I do not **currently** require any expensive drugs and/or medical procedures, why should I pay for what I do not use? I'm just not up for the extra bills."

I told them that the vast majority of people who skimp on health care in planning and managing their retirement end up regretting it later. The risks of financial devastation are simply too great. I urged them both to think about the costs of an extended hospital stay.

Prescription drugs can also eat away at client cash flow. That's why I recommend that clients purchase Part D.

Illustration 4

Medicare Advantage

As I've said, lots of seniors go for the cheaper Medicare Advantage plans, or Part C, which replaces Medicare Parts A and B. Over 70 percent of these plans replace all or some of Medicare Part D coverage.

But here's what clients need to know:

- Not all plans are alike in what is covered, cost, and coverage areas. What medical services are available will differ from county to county as well as from year to year.
- Medicare Advantage plans are available only in the specific county or region in which one resides.
- Hospitals in an area may choose not to participate or to "opt out" of Medicare Advantage plans, preventing anyone from selecting a Medical Advantage plan in that county.
- As these plans are typically renegotiated each year, the availability of doctors and medical facilities may change each year. In some extreme cases, the Medicare Advantage plan for an area could cease to exist.
- Medicare Advantage plans only offer nationwide coverage for emergency care, urgent care, and renal dialysis.
- PPOs often provide more flexibility than HMOs. With a PPO, clients can choose their own doctors and hospitals, and they don't need a referral to see a specialist.
- Medicare Advantage plans typically do *not* provide coverage for large deductibles and the co-pays that result when a patient requires critical care.
- HMOs or insurance companies receive payment from

the US government to provide the Medicare services for Medicare Advantage participants. HMOs and insurance companies both typically receive more than 100 percent of the government's expected costs (from paying Medicare providers) and have lower costs due to a limited network of "preferred providers" (PPOs). HMOs control costs by directly providing the service through their facilities. Private-fee-for-service plans (PFFS) limit costs by limiting both networks and service area.
- If the Medicare Advantage plan doesn't have drug coverage, clients can't buy Medicare Part D due to regulations.

I always advise clients to carefully research and consider their unique health needs, their choice of retirement areas, and their financial means in selecting a Medicare Advantage plan.

What's usually covered with lower deductibles and co-pays in most cases is:

- Hospital stays and doctor visits
- Usually prescription drugs
- Preventive services
- Sometimes vision, hearing care, and health club memberships

Medicare Advantage enrollees may "go outside" the identified network of providers, but the enrollee may pay a much greater percentage of provider costs. Emergency health care service may be received outside the geographical area and provider network, but to receive normal health care service with minimal costs, enrollees are limited to preferred providers within the designated geographical area.

Medicare Advantage HMOS, private-fee-for-service plans (PFFS), or insurance companies typically provide more services at a lower cost to Medicare enrollees than would result if the Medicare enrollee simply added Part D to Medicare Parts A and Part B. Plus, clients can generally enroll with preexisting conditions. The only exception is end-stage renal (kidney) disease. However, deductibles and co-pays from a Medicare Advantage plan, especially during extended hospital stays, may result in higher costs than a Medicare Supplement plan combined with Medicare Parts A, B, and D. Clients should also bear in mind that an increasing number of doctors have chosen not to participate in Medicare. Others may participate but are out-of-network providers for a particular Medicare Advantage plan. That can also make choosing a Part C approach a bit sticky.

Important point: Before clients choose a Medicare Advantage plan, they should ensure that their preferred doctors and hospitals are participants in the Medicare Advantage plan or "in network" to avoid extra charges for going outside the network for medical service. Clients should also make sure that their specific prescriptions are on the plan's covered drug list. The risk of Medicare Advantage plans is the significantly greater cost exposure as the taxpayer gets older and increasingly frail. Thus, I generally suggest Medicare Supplement plans where either needs appear imminent or where financial means to pay higher premiums exists.

Illustration 5

Medicare Supplement plans with or without Part D drug coverage

Medicare Supplement plans, also known as Medigap plans, may initially appear more costly than Medicare Advantage plans, but they are far more flexible, may have more coverage, and reduce the out-of-pocket costs in co-pays and deductibles. The cost of a premium Medicare Supplement plus Part D coverage is about $200 per person per month in 2014. A Medicare Supplement plan can help protect your clients against exposure to extreme financial risk. I recommend that clients give the best of these plans serious consideration before choosing options that only seem less expensive in the short-term.

Medicare Supplement plans work in *conjunction* with Medicare Parts

A, B, and D, which means clients still pay for Part B and Part D for the best possible coverage, including payments for prescription drugs. By contrast, Medicare Advantage plans *replace* Medicare Parts A, B, and D. Many seniors choose Medicare Advantage plans because they provide coverage at little or no cost beyond paying the required Medicare Part B cost. The Medical Supplement insurance helps pay for Medicare deductibles and co-pays.

Eligibility: Medical Supplement insurance becomes more costly the later it is elected and may even be unavailable subject to insurability issues if delayed beyond the initial three years of Medicare eligibility.

Medical insurability for all parts is generally not required in the first three years of Medicare eligibility. Those delaying coverage may encounter eligibility issues. However, I caution that insurability standards for Medicare may be much easier to meet than individual health insurance standards even when there is delayed enrollment. If a participant can afford the relatively low additional costs to buy *both* a Medicare Supplement plan *and* a Part D drug plan (typically $200–300 per month), the benefits greatly exceed the costs.

Benefits include substantial reduction of the potential for financial ruin that typically accompanies extended hospital stays, and protection of a participant's spouse from financial ruin when one must endure an extended hospital stay. Most working individuals will recognize that even the highest quality Medicare Supplement plan (Plan F for most participants) plus Part D drug coverage is both much less expensive and higher quality than all but the very best corporate plans. That's why when enrollment time comes along, your clients need to be totally up to speed.

Important point: Buying a premium Medicare Supplement plan plus Part D coverage maximizes the chances that unforeseen medical events will restrict client cash flow during retirement.

In my view, the approximately $200 per person per month for a top

Medicare Supplement plan and Part D, in addition to the costs of premiums for Medicare Part B, is still meager compared to the value. If your clients balk, work in the psychological peace of mind they'll feel because they'll know they're covered. Psychology influences a great deal of retirement planning.

You ask, "How much is peace of mind and financial protection worth?"

If you've presented a reasoned argument, complete with the facts to back it up, chances are your clients will see the wisdom of purchasing the best health care options to fill in the gaps Medicare doesn't cover. The coverage reduces or eliminates one of the major risks of retirement, those unforeseen health costs that can tip everything upside down in a hurry.

A word on timing

Clients can only make the change to a medical supplement plan during open enrollment dates for that year. In 2013, the open enrollment period was October 15 to December 7 of 2013. Therefore, the best time for a Medicare eligible person to make the decision to buy a Medicare Supplement plan is in the year of initial eligibility when they have the seven-month window, beginning three months prior to their birth month and ending three months after their birth month.

As you discuss Medicare costs and coverage options with clients, it may be handy for you to present the comparison table below when it comes to a discussion of what's best in terms of hospitalization coverage.

Table 1

Medicare Plan Comparisons for 2012

Doctor and Hospital Choice is any doctor or hospital that will accept the patient for Medicare Parts A and B and Medicare Supplements. Restrictions to in-network can be pretty restrictive for Medicare Advantage.

	Medicare Part A & B	Medicare Advantage	Medicare Supplement
Hospitalization			
Days 1–60	All but $1,156	$295 per day	What A & B doesn't
		Co-pay first 5 days	
		What A & B doesn't	
		Days 6–60	
61–90	All but $289/day	What A & B doesn't	What A & B doesn't
91–60 days lifetime is used up	All but $578/day	What A & B doesn't	What A & B doesn't
After using 90 days plus lifetime 60 days	Nothing	What A & B doesn't	All for one year
Blood			
First 3 pints	Nothing		For 3 pints
Hospice Care			
	Nearly all		The rest
Medical Services Including Doctors			
First $140 of Medicare approved amounts	Nothing		The rest
Remainder of Medicare approved amounts	Generally 80%	The rest	The rest
Part B Excess Charges (above Medicare approved amounts)			
Blood—first 3 pints	Nothing		The rest
Durable Medical Equipment			
First $140 of Medicare approved amounts	Nothing		The rest

186 | *Roger Roemmich*

Remainder of Medicare approved amounts	Generally 80%		The rest
Foreign Travel			
First $250 per calendar year	Nothing		Nothing
Remainder of charges	Nothing		80% up to $50,000

Parting words: Medicare is often misunderstood, but it doesn't have to be. If its various component parts are clearly explained, clients will get what's at stake. Hopefully, they'll see the benefit of buying a platinum combo of Part A, Part B, Part D, and a premium Medicare Supplement plan to reduce or eliminate long-term risk exposure due to prolonged hospital stays and the erosive impact of rising drug prices on cash flow. The good news is that Medicare was designed to be as flexible as possible to give people in a wide expanse of income ranges the opportunity to buy the coverage they need during their retirement.

As with alternative investments and Social Security timing, you may experience pushback from clients when you present what you believe are the best possible options on all fronts, Medicare included. Just know that the integrated approach you are bringing to the table will do your clients good during the remainder of their financial lives. Remind yourself that we're not just focused on assets, liquidity, principal preservation, cash flow, maximized Social Security benefits, or Medicare in a single context. No, we're focused on the entire gamut of issues that can and will make a potentially grand difference for your clients.

10

Elephants in the Room
A Case for Long-Term Care

> Age is an issue of mind over matter. If you don't mind, it doesn't matter. —Mark Twain

FEW THINGS STRIKE MORE fear into people than the idea of spending the last days of life warehoused in a nursing home. In fact, seniors say they fear that more than death, according to data from the classic 2007 study *Aging in Place in America*. The study was commissioned by Clarity and the EAR Foundation to examine fears among the elderly and their kids related to aging, and it found that the majority of respondents said loss of independence topped the list in terms of scare factors.

No matter how much we fear it, the cold, hard reality is that 70 percent of people over the age of sixty-five are going to require some form of long-term care at home or in a skilled-nursing facility, says the US Department of Health and Human Services. And yet only 9 percent of Americans have any sort of long-term care protection, leaving the vast majority of retirees exposed to the risks of potential financial ruin in the event of a long-term care event arising from stroke, heart attack, Alzheimer's disease, or some other malady. Genworth's 2012 Cost of Care Survey pegs the median annual expense of full-time skilled-nursing care at $81,030, and the price is much higher than that in many metropolitan areas across the country. The American Association for Long-Term Care Insurance reports that the average duration of long-term care is 1,040 days, or 2.8 years, so you can clearly see that most people simply can't afford to self-insure.

In my experience as a financial advisor, I have found that long-term care is the one area where clients are typically the weakest. Many have fabulous CAMP Scores, until we factor long-term care liabilities and protections into the mix, and then the water gets muddy. If clients haven't taken steps to protect themselves financially from a long-term care perspective, they really aren't in a position to retire with confidence. The pushback you'll get on the long-term care issue is going to be tough to take, but you'll need to stay firmly assertive when *gently* laying out the reasons why long-term care cannot be ignored. Clients must *never* play the role of the ostrich. If they do, they'll quite possibly never get their heads out from under the sand.

Affordability

Whenever long-term care insurance comes up, the first thing clients will usually say is that they don't need the coverage. After you point out the basic statistics, clients should see the need for long-term care protection, but then the issue of price will come up. Clients will say they can't afford to buy coverage. They may well be right!

Traditional long-term care insurance is very expensive, and your clients may not be able to afford full or even *any* coverage. In fact, the nonprofit Life and Health Insurance Foundation says that if assets, other than a home, are $30,000 for a single person or $80,000 for couple, long-term care insurance is probably not something the client can afford, regardless of the risks of not having any coverage. Remember when I cited the study from the National Institute of Retirement Security that said most Americans don't have any money saved for retirement, and of those nearing age sixty-five most have saved only about $12,000? Those statistics make the LHIF figures sound great! A couple with eighty grand sounds like they're in the winning seat compared to the NIRS findings. So, what I'm saying is we have to take studies with a grain of salt. My big point here may seem a bit obvious: if people don't have money, they can't protect themselves against the financial liabilities a long-term care event can trigger, but you should try to help them figure out a way to at least mitigate the damages.

Medicaid is about the only recourse for low-income people. Forty percent of Americans who need LTC are below 150 percent of the federal poverty level and therefore must rely on Medicaid. The Long-Term Care Price Index in 2013 put the premium costs per year for a couple age fifty-five for coverage of $162,000 each with a three-percent inflation option at $3,725, but there are ways to lower the costs. For example, lowering the benefit threshold can reduce the price while still allowing for some protection.

Important point: Rates for traditional long-term care insurance are calculated based on the age of the insured. If clients buy policies when they're young, the cost of coverage will be lower than if they delay purchasing coverage. Purchasers of traditional long-term care insurance are an average of fifty-seven.

Long-term care expenses are the leading cause of poverty among seniors who would otherwise have been comfortable in retirement. The issue is that serious. If clients fail to take steps to buy at least some level of coverage, they're exposing themselves and their families to incredible financial risk. As many as 10 million people over the age of fifty are currently taking care of elderly parents, and the wage losses over time of these caregivers amount to $324,000 for women and $283,000 for men. Aging in America has definite costs, and not all of them are related to dollars and cents.

Complex factors influencing long-term care (LTC) costs include:

1. Length of LTC needs

2. Quality of LTC assistance

3. Severity of LTC needs

4. Region of the United States

LTC costs frequently escalate during periods of physical frailty. Increasing physical frailty is almost inevitable when we live extended lives. Ironically, medical advances that prevent premature death also increase the likelihood for needing LTC assistance. It's important to note that long-term care differs from medical care. Long-term care is for assistance in what are known as the six activities of daily living. An understanding of ADLs, as they're called, is absolutely necessary to achieve prior to any further discussion of long-term care options.

Check out the following list. It's what doctors will use to determine if you are eligible to collect on any long-term care benefits you may have.

Activities of daily living

1. Eating

2. Continence (the lack of control of bodily functions both urinary and fecal)

3. Dressing

4. Bathing

5. Toileting (requiring assistance with elimination needs)

6. Transferring (walking)

There is a distinction between the medical definitions of toileting and continence. Toileting refers to assisting a person who may be able to control bodily functions but needs help with any of the following:

1. Ambulatory assistance

2. Bedpan

3. Urinal

4. Diaper

5. Catheter

Continence refers to lack of control of bodily functions.

Important point: Long-term care is defined by the need of assistance with ADLs.

Depending on the nature of your client's long-term care coverage, assistance with ADLs can occur at home, in an assisted-living facility, or in a skilled-nursing setting, such as a nursing home. Most long-term care benefits are paid-for services rendered at home, and most services are not medical. They're custodial. That's important because clients need to understand what kind of coverage they're getting and why they need it.

Medicare myths

Clients may think that Medicare will cover long-term care expenses, which is another reason they'll say they don't need coverage. Medicare does not cover long-term care. It will pay for skilled-nursing care for up to one hundred days as long as a three-day qualifying hospital stay requirement is met, but if the patient does not show improvement in their condition, Medicare benefits stop. Medicare does not pay for custodial care, which is the most common type of long-term care service. The vast majority of benefits paid to the 13 million Americans currently receiving long-term care are paid-for services at home to assist with activities of daily living.

Although long-term care assistance is defined as a deductible medical cost for federal tax purposes, it is defined as a personal care cost and *not* a medical cost for both Medicare and insurance purposes. The distinction is hugely important. Medicare eligible expenses must be medical needs. Therefore, long-term care needs only qualify if they are both:

1. Medically caused and

2. Temporary.

Both tax deductibility and insurance policies require at least standby assistance needs with two or more of the six ADLs. Standby assistance means that someone must be nearby in case assistance is needed. Persons with certain cognitive or mental impairments qualify without establishing either the need for hands-on assistance (a higher standard) or that they need assistance with two or more ADLs. As you can see, things can get complicated fast.

Medicare is designed to pay for acute, short-term illnesses. Services are only available to those who need skilled-nursing care or therapies. Note that Medicare pays only for medical assistance from qualified medical personnel. After a three-day hospital stay, Medicare will pay for skilled-nursing care for a maximum of one hundred days. After the first twenty days, the amount Medicare pays reduces sharply. Even in the first twenty days, it *must* be determined that the skilled-nursing care will restore the patient's capabilities. If restoration of capabilities is not expected, then Medicare can't be expected to pay. This is yet another critical consideration. If your client is diagnosed with Alzheimer's disease, Medicare won't pay a dime for any custodial services!

Unfortunately, very few people adequately address the potential financial disaster that can result from needing assistance with the six activities of daily living. The six activities of daily living are critical because they both define the conditions that must exist for long-term care insurance to cover costs and they define conditions for deducting costs as medical expenses on federal tax returns.

The hidden costs of long-term care

As I've said, failure to adequately provide for the possibility of significant LTC needs risks not only the quality of life of the person with needs. Spouses and family members may suffer even more due to the following three factors:

1. Financial assets may be strained or evenly totally decimated.

2. Stress of caring for the frail person may physically impair other family members and friends.

3. Emotional distress due to the condition of the beloved family member.

Few individuals or couples have the resources to pay for all potential LTC costs from either cash flow or assets. Even those who have either the cash flow or the assets to pay for LTC would not be advised to choose to self-insure or accept the risk. The risk far outweighs the potential savings from self-insuring!

Important point: Seniors should rely on income from assets to pay for LTC only if the income is *not* necessary to pay for day-to-day cost-of-living needs. Self-insurance is enticing, but only those with very substantial assets should choose to totally self-insure.

Some sources figure the costs of LTC and medical expenses at over $10,000 per month. Thus, receiving an annual income of 5 percent on investment assets of $2,400,000 would be required just to meet the projected annual LTC costs of $120,000! Additional assets would be required to meet other costs and needs. Obviously, I believe few clients will have sufficient assets to totally self-insure. Few clients have a net worth substantially in excess of the $2,400,000 necessary to pay for possible LTC expenses of $120,000 or more plus meet their other needs.

Even those who do have sufficient assets seldom want to use all their accumulated assets. The two critical reasons are:

1. First, they do or should worry about outliving their life expectancy.

2. Secondly, most clients want to protect their spouse or heirs from receiving nothing due to a prolonged LTC need.

Assets that need to be dedicated to earning the required expenses for meeting potential LTC needs should not also be counted when considering assets available for meeting other retirement cash flows. Double counting is quite common, and it's something we need to avoid as financial professionals. When determining cash flow for long-term care or long-term care protection, make sure you haven't counted on the cash for anything else. One of the most common retirement planning mistakes is asking investments to both provide needed cash flow **and** emergency capital. That's just plain silly, and yet it happens all the time.

Long-term care options

Paying for some kind of long-term care coverage is very difficult for many clients, but they do have options. The five options are as follows:

1. Traditional long-term care insurance

2. Variable annuity with long-term care rider

3. Lump-sum life insurance policy with long-term care rider

4. Annual-payment life insurance with long-term care rider

5. Reverse mortgage

Lower income individuals can increase their preparedness for LTC needs with an annuity with an LTC rider. These typically double the promised annual income for the time the LTC need persists. Typically they run for the remainder of a person's life. Another viable method is to buy life insurance with a LTC rider. Costs are typically only 10 percent to 20 percent higher than life insurance without the rider. The reason the costs are that little amount greater than straight life insurance is the insurance company pays the benefit either as a death benefit or a LTC benefit. The disadvantage to the life insurance company is that the benefit is paid sooner, not that the benefits paid are higher.

Policies that require institutionalization frequently fail to meet family needs and desires. Policies that exclude vital services just to lower the premiums typically leave clients hanging when they most need the coverage. That's why it's very important for you as the financial professional to really drill down when it comes to looking at the long-term care products you sell.

Important point: Look for policies that have a strong home health care component. Home-based long-term care services are the way of the future. In the past, many policies required institutionalization before benefits would be paid. Some companies still insist on it, but the industry is moving away from that in favor of allowing seniors to receive care at home.

Option 1: Traditional LTC

Purchasing a traditional LTC policy is a viable option for some clients, but they have to meet certain conditions. Many retirees put off buying a traditional long-term care insurance policy until they reach age sixty, according to the National Clearinghouse on Long-Term Care, US Department of Health. Other sources indicate that the age of the average purchaser is slightly lower. But the bottom line is delaying raises the overall cost of the policy, and it increases the odds that something will come up that will make it impossible for the client to buy any long-term care insurance at all. Fortunately, the average age of people buying long-term care insurance offered at work is fifty, meaning members of Generation X are starting to guard against the risks of exposure to the costs for long-term care when they are younger.

It's important to explain to clients that they will not receive underwriting for traditional long-term care insurance if any of the following apply:

- You already need long-term care services to meet two or more ADLs
- If you have AIDS or AIDS Related Complex (ARC)
- You already have any form of dementia or cognitive dysfunction, including but not limited to Alzheimer's disease
- You have multiple sclerosis, Parkinson's disease, or any other progressive neurological condition
- You have metastatic cancer (cancer that has spread beyond its original site)
- Any other health condition the underwriter says makes you a bad risk

Costs for traditional long-term care insurance are skyrocketing due to steady increases in health care and medical services, and due to skyrocketing numbers of insured making claims on their long-term care policies. Under certain scenarios, clients get priced right out of the policy due to premium increases, forcing them to let the policy lapse when they need it most. The annual increase in premiums is a major problem with traditional long-term care insurance, and the industry needs to address it with the creation of a more stable product that enables clients to predict the long-term costs. Failure to do so will prompt other entities to come up with better products, and the pool of potential buyers will migrate to those better products. That is already happening, and I, for one, applaud the improvements that are currently under way.

Illustration 1

The following is data for an individual who buys his or her long-term care policy at age sixty-five. Remember, the longer clients wait, the more expensive the insurance gets.

Scenario 1: The annual cost is $2,028 for a maximum daily benefit of $100 for a three-year benefit period. The individual is single, and the standard "health rate" (not the preferred rate or rate with spousal discounts, etc.) applies.

Scenario 2: The annual cost is $4,867 for a maximum daily benefit of $240 for a three-year benefit period. The individual is single, and the standard "health rate" (not the preferred rate or rate with spousal discounts, etc.) applies.

Recent US Department of Health and Human Services data indicates that the average daily cost of a semiprivate room in a nursing home is $198. So, the client in Scenario 1 is partially insuring. Hopefully, the client will have other assets that can produce income to pay the difference. As noted earlier, it's important that income from those extra assets not be counted on for meeting other expenses. The individual in Scenario 2 is insuring for a private room and hedging against other unforeseen expenses.

Important point: Most long-term care insurance companies offer an inflation protection component for an extra fee. I always recommend protecting against inflation whenever possible, and long-term care is no exception.

As the data suggest, premium rates are escalating because insurance companies underestimated costs. Several major LTC insurance companies stopped selling new policies in recent years. MetLife left the market in 2010, and Prudential announced its exit from selling new business in early 2012. Major insurers are also increasing premiums. John Hancock announced in late 2010 they would ask state regulators for an average increase of 40 percent per year. At present, the trend continues. The shortcomings of traditional long-term care insurance are driving people away from long-term care insurance polices that fail to assure policyholders of predictable prices for premiums during the lifetime of the policy, and that fail to allow for homecare while still paying benefits. Most buyers understand that premiums can rise due to certain conditions, but fewer and fewer these days are willing to write insurance companies a blank check.

Once insurers sell LTC insurance, they must receive permission from appropriate authorities within *each* state to increase premium costs. Thus, some states may grant rate increases while other states either deny increases or grant lesser increases. Policyholders who get hit with hefty premium rate increases naturally become quite upset. Nevertheless, if a client is already signed up with a reputable long-term care insurance provider, it is seldom right to cancel an existing LTC policy even if the premiums are getting out of hand. You and your client need to make some hard decisions. For example, if the insured won't qualify for another traditional long-term care policy, or if the insured won't pass muster with other underwriters, that client may well be stuck holding the bag. At any rate, look at the long-term care situation with a cool head. Don't rush to judgment, even if you and the client are really annoyed.

Existing LTC policyholders have several options when faced with premium increases. They can:

1. Pay the higher premium and maintain the benefits they originally purchased.

2. Allow the benefit period to be reduced but maintain their cost-of-living increases and daily or monthly limits.

3. Reduce future cost-of-living increases.

4. Reduce their daily benefits while maintaining both their benefit period and their cost-of-living features.

I seldom advise anyone to base **all** their future LTC protection in a traditional LTC policy. My major concern is that escalating costs may force them to abandon coverage just when they need it most. The maximum benefit coverage in these policies is typically about fifty to eighty times the annual premium. This multiple is called the **leverage** in LTC policies. Because the median cost of care is $81,030 per year, it is **very important** to cover the LTC exposure! It's just a matter of how the job gets done.

Option 2: Variable Annuity with LTC rider

An increasing number of financial professionals are moving toward these products for long-term care. Clients can use tax-deferred retirement assets (IRAs) to purchase a variable annuity with a LTC rider. The LTC rider provides for double income when a qualifying LTC need occurs after the contract has been in force for three years. This policy requires qualifying for LTC (needing at least two of the six activities of daily living), but it is not indemnity. Thus, if they received double benefits, they would not need to prove the level of LTC expenses.

This investment is very attractive for protecting cash flow without receiving the double income for LTC. Because this investment includes the insurance company's guarantee of future income growth, it also helps provide purchasing power and inflation protection.

Important point: There is no underwriting requirement for this option.

Option 3: Lump-Sum life insurance with LTC rider

The third alternative is clearly my favorite for all clients who can find the initial lump sum necessary to fund it. A single lump-sum life insurance purchase will typically purchase LTC protection of 2.5 to 4.0 times the amount of the lump sum. This type of policy allows the policy owner to redeem at no cost any time prior to beginning to draw benefits. The real cost of this type of policy is the lost earnings from the policy.

Advantages of this type of policy are:

1. The ease of qualifying for LTC protection.

2. Payment for the coverage is the loss of future earnings on the deposit. Remember you can get your money back on request.

3. Purchase of LTC benefits with lost earnings, **which are never taxed.**

4. A small life insurance benefit to keep the policy legally qualified as life insurance (i.e., a $100,000 lump sum may buy $130,000 of life insurance coverage for a sixty-two-year-old male).

When clients have sufficient cash reserves to purchase a life insurance policy with a LTC rider, that is preferred. The underwriting requirement for this option is moderate, meaning the demands that your clients meet specific conditions are less than they would be if the clients were seeking to buy traditional long-term care insurance.

Option 4: Annual payment life insurance with LTC rider

The Pension Protection Act of 2006 allows life insurance companies to provide life insurance with LTC riders. Favorable tax rules make this a very attractive alternative. I find the cost of coverage typically is about 10 to 15 percent greater than the cost of straight life insurance. Practically, the LTC coverage simply allows benefits to be paid to the insured rather than to beneficiaries after the insured's life. Naturally, if the insured uses most of the benefits, there are less legacy assets (assets left to heirs), but the LTC exposure has been nicely covered.

Many seniors find life insurance with a LTC rider attractive because it guarantees "someone in the family" will receive benefits. The portion not used to pay LTC costs of the insured is paid as a life insurance benefit to heirs. Long-term care partnership state rules provide that Partnership LTC policies provide Medicaid asset protection. For every dollar that a LTC Partnership policy pays out in benefits, a dollar of assets can be protected from the long-term care Medicaid limit. Partnership policies must meet the rules for tax-qualified plans under federal law.

Pointer: Strict underwriting requirements apply to this option.

Option 5: Reverse mortgages

Obviously, reverse mortgages aren't a long-term care option. They are a possible source of cash to fund one of the four options above. Reverse mortgages for long-term care coverage aren't for everyone, but if your clients have no other assets available, they might want to consider one. The reverse mortgage could allow for a financial margin of safety as well as a hedge against long-term care liabilities.

A reverse mortgage may meet government standards for homeowners over age sixty-two. The Internal Revenue Code even has provisions detailing tax treatments when reverse mortgages provide the means for meeting cash flow deficiencies for taxpayers age sixty-two and older. At this time, reverse mortgages are not available to younger people. A reverse mortgage either:

1. Provides an immediate lump sum of no more than 50 percent of a home's net investment equity; or

2. Provides a monthly cash flow for the period the homeowner continues to live in the home.

When the homeowner either moves or leaves the home permanently to receive greater care in a nursing home or assisted-living facility, the mortgage is settled. There may or may not be any residual equity or principal for the homeowner or their heirs.

Important point: Reverse mortgages work best for single persons with no one dependent upon them for income support. Reverse mortgages should be used only after very careful research and thought and even then not in situations where the homeowner may not be able to remain in the home at least five years. The decline in real estate values over the past five years has made a reverse mortgage far less attractive than it used to be.

Prefer a lump-sum withdrawal of homeowner equity to purchase a lump-sum life insurance policy with an LTC rider to relying on the home to provide required assets when LTC needs arise. Reverse mortgages do have some appeal as a means of providing for LTC needs, but, as I think you're starting to gather, I generally do not like reverse mortgages for the following reasons:

1. Fees and rates are higher than for conventional mortgages.

2. There is no leverage with reverse mortgages. Every dollar of costs is borne by the borrower. No insurance pays part of the cost.

3. Reverse mortgages are frequently poorly explained to confused seniors.

Most forms of LTC protection allow taxpayers and their heirs to retain some assets when state and federal LTC assistance is needed. These LTC Partnership rules generally do not give favorable treatment to reverse mortgages. I typically view reverse mortgages as viable only if they meet a need that would not be able to be met without taking a reverse mortgage. Examples:

1. Purchasing long-term care insurance

2. Purchasing Medicare Supplement coverage

3. Buying an annuity that promises a greater income and residual value than the reduction in net housing value

4. Meeting minimal monthly cash flow needs

Important point: Given increasing life expectancy for seniors, I think care should be taken not to utilize a reverse mortgage prior to age sixty-five or seventy.

Table 1

The comparison table below is a useful guide to long-term care options.

Table of LTC Alternatives

Feature	Traditional LTC	Annuity With LTC Rider	Lump-Sum Life Ins With LTC Rider	Annual Payment Life Ins With LTC Rider
Initial Payment	Annual Premium	Initial Investment	Lump-Sum Payment*	Annual Premium
Premium Increase Potential	High	Little or None	Little or None	Little or None
Leverage	Typically 30+ Times Premium	Income Doubles (i.e., 5% to 10%)	Typically 2 1/2 to 4 Times Lump-Sum	Typically 30+ Times Premium
Ease of Qualification	Strict Underwriting	No Underwriting	Moderate Underwriting	Strict Underwriting
Cost If Don't Ever Need	Loss of Premiums	Slightly Lower Return	Lose Potential Earnings on Lump-Sum	Minimally Higher Premium**

Cost-of-Living Coverage Increases	Available for a Cost	No But Investment Base May Grow	Yes	Not Typically
Type of Benefits	Daily or Monthly Based Upon Qualification and Reimbursement	Double-Income Monthly Based Upon Qualification	Monthly Maximum For Specified Period Until Benefits Are Used Up	Monthly Maximum For Specified Period Until Benefits Are Used Up
Major Advantage	Lower Initial cost and Cost-of-Living Increases	Investment Can Grow and be Used if no LTC Need	LTC Protection Provided For Using Investor's Money Life Insurance Excess Over Initial Premium Is Small	Lower Initial Cost and No Premium Increases Life Insurance Benefit If Not Needed for LTC
Major Disadvantage	Substantial Premium Increases Are Likely	Investment Value Must Be Greater	Large Initial Deposit Required to Get Sufficient Benefits	No Cost-Living Feature

Don't Let Your Clients Eat Dog Food When They're Old!

Long-term care tax deductions

If your clients are paying for long-term care, it's possible to deduct some of the costs of that care from federal income taxes. Let's take a look at how.

Illustration 2

Bill is paying a lot of money to help with his mother's medical bills. Bill's accountant and I helped carefully structure Bill's tax situation to offset part of Bill's mother's costs, by deducting her medical expenses on his return. Qualification for deducting a dependent requires:

a. a relationship test (i.e., a qualifying child or relative)

b. providing more than one half the dependent's support (that's a very big requirement)

c. the dependent earns less than the current-year personal exemption amount (social security benefits not generally included)

d. dependent is a US citizen or resident alien

e. must live with the taxpayer (that's another big requirement, and many kids won't meet it)

Observe that Bill's mother appears to fail several dependency tests. She does not live with Bill, and her interest, dividend, and pensions exceed the personal exemption amount. However, when a taxpayer may not claim a dependent due to the gross income test, taxpayers may utilize an exception that exists to allow taxpayers to claim medical expenses they pay for their parents.

If a taxpayer could claim a parent as a dependent, but the dependent's gross income exceeds the personal exemption amount, the taxpayers may still claim the parent's medical expense on their own return. The taxpayer *must* provide over half the parent's support. However, the parent need not live with the taxpayer.

I noted earlier that Bill's accountant deducted his mother's medical expenses. Clearly, based upon my discussion, this is a reasonable position. The problem occurred when Bill's mother's accountant disputed Bill's right. This accountant strongly argued the IRS would both deny the deduction and impose penalties on Bill's return. Bill asked me to intervene and tell him the appropriate position. Phil (Bill's accountant) seldom takes a bad position. The mother's accountant forcefully took a badly informed position. Unfortunately, this accountant's misunderstanding is often a majority position for tax accountants and fails the client's best interests.

Important point: Many if not most tax preparers do not know the medical expense exception that allows a taxpayer to deduct medical expenses they pay for their parents. They must pay the expense directly to institutions and/or care providers. They must also provide at least half the parent's support.

These expenses can be deductible but only if paid directly to care providers and/or institutions. As noted, the payer must pay at least half the total expenses of the parent with some parent income able to be excluded. Only one child in a given tax year can claim these deductions, but the good news is siblings can alternate claiming the dependency exemption and paying and deducting a parent's medical expenses. Caution dictates careful structuring and documenting the payments and the process.

Your clients can also benefit from tax deductions for fees paid to caregivers, but only if certain criteria are met. The criteria for eligibility for the tax deduction are twofold. The first is contingent upon the recipient of the care being unable to perform two of the six activities of daily living, and a physician has to sign off on that in writing. Again, if a doctor confirms that the recipient of the long-term care services cannot perform two of the six activities of daily living, your client has met the first requirement.

The caregiver must be a valid employee

The recipient of the care or any other party that contributes financially to pay for the care will meet the second requirement for the tax deduction if the caregiver is an employee and all mandatory taxes are withheld.

Scenario 1: If the family has hired a licensed, certified home care company that is issuing a W-2 to its employee that provides the care, no further action is required on the part of the person or persons claiming the deduction. Obviously, good records will need to be kept to keep track of payments and to delineate what services were performed on the part of the caregiver.

Scenario 2: If the family has hired an individual as a domestic employee, the earnings must be reported on a W-2 Form. Use Schedule H at the end of the year to pay the employee's FICA and withholding tax. The key is that all Social Security and Medicare taxes must be paid, amounting to 15.3 percent of the reported wages.

Many clients may object to having to pay the taxes, opting to pay the caregiver under the table instead. Those who do so lose their ability to take a tax deduction typically worth far more than the 15.3 percent of Social Security and Medicare taxes. Further, they expose themselves and you to potential legal and financially ruinous consequences. We'll discuss the liability issue a little later.

Some individual caregivers may object to receiving a W-2 Form, correctly assuming that they will have to pay taxes. Advise your clients to work out the issue with the caregiver. For example, the client could offer to boost the proposed hourly wage enough to pay the Social Security and Medicare taxes in full. Paying the caregiver's Social Security and Medicare taxes is worth it if the tax deduction is high enough, and it usually is when you're talking about expenses for long-term care. If the caregiver still objects to receiving a W-2, then you should advise your client to look for another provider. It is quite likely the caregiver wants to be paid under the table to remain in programs like Section 8 housing or food stamps that set limits on income.

Scenario 3: In most cases, issuing a 1099 Form won't be a viable alternative to the W-2 Form. An independent contractor is very strictly defined as an individual or company that uses its own equipment, sets its own hours, and provides a service to more than one person or business. If the caregiver uses the recipient's equipment, the recipient sets the hours, and the caregiver provides services only for the recipient, the caregiver is a domestic employee.

Long-term care tax deductions for the recipient of the care and/or for anyone contributing financially to pay for the care can be substantial. Those over the age of sixty-five will have to meet a 7.5 percent deductible, and a deductible of 10 percent for those under the age of sixty-five, based on new provisions of the Affordable Care Act. Even if your client pays the full 15.3 percent of the Social Security and Medicare taxes for the employee, and even if the deductible for medical expenses claimed on Schedule A is 10 percent, it's still very likely that the tax deduction could amount to tens of thousands of dollars, a potentially valuable deduction for a person earning a high income.

In spite of the tax benefits of playing by the rules, the majority of paid caregivers are off the books. The results of this are far reaching.

First, the caregiver is failing to contribute to the Social Security and Medicare programs. This reduces benefits for the caregiver when they are elderly, and, in a case where a caregiver remained off the books throughout his or her work life, it means the caregiver receives no benefits at all. This in turn bloats the Medicaid program, costs hospitals in added medical expenses, and otherwise ripples through the economy.

Getting caught: Here's what could happen to your client if earnings of a domestic employee go unreported, or if they are improperly reported, and the situation comes to the attention of the US Department of Labor. Say the caregiver goes to the local Social Security office. He or she is told no Social Security payments will be made, or he or she finds out that because no contributions have been made in years, the benefits are almost zilch. Naturally, the caregiver is going to say that he or she worked for your client! The Social Security office would probably refer the matter to the US Department of Labor. That's when the trouble will start for your client, and it will come back to bite you as well. Ask yourself, is it worth the risk to not play by the rules? Just how good is your error and omissions insurance?

The US Department of Labor can force the recipient of the care and/or his or her family to pay big bucks for the following:

- All the worker's unpaid FICA, Medicare, and income taxes
- Back overtime wages for the caregiver
- Penalties and interest on the caregiver's unpaid FICA, Medicare, and income taxes
- Reimbursement to the government for Medicaid expenses paid for the caregiver as a result of the worker not having Social Security or Medicare because you failed to report the wages
- 125 percent for punitive damages

The US Department of Labor is not subject to the usual legal encumbrances in place in a court of law. The Department can levy fines and otherwise take whatever action it deems fit on a case-by-case basis. Play by the rules. You and your clients will come out on top!

Aging in place

Numerous studies indicate that the vast majority of seniors want to age in place. In other words, they envision spending the last days of life in familiar surroundings, as opposed to an assisted-living facility or a nursing home. Chances are your clients feel the same way.

As you help clients plan for their retirement, it's important to include the concept of aging in place in the context of your conversation about long-term care. As I've said, most long-term care these days is received at home, not in a skilled-nursing facility. That means your clients need to be ready to age in place, and that is going to require taking steps to modify the home to make it more senior friendly.

Most homes in America are still designed around the Peter Pan principle, where the architects envision families occupying the space. Nobody is expected to get old in the house. That can be a problem when it comes to aging in place. Studies from the MetLife Mature Market Institute, a leading research organization on the elderly, show that preventing falls should top the home-modification priority list. Falls cause 75 percent of all accidental deaths among people over the age of sixty-five. For less than $1,000, seniors can install grab bars and grips in bathrooms, handrails on both sides of stairs, and path lighting in bedrooms for ease of mobility at night. Getting rid of area rugs and other trip hazards is also vital.

No-step entries for wheelchair-accessible showers, widened bathroom and hallway doors to allow for wheelchairs, seated multilevel food preparation areas in kitchens, and ramps or no-step entries to front and back doors are just a few more examples. Costs vary based on homes and location, but MetLife estimates that the average single-story home can be made more senior friendly for $9,000 to $12,000. More complicated modifications involving chair glides or ceiling lifts can cost well over $10,000 alone.

With demographic projections putting 8.7 million seniors at eighty-five or older by 2030, home modifications for aging in place have become big business. The National Association of Homebuilders estimates that the market for remodeling existing homes to better accommodate aging boomers is between $20 and $25 billion, or about 10 percent of the current $214 billion home improvement industry. No doubt that figure will increase in the coming years.

Addressing the financial planning for aging in place is not a subject that comes up very often among financial professionals and their clients. But it should. It's just another example of how we all need to approach the subject of retirement with a new philosophy.

Parting words: Long-term care protection is as important as having the right health care coverage to augment Medicare. Both are vital to preserving the financial lives of clients as they seek to enjoy retirement in comfort and dignity. The long-term care discussion is one you should have with clients very early on in your relationship. Even if the clients are young, it still won't hurt to go over the basic options they have. If the clients are in the last years of the accumulation stage, then they absolutely need to understand the choices they have, and they need to act to get at least some coverage in place to help mitigate the financial risks of a long-term care event. Aging in place should also be part of the conversation.

Long-term care is a difficult subject for most people. Don't be surprised if clients would prefer not to talk about it. As a financial professional, it is up to you to steer clients toward making the best possible decisions as they go forward into retirement. Understanding how long-term care works, what it costs, how it can be paid for, and why it's so necessary is a cornerstone of sound retirement planning.

11

Concepts in Play Case Studies

Money is better than poverty, if only for financial reasons.
—Woody Allen

Now that we've discussed the various components of an integrated approach to retirement planning, it's important for us to see the concepts play out in a number of scenarios. As you are no doubt aware by now, each decision impacts another aspect of planning. For example, Social Security timing goes hand-in-hand with retirement timing. Generally speaking, clients tend to see both as simultaneous events when in fact clients can retire and defer Social Security, or one spouse can start collecting at full retirement age and the other spouse also of full retirement age can collect spousal benefits. Long-term care discussions should also include aging in place, including a look at financial outlays that will be required to make the home more conducive for seniors to live as independently as possible. Medicare figures into cash flow planning in perhaps a bigger way than you imagined before learning more about its complexities and costs. Taxes and investments are obviously important as well. Everything fits together like a big jigsaw puzzle!

Let's take a close look at some retirement planning strategies derived from my own practice.

Illustration 1

Variable annuities

Bonnie called when she was a victim of downsizing by Big Tech Company during the summer of 2004. Her investment pool totaled slightly more than $1,100,000. Bonnie chose early retirement at fifty-five. Bonnie's investments included a huge concentration in Big Tech Company stock. We agreed she would maintain that concentration. On October 1, 2004, those shares were worth $167,760. Eight years later, Bonnie's Big Tech Company shares had depreciated to $135,040. Bonnie's experience shows why financial advisors fear concentrated stock and/or land holdings. Diversified portfolios don't guarantee economic prosperity, but they minimize concentration risks.

Nondiversified investments have the potential to score tremendous investment returns for their owners. If these investments do not do well, they also risk quality of life for these seniors. Very often, the key is timing. If the investment is good and the senior's needs permit patience, very good things often result.

Bonnie and I still believe holding Big Tech Company's stock will prove a wise investment. I assured Bonnie we have both the time and patience to wait for the recovery of Big Tech Company's stock.

Important point: Diversified portfolios *do not guarantee* either better investment performance or less portfolio volatility.

Professor Harry Markowitz received a Nobel Prize in Economics for his pioneering Modern Portfolio Theory. However, diversified portfolios increase the potential for maximizing expected return for a given level of risk. A retiree's acceptable risk level should always contemplate whether cash flow needs are met. Taking more investment risk may be necessary to meet their cash flow needs.

The goal of retirement portfolio allocations should be to maximize return potential for a given level of risk. Risk tolerance defines both the appropriate investment mix and the potential cash flow and asset growth. Ironically, Markowitz's risk/reward ideas seemed radical when originally presented. During Markowitz's dissertation defense in 1955, Milton Friedman argued that his ideas were not economics.

Fortunately, we applied Markowitz's portfolio optimization ideas when Bonnie's original allocation was constructed. Markowitz (now in his eighties) still believes strongly that portfolio optimization helps develop a more efficient portfolio that maximizes return for a given level of risk. Markowitz has been very critical of regulators and others who suggest incorporating only stocks, bonds, and cash in a portfolio.

Jim Sharp acquainted me with variable annuities and living benefit features during mid-2004. Jim's explanation struck a chord with me. Jim made the following key points that allowed me to help Bonnie. Jim's company offered the following benefits:

1. Income for life beginning in ten years based upon a guaranteed value of 200 percent the original deposit or the market value of our chosen mutual fund portfolio.

    He illustrated as follows:

    Invest $100,000 today.

    Begin income ten years later based upon $200,000 (200 percent of $100,000) at the given percentage of 5 percent (the contractual percent for Bonnie's age when she begins drawing benefits). The computed annual payout would be $10,000.

    OR

Begin income ten years later based upon the highest annual value for our chosen investment fund. Assume Bonnie's fund had a highest annual value of $220,000 during the ten-year accumulation period that would become the basis for annuity payouts. Note that $220,000 is greater than $200,000 (200 percent of $100,000). Thus, the given percentage of 5 percent for Bonnie's age when she begins drawing benefits results in an annual payout of $11,000.

2. Ability to walk away or cash-in the annuity in ten years with the mutual fund value at the time of withdrawal. Note that unless the highest mutual fund value is the ending mutual fund value, the cash flow from any replacement investment would be based upon a lower value.

   Note that liquidating the fund provides the investor only the ending mutual fund value. Drawing income based upon the contract yields cash flow based upon the "locked-in" highest value.

Bonnie and I discussed the advantage to Bonnie and the insurance company if she draws income at the end of the ten years. Bonnie's income is higher because she draws 5 percent of the locked-in value, and the insurance company profits because she continues her investment in their contract. This has been one of life's win-win scenarios.

Jim Sharp lived up to his name! He suggested splitting our investment into several contracts. Jim noted that this would be superior to one contract with an investment allocation in several different mutual funds, *if* one or more mutual funds more than doubled while at least one chosen mutual fund did not double. Jim noted that funds that more than doubled at any valuation date would draw income off the highest annual value, and funds that failed to double would utilize the guarantee of double the original investment for calculating annuity payouts. Note that if the fund investments had been aggregated, the best performers would be reduced by the underperformers. Buying separate contracts results in optimal value from the insurance company guarantees.

I found Jim's ideas and his company's product fascinating. I asked

Jim to show me more. We laughed because I was the only member of Jim's audience that showed any interest in his product. The underlying mathematics and concept were just too new and different! I felt the single most fascinating idea Jim proposed was investing aggressively and *not* diversifying! We would apply Markowitz's portfolio optimization ideas in a modern way!

Annuities with living benefits generally provide a growing, guaranteed future income base but do not guarantee future asset values. Investors should fully utilize the insurance company promise they pay for. This means they should:

1. Invest aggressively because if the investment does not perform, then income will be based upon the minimum guaranteed growth.

2. *Do not* diversify. Each chosen investment should stand on its own! The income guarantees protect against the lack of diversification.

3. Select initial bonuses offered if they are part of the guaranteed growth.

Bonnie was the ideal client. She grasped my explanation and was ready to choose the investments. We decided $200,000 total would be allocated to Jim's variable annuity with living benefits. Notice that all of our choices were aggressive. We chose all of the following funds:

1. Technology

2. Finance

3. Emerging world

4. Biotech

5. Health care

Don't Let Your Clients Eat Dog Food When They're Old! | 217

Bonnie's investment in each fund was $40,000. We opened a separate account for each fund. Remember Jim's powerful suggestion was to put each fund in its own contract. Bonnie paid the insurance company for assuming downside risk on her chosen investments by "paying a risk premium above the normal mutual fund and insurance company administrative costs." Bonnie was my first client to receive the benefit of Jim's advice and one of the first within the retirement industry. I quickly received questions from compliance personnel, asking if I realized there was a state contract charge of $30 per contract per year for variable annuities. Separating Bonnie's investment into five contracts added $120 per year to the internal contract charges. I replied that I did know about the state contract charge and felt the additional return more than justified the extra cost.

Any new product/idea will be and should be closely monitored by bank, insurance company, or broker dealer compliance personnel. Compliance functions help ensure that client needs receive primary focus. If investments do not meet client needs, they should never be made. I explained that Bonnie's future cash flow concerns were best met by Jim Sharp's product.

Variable annuity with living benefits costs cover all of the following:

1. Risk premium to the insurance company for "guaranteeing" future cash flows based upon an income base that may increase if the underlying mutual funds appreciate but can never decrease

2. Mutual fund costs

3. Insurance company administrative costs

My explanation for using five variable annuity contracts emphasized the following:

1. Variable annuity contract charges are taken from client accounts not paid by check or cash.

2. Insurance company guarantees are net of fees! If investments do not do well, clients receive cash flow based upon guarantees. Thus, ultimately, if the client's return is reduced by the contract charges, the client receives extra income.

I explained that if Bonnie received just the guaranteed 7 percent income growth prior to cash flow withdrawals, there would be no reduction for either the state $30 per contract charge or any insurance company contract charges. These charges reduce only the client's potential for excess returns! Remember, guarantees are based upon original investment plus bonuses and are "net of fees."

Compliance also questioned my decision to use a 5 percent bonus. Compliance asked the right question. The insurance company charges are increased on contracts that include a bonus. I noted the fact that guarantees included bonuses! For this reason, I generally counsel the client to choose a bonus. I do not believe those advisors who never take bonuses for fear long-range accumulation might be slightly less. Understand that cash flow and cash flow guarantees are more important to retirees than maximizing potential accumulation. Thus, Bonnie was guaranteed 5 percent income on $420,000 ($200,000 investment plus $10,000 bonus times two) in ten years.

Investment allocation reduces volatility and chance of disastrous loss. Eight years later, on September 1, 2012, the results showed the merit of Jim's suggestions and our choices.

Type of Investment Fund	Initial Investment	Initial Bonus	Base for Guaranteed Double	Current Value	Projected Income Base (2014)
Emerging Markets	$ 40,000	$ 2,000	$ 42,000	$ 86,890	$ 109,315
Health Sciences	$ 40,000	$ 2,000	$ 42,000	$ 56,900	$ 84,000
Small-Capitalization	$ 40,000	$ 2,000	$ 42,000	$ 49,698	$ 84,000
Technology	$ 40,000	$ 2,000	$ 42,000	$ 49,598	$ 84,000
Financial	$ 40,000	$ 2,000	$ 42,000	$ 45,155	$ 84,000
Totals	$ 200,000	$ 10,000	$ 210,000	$ 288,241	$ 445,315

Bonnie and I appreciate Jim's advice today even more than ten years ago! Her investment value has grown from $200,000 to $288,241. Since the last eight years haven't been kind to investors, we would be pleased with that growth, but we recognize that $288,241 *is less than* the value on September 1, 2007! Bonnie's investment value declined slightly over the last five years! All of the growth occurred in the first three-plus years! More significantly, Bonnie's total ($200,000) investment has little chance of doubling in ten years. Bonnie has profited handsomely from Jim Sharp's advice.

The merits of Jane Bryant Quinn's comments, that variable annuities with living benefits offer promise of providing stock market gains without market risks, shine through in Bonnie's case. One of Jane Bryant Quinn's more famous quotes says it all: "I know what you want in a retirement investment: terrific stock market gains without any risk of loss and a steady stream of retirement income."

Jim's variable annuity has given Bonnie more market gains than we could have ever expected given the bad economic climate. I remember that when we chose the investments, we expected three or four of our chosen five funds to double in ten years. Each of the funds had a solid record suggesting they would *more than* double in ten years. Note that only one of the funds had proven as we approached the ten-year decision point in 2014 to have more than doubled, and even that fund was nowhere near its high.

However, there is a reason each investment sponsor issues a disclaimer that there is no guarantee that the past will be repeated in the future. Few experts anticipated the disappointing investment performance of the last ten years. Jim's variable annuity allowed us to:

1. Invest aggressively with the potential for favorable gains while reducing our risk by giving us the opportunity to seize the future income guarantees offered for investments that failed to double.

2. If any of the five funds were above the guaranteed growth value at ten years, we could walk away/cash-in and choose a new investment product.

3. Protect Bonnie's future income.

Bonnie was sixty-five in the fall of 2014. We began her income/cash flow from Jim's variable annuity. Her expected income will be 5 percent of $445,315! Bonnie can project with almost certainty the $22,265 annual cash flow for the rest of her life. Bonnie projects her annual cash flow needs approach $65,000. Her initial retirement allocation of 18 percent to Jim's variable annuity should provide 34 percent of her needed retirement cash flow!

Note that the projected $22,265 cash flow is 11.13 percent of Bonnie's original investment. It is also 7.72 percent of the current value of $288,241! Remember even five-year CDs currently pay less than 1 percent.

When Jim Sharp's presentation impressed me in 2004, variable annuities with living benefits were considered risky and too costly. Surprisingly, today there are still very few experts other than Jane Bryant Quinn, Ben Stein, and Moshe Milevsky that seem to appreciate the contribution variable annuities with living benefits have made to retiree security and quality of life.

New financial vehicles are frequently viewed as too risky and complex when first introduced. Within a few years, study and experience may show they fit an investor need. Niche investments generally arise because there is a need. Many new investments would have been accepted and utilized more quickly if the financial press and financial advisors were focused more on cash flow and less on liquidity.

During my PhD studies at Michigan State University, I wandered down a hallway one day and peeked into a classroom that piqued my interest because the Economics professor was shouting to his class. The professor's flamboyant delivery made me hear his important message. He was screaming, "John Maynard Keynes dared to dispute widely accepted economic theories of the day. How dare he dispute the establishment ideas!"

John Maynard Keynes was a noted British economist famous for his ideas on the causes of business cycles. He advocated fiscal and monetary measures to mitigate the adverse effects of economic recessions and depressions. *Time* magazine named Keynes one of the one hundred most important and influential people of the twentieth century. Keynesian Economics declined between 1979 and 2007. Noted University of Chicago economist Milton Friedman and others questioned government's ability to control economic cycles. However, during the financial crises of 2007–2014, the governments of George W. Bush and Barack Obama returned to use of Keynesian methods to control the severity of the economic cycle. Ironically, former Federal Reserve Chairman Ben Bernanke remains one of the world's foremost economic scholars on depressions and recessions.

When a financial need arises, solutions emerge that meet that need. Variable annuities with living benefits fill seniors' need for regular, reliable cash flow during retirement. They give seniors some opportunity to participate in market gains without risking their cash flow. Purchasing-power risk is mitigated by the potential for increasing (but not decreasing) income.

Professor Moshe Milevsky, associate professor of Finance at York University in Toronto, emerged early in the twenty-first century as one of the leading retirement scholars. Ironically, Milevsky testified as an expert witness *against* variable annuities during the late twentieth century. His more recent work suggests that declining corporate pensions make it advisable that many people "purchase a personal pension" to minimize the potential for "running out of money." Variable annuities with living benefits are one of both Milevsky and Jane Bryant Quinn's suggestions for "providing the personal Pension," ensuring that seniors will have cash flow to meet retirement living expenses.

Variable annuities with living benefits provide retirement cash flow at a cost! Insurance companies provide downside protection in some combination of the following ways:

1. Consistent cash flows that can grow but never decrease are promised.

2. Insuring against loss of principal. Principal can grow but not decrease.

3. Allow investors to share in investment gains.

The costs are:

1. Investor gains may be capped (no more than an upside limit).

2. Investors share in gains, but only if the excess of market gains over guaranteed rates is more than 4 percent.

   Example: The underlying mutual fund goes up 14 percent. The investor income base is guaranteed to grow 5 percent if no withdrawals are made that year. The insurance company costs and profits total 4.25 percent. The investor gets 4.75 percent plus their cash flow (if they draw the 5 percent) or 9.75 percent if they defer cash flow.

3. Investor investment choices are limited to select mutual funds to prevent excess insurance company exposure.

Naturally, some variable annuities with living benefits are better than others. The enormous variety of choices in contract options and features makes it very important for you to find an appropriate vehicle that meets the needs of your clients.

A few words on costs

Cost should never be judged in a vacuum. Is a football game between two losing teams as appealing as the national championship game? Of course not. Costs should always be viewed against benefits. Neither Bonnie nor I worried that Jim Sharp's company limited sharing in market gains. Their costs prior to allowing Bonnie to share in excess returns are approximately 4 percent (a typical amount). However, note that their share is taken from market returns greater than the guaranteed growth!

Insurance companies charge approximately 4 percent prior to allowing investors to share in excess returns. These charges do not apply against guarantees. Seniors frequently focus on limiting downside. They like having some upside and are willing to sacrifice part of their upside potential.

Financial writers, financial talk show hosts, and even some advisors view controlling costs as the most "important variable" for selecting investments. They are both right and wrong. The key distinction is whether the investment is a standardized product or a unique product or service.

When Bonnie invested in Jim Sharp's company's variable annuity with living benefits, it wasn't the cheapest or only variable annuity with living benefits available. It was, however, easily the best at that time. No annuity company currently offers a contract with the features Bonnie got in 2004. Thus, a key tenet for all seniors and those who care about them is: Many complex financial products are the financial equivalent of a high-powered car. Not everyone can drive the high-powered car properly, and not every advisor helps clients take full advantage of the financial product's key features once the client buys the product.

Illustration 2

Long-term care

In the late summer of 2007, my business associate and I identified three of my clients who seemed likely to need long-term care (LTC) assistance in the future. One client had multiple sclerosis (MS), the second had significant back problems, and the third had been drawing disability benefits since his midforties due to a major heart-related stroke. None of the three qualified to buy conventional LTC. However, I had identified a life insurance company offering a fixed annuity (no principal risk) with a unique feature (they are still rare) that doubles annuity income if the owner requires LTC assistance. The LTC standard was the need for assistance with two of the six activities of daily living utilized in qualified LTC contracts. There was also no requirement that the care be received in a nursing home (which was generally required in competing contracts). All three invested a fairly significant amount because the need was very likely to be there.

I am very happy to report "The Rest of the Story" as the late radio great Paul Harvey would say. It is now five years later. All three have seen their investment grow. The client with MS continues to get worse. He clearly qualifies to receive 10 percent of his investment value for the remainder of his life. The back patient is doing well with therapy but may eventually have a need. The former heart patient is doing well. It now seems less likely that he will need the policy.

We are assisting the MS patient to begin benefits. The back patient has been advised to continue the policy, and we suggested to the heart patient that it is time we seek a better choice for him. The heart patient luckily made money on the policy during one of the roughest five-year periods in recent financial history.

I also find the second example very rewarding. About fifteen months after we helped the first three clients buy the fixed annuity with the double the income for LTC needs, Brandon Best told me about a new variable annuity with living benefits his company was introducing. Brandon's company provided a very solid variable annuity with the option to add a rider that would double the income for LTC needs. Brandon had my interest!

I have a Florida client that retired early because of physical disabilities. I knew this client's condition would deteriorate over time. Brandon's company's contract provides double the income for LTC needs in addition to:

1. Guaranteed income growth prior to beginning withdrawals
2. Potential for stock market gains
3. Death benefits for the client's heirs if principal is not exhausted

Brandon's variable annuity with living benefits best met this client's needs. I encounter many clients with no LTC coverage or inadequate LTC coverage. Brandon's company had developed the ideal product for these clients!

The best retirement cash flow vehicle for any need may change over time. If enough people have the need, competitors will consider developing a better solution. Brandon's variable annuity with living benefits remains the only solution for meeting both growth of cash flow goals and LTC protection. Not surprisingly, Brandon's company has maintained an over 50 percent market share since bringing this product to market.

I laughingly note that Ralph Waldo Emerson said, "If a man has good corn or wood, or boards, or pigs, to sell, or can make better chairs or knives, crucibles, or church organs, than anybody else, you will find a broad, hard-beaten road to his house, though it be in the woods."

We frequently get new clients who "bought the Ferrari" but have never driven it because their former advisor lost interest after the sale. The talk show hosts, etc. are right where even the most-suitable product is bought and not used properly. The two most important questions for choosing investment products are needs and suitability. Unfortunately, many writers, talk show hosts, and regulators focus on liquidity and costs.

I believe deciding strictly based on liquidity and costs is similar to diagnosing and treating a cancer patient based solely on a telephone interview. If my loved ones have a serious medical condition, I want the best care for them whatever the cost! Both Moshe Milevsky and Jane Bryant Quinn repeatedly demonstrate flexibility and recognition that the treatment must fit the ailment. Brandon's company recognized a need and designed a product to meet the need.

Illustration 3

Nontraded REITs

During July of 2008, I suggested Bonnie reallocate $45,000 of her IRA to a nontraded public REIT. Once again, Bonnie proved to be the perfect client! We discussed the investment thoroughly before Bonnie agreed to make the change.

Bonnie's 2008 tax status provided us an opportunity to make a strategic move. Remember that in 2008 Bonnie had retired but was not drawing any corporate pension, Social Security, or IRA withdrawals. Bonnie's needed $65,000 of cash flow was produced by utilizing her after-tax investments. Since she had virtually no taxable income, we chose to convert $45,000 of her IRA to a Roth IRA prior to investing in a nontraded public REIT. Bonnie's tax cost for the conversion was small (she had virtually no other taxable income). When Bonnie eventually chooses to withdraw the income from the REIT, it will be nontaxable. The most recent value for Bonnie's nontraded self-storage REIT is over $95,000. Thus, $50,000 of Bonnie's gains will never be taxed.

When a client's current taxable income is substantially lower than future taxable income, consider converting part of existing IRAs to a Roth IRA. The current tax cost is justified by future tax savings. Take extreme care in choosing investments for Roth IRAs. Investments should not risk loss and should have the opportunity for substantial growth.

I was introduced to nontraded public REITs in 2007 and 2008 by a REIT wholesaler I will call Tom Terrific. Tom Terrific was a character in an animated cartoon that appeared on *Captain Kangaroo* from the mid-1950s to the 1970s. Tom Terrific could transform himself into almost anything, thanks to his "magic, funnel-shaped thinking cap." The magic, funnel-shaped thinking cap increased Tom's intelligence.

My modern Tom Terrific's nontraded public REIT helped me appreciate a critical principal for retiree financial planning. This principle is: The ideal retirement investment produces substantial cash flow with little or no risk of loss of principal. Some degree of liquidity can more easily be sacrificed if there is no need for using principal to meet cash flow needs.

The cartoon Tom Terrific had an arch-foe named Crabby Appleton. Crabby Appleton's motto was "I'm rotten to the core!" My modern-day Tom Terrific and those who love his nontraded public REIT encounter our own CRABBY Appletons in the form of financial journalists, regulators, and retirees who refuse to read and think. If only we could give them Tom Terrific's hat. If they had Tom's hat, they would realize that the number-one characteristic retirement investment vehicles need is cash flow. Investments providing substantial cash flow reduce pressure caused when principal must be consumed to meet retirement cash outflows.

Skeptics (our modern-day Crabby Appletons) may say that the nontraded public REIT contained substantial risk, but let's examine the facts. The self-storage REIT Bonnie bought:

1. Paid a 7 percent annual yield.

2. When dividends were reinvested, it bought new shares at a 5

percent discount to the $10.00 share price. This reinvestment results in an immediate 5 percent return assuming the share price remained constant.

3. Self-storage REITs historically have performed both consistently and paid healthy dividends.

Substantial dividends reduce investment risk by reducing the unrecovered investment cost each year. Note that risk is greatest when cash flows are postponed.

Discounted cash flow models value investments based upon current and future cash flows. Current cash flows receive the greatest weight because they are both certain and may be reinvested quicker to earn greater future returns. Over time, investors are willing to pay for cash flow.

Your retired clients should place greater emphasis on cash flow than stock appreciation. Cash flow is more reliable, and it pays the bills in the near term. Bonnie and I chose the nontraded public self-storage stock because we were seeking long-term cash flow. As shown below, her self-storage stock has paid the 7 percent dividend each year for four years and was recently revalued at $10.79. Thus, in addition to 7 percent annual dividends, Bonnie's stock has increased in value. We sacrificed liquidity and potential appreciation for greater cash flow and less volatility.

Note that Bonnie's nontraded public REIT pays over twice the annual dividends of the two large-stock-exchange-listed self-storage stocks.

Initial investment	$45,000
Share price	$10.00
Annualized interest rate	7%
Discount for reinvested dividends	5%

The stock value of Bonnie's self-storage REIT increased from the original $10.00 per share to $10.79 per share on June 1, 2014. Thus, Bonnie's original investment of $45,000 in July of 2008 appreciated to approximately $95,000 in six years. Bonnie's investment has returned about 105 percent in a stock market that has failed to appreciate substantially!

The nontraded REIT I suggested had a dividend rate of 7 percent annually paid 1/12 of 7 percent on the fifteenth of each month. I explained to Bonnie that the nearest equivalent REIT listed on the New York Stock Exchange paid approximately 3 percent.

Bonnie started receiving Social Security benefits upon reaching age sixty-two (ten months earlier). Bonnie's Social Security benefits netted her $1,500 per month. I now felt it was a mistake for Bonnie to begin benefits. I certainly understood Bonnie's concern that she needed $5,500 monthly and had apparently reduced her retirement principal from an original approximately $1,200,000, but I felt she was in great shape. Her current assets were:

	Stated Value	IRS Value
Variable Annuities	$ 288,241	$ 380,000
Traditional IRA	$ 195,670	$ 195,670
Self-Storage Roth IRA	$ 64,904	$ 64,904
Individual Account	$ 87,522	$ 87,522
Total	$ 636,337	$ 728,096

I explained the IRS value incorporates the value of the guaranteed cash flow from variable annuities with living benefits. The IRS reasoning reflects their assumption that a rational person will always choose the higher real value between the liquidation value and the cash flow value. I agree with the IRS logic. If taxpayers could convert traditional IRAs invested in variable annuities with living benefits based upon their liquidation value, I would use this strategy for clients over and over! I would love for my clients to invest their IRAs in variable annuities with living benefits, and just prior to beginning to draw living benefits, be able to convert the traditional IRA to a Roth IRA, making the income tax-free! However, the IRS recognized that mathematically actuaries view the "real" value as the time-weighted expected return from retirement cash flows.

I knew I would further confuse Bonnie by telling her that her variable annuity with living benefits would grow from $455,315 to at least $600,000 if we waited until age seventy to begin benefits. Bonnie wondered how I expected her to meet her cash flow needs in the next seven-plus years (remember, she is nearly sixty-three). She had patiently waited eight years to begin cash flows from the variable annuity with living benefits! Now I wanted her to consider waiting even longer to begin the cash flow. I had some explaining to do!

Illustration 4

Home equity to defer Social Security

Sometimes it's best to use home equity to meet cash flow needs in early retirement if the home equity allows clients to defer taking Social Security and other investments that continue to grow when benefits are deferred. Yes, I know this may sound a little crazy to you, but hear me out. I do not believe in using home equity unless there is a very good reason. That good reason occurs much more frequently in recent years because:

1. Interest rates on equity loans are at sixty-year lows.

2. Social Security increases for deferring retirement benefits have increased to 8 percent per year between full retirement age (currently sixty-six) and age seventy.

3. Variable annuities with living benefits and pensions generally guarantee increased cash flow payments if benefits are deferred.

4. Reinvestment rates in nontraded public REITs typically significantly exceed interest rates on equity loans.

Note that Social Security, variable annuities with living benefits, and nontraded public REITs all generate cash flow growth that significantly exceeds the cost of equity loans on home equity.

Home equity loans may provide a means to delay drawing:

1. Social Security
2. Variable annuities with living benefits
3. Cash flow from nontraded REITS

I provided Bonnie with the following timeline for projecting her cash flow for ages sixty-three to seventy:

Bonnie's Age	Social Security	Variable Annuity(4)	Best Variable Annuity(1)	Nontraded REIT	Investments or Home Equity	Needed Cash Flow
63					$ 5,500	$ 5,500
64					$ 5,665	$ 5,665
65				$ 434	$ 5,401	$ 5,835
66	$ 1,000		$ 455	$ 434	$ 4,121	$ 6,010
67	$ 1,030		$ 455	$ 434	$ 4,271	$ 6,190
68	$ 1,061		$ 455	$ 434	$ 4,426	$ 6,376
69	$ 1,093		$ 455	$ 434	$ 4,586	$ 6,567
70	$ 2,721	$ 2,000	$ 455	$ 434	$ 1,154	$ 6,764

I explained my timeline to Bonnie as follows:

1. Social Security grows 10 percent per year from sixty-three to seventy if she defers receiving Social Security. Ten percent per year growth without risk!

2. Her variable annuity with living benefits guarantees:

    a. Five percent per year based upon double the original investment after ten years (her age sixty-five) and triple the income after fifteen years (her age seventy). Bonnie invested $40,000 each in the five contracts. I suggest she take advantage of the guaranteed triple on four of the five contracts. The variable annuity with living benefits grows 10 percent per year from sixty-five to seventy. Ten percent per year growth without risk!

    b. However, since one of the five contracts has grown to $109,315, the guarantee would only increase the cash flow base by $10,685 in five years. This is a compound growth of less than 2 percent per year. There is no reason to defer at age sixty-five.

3. The nontraded REIT reinvestment rate results in an increase of 7 percent per year in cash flow with very little risk. Bonnie should expect to begin income at 7 percent in two years at age sixty-five. The base is expected to be just under $75,000 at that time.

4. The cost of an equity line would cost much less than 10 percent per year. Thus, the cash flow from Social Security and variable annuities with living benefits growing 10 percent per year justifies an equity line.

5. The cost of an equity line would cost much less than 7 percent per year. Thus, the cash flow from growing 7 percent per year justifies an equity line!

Bonnie's head was swimming after all the information I provided her. I reminded her that retirement planning is a process rather than a project. The only critical immediate action was to repay the Social Security benefits she had received before she had exceeded the twelve-month limit. After Bonnie gave my analysis some additional thought, she saw the wisdom of deferring Social Security and withdrawals from her variable annuity and her nontraded REIT.

As noted throughout this book, retirement cash flow management requires an integrated approach these days. Investments are just one piece of the puzzle.

Consider all of the following as cash flow sources and therefore part of the retirement allocation process:

1. Cash flows from investments
2. Cash flow from Social Security
3. Cash flow from corporate or government pensions
4. Cash flow from full or part-time work
5. Cash flow from equity credit in their home

Consider the cost of all cash flow sources, including home equity loans and drawing down investments, before deciding which sources to utilize first in meeting cash flow needs.

Parting words: The solutions to your client's retirement problems exist, even if it appears that no options are obviously available. All it takes is a bit of creativity and an open mind. Get set to embark on a new and innovative way of helping your clients. The future is now, and the rewards for you and your clients will continue to pay for many years to come!

12

Appendix
Quick Facts at a Glance

Rule No. 1: Never lose money. Rule No. 2: Never forget Rule No. 1. —Warren Buffett

OVER THE DECADES AS a financial professional, I've found that it is often very helpful to have a handout ready to show clients as I make my points. This appendix contains tools that will assist you as you discuss the importance of tax-deferred investments, the power of compounding interest, Social Security timing, Medicare, long-term care, and much more! The text is written for the client and is meant to serve as a primer on any given issue associated with an integrated approach to retirement planning and cash flow management. The idea is that you can hand clients the pages on a specific issue to use for the purposes of your discussion, and then the client can take the primer home for further review.

You can also find these primers and much more on our company website: www.retirementcashflow.com. Feel free to download whatever you may need. You can also learn more about how you can use the CAMP Score to assess client retirement readiness, harnessing this powerful algorithm to enhance your business and brighten the financial lives of your clients. The automated calculator is unique in that it factors in the entire gamut of issues that are important to making certain your clients have sufficient cash flow during their retirement years.

At the very least, you now have a solid platform of knowledge about retirement cash flow planning and management. You're one up on most of your competitors!

Cash Flow is King

Always guard against inflation

As you work with your financial advisor to plan your retirement, keep in mind that inflation of 2 to 3 percent has been historically common. You want cash flow vehicles that can increase your stream of dollars to keep up.

The following tables show you the mix of cash flow vehicles that can increase revenue over time. Table 2 shows you why this happens.

Table 1

Type of vehicle	Potential for increasing cash flow
Social Security	Yes
Stocks	Yes
Corporate bonds	No
Treasury bonds	No
Treasury inflation protected bonds	Yes
Federal pensions	Yes
State pensions	Maybe
Local pensions	No
Stock mutual funds	Yes
Bond mutual funds	Maybe
Fixed annuities	No
Variable annuities	Yes
Nontraded REITs	Yes

Table 2

Retirement Vehicle	Cash Flow Increases When This Happens
Social Security	Inflation Occurs and/or Benefits Are Delayed
Stocks	Corporate Revenues Grow Increasing Dividends
Corporate Bonds	Almost Never
Treasury Bonds	Never
Treasury Inflation Protected Bonds (TIPS)	Cash Flow Doesn't Increase but Principal Grows with Inflation
Federal Pensions	Inflation Occurs and/or Benefits Are Delayed
State Pensions	Inflation Occurs and/or Benefits Are Delayed (No Index in Some States)
Local Pensions	A Very Few Are Inflation Indexed
Corporate Pensions	A Very Few Are Inflation Indexed
Stock Mutual Funds	Corporate Revenues Grow Increasing Dividends
Bond Mutual Funds	Slowly When Interest Rates Rise But Principal May Be Lost
Fixed Annuities/ CDs	Slowly When Interest Rates Rise
Variable Annuities	Cash Flows Rise Based Upon Delayed Receipt and Increasing Mutual Fund Values
Nontraded REITS	Rents Grow and Dividends Are Reinvested Increasing Future Dividends

The Power of Compounding Interest

Compounding interest works for and against you

Compounding interest is still a powerful tool even in this present low-interest economy. But it's even more negatively powerful when it comes to debt. Check out the numbers below that illustrate compounding at 1 percent per month on a debt of $1,000.

Table 1

Month	Beginning Principal ($)	Interest ($)	Ending Principal ($)	Compound Annual Rate
0			1000.00	
1	1000.00	10.00	1010.00	
2	1010.00	10.10	1020.10	
3	1020.10	10.20	1030.30	
4	1030.30	10.30	1040.60	
5	1040.60	10.41	1051.01	
6	1051.01	10.51	1061.52	
7	1061.52	10.62	1072.14	
8	1072.14	10.72	1082.86	
9	1082.86	10.83	1093.69	
10	1093.69	10.94	1104.62	
11	1104.62	11.05	1115.67	
12	1115.67	11.16	1126.83	**12.68%**

Even the best of investments don't earn 12.68 percent per year over the long run. If the cost of a debt is more expensive than the rate than can be earned on an investment, then paying off the debt is the preferred investment!

Don't forget the taxman!

The taxation of most investments is either ordinary income (currently federal tax rates of up to 39.6 percent) or capital gains (currently federal rates up to 23.8 percent). If you're in the 10 to 15 percent tax bracket, your capital gains are not taxed. Ordinary income is taxed, so interest on a CD or for a money market fund would incur a tax liability.

Keep taxes in mind when deciding whether to pay off high-cost debt. If you're getting a return that's taxed, chances are paying off the debt is a better deal.

Table 2

Month	Beginning Principal ($)	Interest ($)	Ending Principal ($)	Compound Annual Rate
0			1000.00	
1	1000.00	10.00	1010.00	
2	1010.00	10.10	1020.10	
3	1020.10	10.20	1030.30	
4	1030.30	10.30	1040.60	
5	1040.60	10.41	1051.01	
6	1051.01	10.51	1061.52	
7	1061.52	10.62	1072.14	
8	1072.14	10.72	1082.86	
9	1082.86	10.83	1093.69	
10	1093.69	10.94	1104.62	
11	1104.62	11.05	1115.67	
12	1115.67	11.16	1126.83	**12.68%**
	Net of Tax		1095.12	**9.51%**

Approximately 80 percent of states tax interest earned. Retirement of debt would compare even more favorably with investments if state income taxes apply. If the state tax is 5 percent net additional cost, then the net of tax interest return is only 8.88 percent.

Your IRA or 401(k)

Deferring taxes even when you're in a low bracket always makes sense

Table 1 shows you what happens when you don't defer taxes in a retirement account. We're assuming here that you're in a combined federal and state tax bracket of 30 percent and that the investment is earning 6 percent. The $700 in the far right-hand column represents the money you'd have left to invest after taxes.

Table 1: Return to Cash

Year	Beginning Principal ($)	Interest ($)	Deferral Part One Return to Cash Ending Principal ($)	Return to Cash Value ($)
0			1000.00	700.00
1	1000.00	60.00	1060.00	742.00
2	1060.00	63.60	1123.60	786.52
3	1123.60	67.42	1191.02	833.71
4	1191.02	71.46	1262.48	883.73
5	1262.48	75.75	1338.23	936.76
6	1338.23	80.29	1418.52	992.96
7	1418.52	85.11	1503.63	1052.54
8	1503.63	90.22	1593.85	1115.69
9	1593.85	95.63	1689.48	1182.64
10	1689.48	101.37	1790.85	1253.59
11	1790.85	107.45	1898.30	1328.81
12	1898.30	113.90	2012.20	1408.54

Note the following about these calculations:

When the initial deferral of $1,000 is made, all $1,000 is earning at 6 percent. Absent the deferral, $300 would have been paid in taxes, leaving only $700 to earn 6 percent. The earnings of $42 after the first year would then have been subject to 30 percent taxes, leaving only $29.40 or 4.2 percent after-tax return. With the deferral advantage the contribution into your tax-deferred retirement account would have $1,060 versus $742. Plus, you would have benefited from a 25 percent reduction in federal tax liability in the calendar year the contribution was made. Obviously, $700 won't earn as much as a $1,000 over a twelve-year period.

Table 2

Some investors think that they'll owe the taxes anyway, so deferrals don't matter. In table 2, we'll look at what happens when you choose not to defer taxes, leaving the $700 of the $1,000 to invest at the same 6 percent earnings rate on the investment itself. However, we'll throw in the fact that the interest on the $700 is subject to the 30 percent tax as ordinary income under our current scenario. The investment growth would be reflected in the following example, which shows that the actual return drops from 6 percent to 4.2 percent because of the tax liability, thereby extending the time it takes to double that same after-tax $700 by five years!

Table 2: Tax liability

Year	Beginning Principal ($)	Deferral Part Two No Deferral Pay Taxes As You Go Interest ($)	Taxes On Interest ($)	Ending Principal ($)
0				700.00
1	700.00	42.00	12.60	729.40
2	729.40	43.76	13.13	760.03

3	760.03	45.60	13.68	791.96
4	791.96	47.52	14.26	825.22
5	825.22	49.51	14.85	859.88
6	859.88	51.59	15.48	895.99
7	895.99	53.76	16.13	933.62
8	933.62	56.02	16.81	972.84
9	972.84	58.37	17.51	1013.70
10	1013.70	60.82	18.25	1056.27
11	1056.27	63.38	19.01	1100.63
12	1100.63	66.04	19.81	1146.86
13	1146.86	68.81	20.64	1195.03
14	1195.03	71.70	21.51	1245.22
15	1245.22	74.71	22.41	1297.52
16	1297.52	77.85	23.36	1352.02
17	1352.02	81.12	24.34	1408.80

The important point is that the interest is taxed, creating less growth and more tax liability over a longer time. Note that per $1,000 deferred into the retirement account, the accumulation is 22.82 percent greater than it is if taxes were paid on the interest.

Dollar-Cost Averaging

Dollar-cost averaging simply means you buy a given investment vehicle, like a mutual fund or a particular stock, on a schedule without trying to time the market. Market timing traditionally has yielded lower returns than disciplined investing. Dollar-cost averaging makes sense during the accumulation stage of your financial life.

Table 1 shows the difference between having volatile investments during a ten-year accumulation period and a ten-year withdrawal period. Note that in this example, the top part of the table assumes investing $10,000 per year while the bottom part assumes that $10,000 per year with an inflation rate of 3 percent is withdrawn.

Table 1

Dollar-Cost Averaging

Yr	Invest	Invest Return	Beginning Unit Price	Ending Unit Price	Units Beginning	Units Bought	Units Ending	Year End Value
1	10000	-9.10%	$10.00	$9.09	0	1,000.00	1,000.00	$9,090.00
2	10000	-11.89%	9.09	8.01	1,000.00	1,100.11	2,100.11	16,820.20
3	10000	-22.10%	8.01	6.24	2,100.11	1,248.56	3,348.67	20,892.94
4	10000	28.69%	6.24	8.03	3,348.67	1,602.78	4,951.45	39,756.12
5	10000	10.88%	8.03	8.90	4,951.45	1,245.46	6,196.91	55,169.58
6	10000	4.91%	8.90	9.34	6,196.91	1,123.25	7,320.16	68,369.41
7	10000	15.79%	9.34	10.81	7,320.16	1,070.68	8,390.83	90,743.94
8	10000	5.49%	10.81	11.41	8,390.83	924.67	9,315.51	106,274.78
9	10000	-37.00%	11.41	7.19	9,315.51	876.55	10,192.05	73,253.11
10	10000	26.46%	$7.19	$9.09	10,192.05	1,391.35	11,583.40	$105,281.89

Yr	Invest	Invest Return	Beginning Unit Price	Ending Unit Price	Units Beginning	Units Sold	Units Ending	Year End Value
0								$105,281.89
1	-10000	-9.10%	$10.00	$9.09	11583.4	(1,000.00)	10,583.40	96,203.11
2	-10300	-11.89%	9.09	8.01	10,583.40	(1,133.11)	9,450.29	75,689.23
3	-10609	-22.10%	8.01	6.24	9,450.29	(1,324.60)	8,125.68	50,697.50
4	-10927.27	28.69%	6.24	8.03	8,125.68	(1,751.40)	6,374.29	51,180.30
5	-11255.088	10.88%	8.03	8.90	6,374.29	(1,401.77)	4,972.51	44,269.08
6	-11592.741	4.91%	8.90	9.34	4,972.51	(1,302.15)	3,670.36	34,280.75
7	-11940.523	15.79%	9.34	10.81	3,670.36	(1,278.44)	2,391.92	25,867.75
8	-12298.739	5.49%	10.81	11.41	2,391.92	(1,137.23)	1,254.69	14,313.95
9	-12667.701	-37.00%	11.41	7.19	1,254.69	(1,110.39)	144.30	1,037.13
10	-13047.732	26.46%	$7.19	$9.09	144.30	(1,815.39)	(1,671.09)	$(15,188.60)

If you had contributed $10,000 per year to your 401(k) with the investment returns from 2000 to 2009, you would have accumulated $105,281.89 at the end of the ten-year period (top part of table 2). By contrast, an investor with an initial investment of $100,000 at the beginning of year one and with no other activity would have ended up with approximately $90,900.

Important point: During the distribution stage of retirement, dollar-cost averaging is generally disastrous for investors. When prices are low, they have to sell more units to get the same distribution. Buying high, selling low doesn't work!

Loss of Principal

It takes years to make up for big losses in the market

Table 1 clearly shows how much it takes for an investment that has suffered a loss to come back to breaking even.

Table 1

If the Investment Loss Is	It Requires Gains of to Return to the Original Balance
20%	25%
25%	33 1/3%
33 1/3%	50%
50%	100%

Understanding Sequence Risk

Loss of principal early in retirement permanently damages cash flow

Although it might sound obvious, it's best to retire when the bulls are running down Wall Street. You want the market to go up, particularly in your early years of retirement, because a series of negative returns will deplete principal and contribute to lower returns later even when the market goes up. This is called sequence risk.

Conversely, you don't ever want to retire when the stock market is heading down. If you do and you're invested in equities, you're virtually guaranteeing loss of principal and future cash flow you probably won't be able to make up later. If you're facing such a scenario, seriously consider deferring your retirement until market conditions improve. Of course, if you don't own any stocks, mutual funds, or bonds, then the point is moot! Chances are you have invested over the years, so take a close look at the examples below. They illustrate the point I'm trying to make about sequence risk.

The following cases show you the difference in assets after a mere five years between someone who retired and got whacked with the bears versus someone who retired and ran with the bulls. The scenarios are based upon investments of $400,000 with annual income needs of $20,000.

In case 1, you saw negative returns in the first three years of retirement. Drawing down principal was required to make up the shortfall between returns and living expenses of $20,000, leaving the retiree with $239,747 left from the initial invested amount of $400,000.

Case 1 Return
Yr 1 -9%
Yr 2 -11%
Yr 3 -22%

Yr 4 +25%
Yr 5 +11%
Remaining assets $239,747

Financial products have been developed to reduce or ameliorate sequence risk, but it's still very real in traditional fixed- or growth-income types of investments subject to market downturns. As you can see, case 1 shows losses for the first three years and positive returns in the last two years of our scenario. Now, take a look at the big difference in how your investments would have performed if you were you to flip the same positive returns gained in the same five-year period, putting the positives into the mathematics at the start instead of at the end. In case 2, we have positive returns of 25 and 11 percent, followed by the same negative returns we had in case 1. All that differs is the order.

Case 2 Return
Yr 1 +25%
Yr 2 +11%
Yr 3 -9%
Yr 4 -11%
Yr 5 -22%
Remaining assets $274,463

Thus, the difference between case 1 and case 2 is $34,716, or 14 percent in case 2. You can see that starting off with returns of 25 percent versus the 9 percent we had in case 1 really made a difference even though we had the same returns of 11 percent in the second year of retirement, and so on down the line.

Early Social Security

Resisting the urge to take Social Security early pays off

Table 1 shows you how much you can grow your Social Security benefits by waiting to collect. As you can see, the difference in the monthly benefit is substantial between age sixty-two and age seventy.

Table 1

Social Security Benefit for Retirees Born Between 1943 and 1954 Assume Age 66 Benefits Are $2,000 Per Month			
Begin Benefits at:		One Year Adds	Total Addition
62	$1,500		
63	$1,600	6.7%	$100
64	$1,733	8.3%	$233
65	$1,867	7.7%	$367
66	$2,000	7.1%	$500
67	$2,160	8.0%	$660
68	$2,333	8.0%	$833
69	$2,519	8.0%	$1,019
70	$2,721	8.0%	$1,221 81%

Don't Let Your Clients Eat Dog Food When They're Old!

Social Security's More Important than Ever

Seniors are suffering in today's low-interest economy

Social Security is only supposed to provide 40 percent of your retirement cash flow, and yet for many retirees it's being asked to provide most or all of the money needed to pay bills. Table 1 shows that in 1990 it was much easier for senior citizens to achieve cash flow with investments like CDs, bonds, and money markets. Not so today!

- • It takes over thirty times the assets invested in CDs in 2013 (versus 1990) to produce less than three times the monthly Social Security income (versus 1990).
- • It takes over ten times the assets invested in ten-year US Treasury bonds in 2013 (versus 1990) to produce less than three times the monthly Social Security income (versus 1990).
- • The S&P 500 Index return varies wildly between decades.
- • A worker who retired at age sixty-five in 1990 with maximum benefits would receive just less than $1,800 in benefits in 2013. The increases have occurred due to Social Security cost-of-living indexes.

The figures in table 1 tell the sad story!

How Valuable Is Social Security?				
	1990	2000	2010	2014
Maximum Social Security (Age 65)	$975	$1,435	$2,191	$2,465
Receiving 2013	$1,792	$ 1,986	$2,309	$2,465

6-month Certificate of Deposit (CD)	7.50%	6.75%	0.75%	0.63%
Assets Required to Match Social Security	$156,000	$255,111	$3,505,600	$4,692,238
10-Year US Treasury Bond	7.94%	6.58%	3.85%	2.40%
Assets Required to Match Social Security	$147,355	$261,702	$682,909	$1,232,500
Return on S&P 500 Index for Last 10 Years	Approx. 18%	Approx. 18%	Approx. 1%	Approx. 10%

Understanding Medicare

Medicare is more complex than you may think.

The most important point about Medicare is that it won't cover everything. There are annual premiums and monthly costs that can add up to more than $1,000 per year for a couple. Costs can be lowered through higher deductibles and plans that don't cover as much, but skimping on coverage risks potentially ruinous bills in the event a long hospital stay is required.

The four key parts of the program are detailed below. Medicare Supplement insurance coverage is included as well.

- Part A covers hospital services.
  This is free for everyone with more than forty quarters of Social Security, but in 2014, you'd pay a $1,216 deductible for every benefit period. Medicare Part A does not restrict benefits paid from a dollar standpoint, but it does limit the time it will pay benefits.

- Part B covers doctor services.
  In 2014, you'd pay an annual premium of $104.90 and a deductible of $147.00.

- Part C covers Medicare Advantage plans.
  These are low- or no-cost plans that replace Part A and Part B, and some plans provide prescription drug coverage (30 percent don't). Costs vary, and these plans can be highly restrictive in services and doctor choice.

- Part D covers prescription drugs.
  Premiums vary with the plan you choose.

- Medicare Supplement insurance fills in the gaps in Medicare Part A, Part B, and Part D, if applicable. For example, without Medicare Advantage or a more comprehensive Medicare Supplement plan, you would be billed for 20 percent of all hospital costs under Part A. These plans are generally the best in our view because they cover most of contingencies.

Table 1 below is an excellent illustration of just how complex Medicare can get. If you choose one option, you end up with less coverage than with more comprehensive plans. Notice how everything can work together, but there are still gaps. Remember, Medicare Part A is tiered based on time, not on dollar amounts spent for medical procedures. Study table 1 before making any decisions on Medicare options.

Table 1

Medicare Plan Comparisons

	Medicare Part A & B	Medicare Advantage	Medicare Supplement
Hospitalization			
Days 1–60	All but $1,156	$295 per day	What A & B doesn't
		Co-pay first 5 days	
		What A & B doesn't	
		Days 6–60	
61–90	All but $289/day	What A & B doesn't	What A & B doesn't
91–60 days lifetime is used up	All but $578/day	What A & B doesn't	What A & B doesn't
After using 90 days plus lifetime 60 days	Nothing	What A & B doesn't	All for one year
Blood			
First 3 pints	Nothing		For 3 pints

Don't Let Your Clients Eat Dog Food When They're Old!

Hospice Care			
	Nearly all		The rest
Medical Services Including Doctors			
First $140 of Medicare approved amounts	Nothing		The rest
Remainder of Medicare approved amounts	Generally 80%	The rest	The rest
Part B Excess Charges (above Medicare approved amounts)			
Blood—first 3 pints	Nothing		The rest
Durable Medical Equipment			
First $140 of Medicare approved amounts	Nothing		The rest
Remainder of Medicare approved amounts	Generally 80%		The rest
Foreign Travel			
First $250 per calendar year	Nothing		Nothing
Remainder of charges	Nothing		80% up to $50,000

An Argument for Medicare Supplement Coverage

Health care costs are a leading cause of financial stress among retirees

Contrary to popular belief, Medicare doesn't cover everything. In fact, retirement experts agree that an average couple will spend in excess of $250,000 in extra costs for health care during retirement. Purchasing the right combination of coverage at the time you enroll in Medicare can save you tons of money down the road. For example, if you don't sign up for Medicare Part D right away, you could be hit with a 10 percent surcharge for every year you wait and don't have comparable, creditable prescription drug cover. About 70 percent of Medicare Advantage plans have Part D coverage, but others don't. The finer details of Medicare are beyond the scope of this primer. Suffice it to say that Medicare Supplement plans are the way to go, if you can afford the best ones.

Why? Because Medicare Supplement plans substantially reduce exposure to large unexpected medical costs. Large unexpected medical costs deplete savings and therefore damage future cash flows for you and your family. These plans also generally have lower deductibles and co-pays than the more restrictive Medicare Advantage plans.

Table 1 below assumes you were wise enough to pay $150 per month ($1,800 per year) for the best Medicare Supplement coverage. If you paid this for five years and never used the coverage, you'd have rung up a bill of $9,000 in expenses you may think you didn't need to pay. This would annoy you, right? However, if you didn't pay the extra money and in year six you got sick and spent eighty days in the hospital to the tune of $40,000 of doctor costs, you'd be even madder! Look at the extremely negative effect of saving $1,800 per year for five years only to get sick in year six.

By the way, I see this happening all the time. A senior goes cheap and gets totally messed up financially because of being penny-wise and pound-foolish.

Table 1

Year	Savings	Earnings on Savings	Cumulative Savings
1	$1,800	$36.00	$1,836.00
2	$1,800	$109.44	$3,745.44
3	$1,800	$185.82	$5,731.26
4	$1,800	$265.25	$7,796.51
5	$1,800	$347.86	$9,944.37
6	$1,800	$433.77	$12,178.14

Less:	
Hospital Costs	$5,780.00
Doctor Costs	$8,000.00
Net Savings/Cost	$(1,601.86)

Note that over six years, the frugal "why pay the extra cost of a *premium* Medicare Supplement plan Medicare enrollee" has cost himself or herself $1,601.86.

Table 2

Year	Savings	Earnings on Savings	Cumulative Savings	Plan Pays	Net Savings
1	$1,800	$36.00	$1,836.00	$1,000	$836.00
2	$1,800	$69.44	$2,705.44	$1,000	$1,705.44
3	$1,800	$104.22	$3,609.66	$1,000	$2,609.66
4	$1,800	$140.39	$4,550.04	$1,000	$3,550.04
5	$1,800	$178.00	$5,528.05	$1,000	$4,528.05
6	$1,800	$217.12	$6,545.17	$1,000	$5,545.17

Less:
Hospital Costs $5,780.00
Doctor Costs $8,000.00

Net Savings/Cost $(7,234.83)

Not paying for the premium Medicare Supplement coverage over six years, with the illness factored into the numbers, would cost you $7,234.93 even if you received only $1,000 in greater annual benefits from the Medicare Supplement plan in years one through five than would be available under the best no-cost Medicare Advantage plan.

Long-Term Care Options

Lack of long-term care coverage is a leading cause of poverty among seniors

With the annual median cost for long-term care coverage in a skilled-nursing care facility at $81,030 in 2013, you can't afford *not* to have some financial protection in place in the event long-term care is needed for you or your spouse. The question is how do you pay for it, and what kind of coverage do you buy? The finer issues of long-term care are beyond the scope of this primer, but this is a great place to start the learning curve.

Five long-term care options:

1. Traditional long-term care insurance
2. Variable annuity with long-term care rider
3. Lump-sum life insurance policy with long-term care rider
4. Annual-payment life insurance with long-term care rider
5. Reverse mortgage
   (Reverse mortgages aren't right for everybody!)

What is long-term care?

Long-term care boils down to assistance with what are known as activities of daily living, or ADLs in long-term care lingo. Many people believe long-term care is mostly received in nursing homes, but in fact most long-term care is received at home for custodial or personal services. Some long-term care options require institutionalizing the recipient before benefits are paid. This is rapidly changing as the trend toward a focus on homecare continues.

The following are activities of daily living:

1. Eating

2. Continence (the lack of control of bodily functions, both urinary and fecal)

3. Dressing

4. Bathing

5. Toileting (requiring assistance with elimination needs)

6. Transferring (walking)

There is a distinction between the medical definitions of toileting and continence. Toileting refers to assisting a person who may be able to control bodily functions but who needs help with any of the following:

1. Ambulatory assistance

2. Bedpan

3. Urinal

4. Diaper

5. Catheter

Continence refers to lack of control of bodily functions.

In order to receive long-term care benefits, regardless of which long-term care coverage you choose, a doctor must certify that you are physically incapable of performing two of the six of these activities of daily living. Coverage can also kick in if you are diagnosed with Alzheimer's disease or some other form of dementia that prevents you from doing two activities of daily living.

Medicare won't pay

Very little long-term care assistance is provided under Medicare. Although long-term care assistance is defined as a deductible medical cost for federal tax purposes, it is defined as a personal care cost, not a medical cost for both Medicare and insurance purposes. The distinction is hugely important. Medicare eligible expenses must be medical needs. Therefore, long-term care needs only qualify if they are medically caused and temporary. So, if you're diagnosed with Alzheimer's disease, Medicare won't pay you a dime for long-term care!

Table 1
Long-term care options and comparisons

As you consider your long-term care options, use the comparison table below as a guide.

Table of LTC Alternatives

Feature	Traditional LTC	Annuity With LTC Rider	Lump-Sum Life Ins With LTC Rider	Annual Payment Life Ins With LTC Rider
Initial Payment	Annual Premium	Initial Investment	Lump-Sum Payment*	Annual Premium
Premium Increase Potential	High	Little or None	Little or None	Little or None
Leverage	Typically 30+ Times Premium	Income Doubles (i.e., 5% to 10%)	Typically 2 1/2 to 4 Times Lump-Sum	Typically 30+ Times Premium
Ease of Qualification	Strict Underwriting	No Underwriting	Moderate Underwriting	Strict Underwriting
Cost If Don't Ever Need	Loss of Premiums	Slightly Lower Return	Lose Potential Earnings on Lump-Sum	Minimally Higher Premium**

Don't Let Your Clients Eat Dog Food When They're Old!

Cost-of-Living Coverage Increases	Available for a Cost	No But Investment Base May Grow	Yes	Not Typically
Type of Benefits	Daily or Monthly Based Upon Qualification and Reimbursement	Double-Income Monthly Based Upon Qualification	Monthly Maximum For Specified Period Until Benefits Are Used Up	Monthly Maximum For Specified Period Until Benefits Are Used Up
Major Advantage	Lower Initial cost and Cost-of-Living Increases	Investment Can Grow and be Used if no LTC Need	LTC Protection Provided For Using Investor's Money Life Insurance Excess Over Initial Premium Is Small	Lower Initial Cost and No Premium Increases Life Insurance Benefit If Not Needed for LTC
Major Disadvantage	Substantial Premium Increases Are Likely	Investment Value Must Be Greater	Large Initial Deposit Required to Get Sufficient Benefits	No Cost-Living Feature